IMAGINING WHO'S TELLING WHO

IMAGINING WHO'S TELLING WHO

*(Useful theories regarding the conscious,
and the subconscious mind)*

GEOFFREY KEANE

IMAGINING WHO'S TELLING WHO

This book is written to provide information and motivation to readers. Its purpose is not to render any type of psychological, legal, or professional advice of any kind. The content is the sole opinion and expression of the author, and not necessarily that of the publisher.

Copyright © 2020 by Geoffrey Keane

All rights reserved. No part of this book may be reproduced, transmitted, or distributed in any form by any means, including, but not limited to, recording, photocopying, or taking screenshots of parts of the book, without prior written permission from the author or the publisher. Brief quotations for noncommercial purposes, such as book reviews, permitted by Fair Use of the U.S. Copyright Law, are allowed without written permissions, as long as such quotations do not cause damage to the book's commercial value. For permissions, write to the publisher, whose address is stated below.

Printed in the United States of America.

ISBN 978-1-951559-05-2   (Paperback)
ISBN 978-1-951559-06-9   (Digital)

Lettra Press books may be ordered through booksellers or by contacting:

Lettra Press LLC
30 N Gould St. Suite 4753
Sheridan, WY 82801, USA
1 303-586-1431 | info@lettrapress.com
www.lettrapress.com

CONTENTS

Forward vii
Introduction.. xiii

Chapter 1:   What We May Reliably Come to Trust About Ourselves .. 1
Chapter 2:   The Conceptual Conscious and Subconscious 22
Chapter 3:   Theorizing, to a More Expansive Degree 43
Chapter 4:   Mentality is Physiology 51
Chapter 5:   Within Us Each, There Appear to be Two Sets of
             Inclinations 63
Chapter 6:   Also, Two Different Sources of Disturbance Within 80
Chapter 7:   Exploring Mental Uncertainties, and Arriving at
             Theoretical Certainties; and Vice-Versa 93
Chapter 8:   Detecting Our Inner Nature 103
Chapter 9:   Governing Yourself, Through Depending
             Upon Theoretical Contentions Regarding the
             Subconscious Mind 116
Chapter 10: Revisiting Morality, From A Different Perspective 121
Chapter 11: Incorporating Conscious-Subconscious Theory
             into an Intimate Relationship 128
Chapter 12: Challenging Our Somewhat Standard Definition
             of What it Means to Be in a "Relationship" 134
Chapter 13: Internal Versus External Recognition;
             Which is Truly More Valuable? 139
Chapter 14: Musical Connections; and Our Commonality,
             in General 142
Chapter 15: Intuiting the Probable Origin of Conscious-Versus-
             Subconscious Lines of Thinking and Feeling 149

References 213

FORWARD

As many of us are aware, using our imagination to try and grasp aspects of what we are not able to personally experience can be very beneficial. For example, we can try to empathize with how we might think and feel if we were to walk a mile in someone else's shoes, so to speak; when we are considering the type of behavior we are observing of them, which doesn't seem entirely sensible or appropriate.

We also know that we can invent concepts, and employ conceptual thinking to help ourselves and others to better-understand various matters of some importance; through associating some principal we do understand in one familiar context, with something we are having difficulty understanding, because it is in the realms of a new context that we are as yet unfamiliar with. This is an example of how our ability to use our imagination can help us to great benefit.

All I mean to accomplish, in pursuing this line of psychologic theory, is simply to use my imagination of how the human mind apparently works, as a mechanism to bring interesting abstract ideas to our awareness in a more tangible sense; so that we might individually and collectively become newly able to embrace some of these potentially useful ideas and concepts; therefore becoming better off for having meaningfully viewed ourselves vis-à- vis these somewhat unconventional theoretical standpoints, perhaps.

Our ability to imagine can sometimes be of the most paramount help to us in dealing with our most difficult and plaguing problems; but I also see that using our imagination can sometimes help us to make creative advances in our understanding of ourselves; and this is too is what I have been attempting to work toward.

Although we cannot be at all certain whether one's possible imaginations, regarding the structure and workings of the human mind, may, or may not actually be a reality of the human condition, it certainly does appear that the product of certain peoples' imaginations can go a long way toward enlightening us, on different matters.

Entertaining certain interesting theories has certainly helped us over the ages, whether some of these theories could ever be proved, or not.

For example, astronomers began looking at the heavens above, some centuries ago, and hearing about their observations, the public at large began to question whether our earth really was the center of the universe, and whether the earth was really flat, as was generally once accepted by all. We didn't have proof, but we began to see mounting evidence to this effect.

As we know from our experiences in the courtroom, we don't necessarily need proof of guilt, in order to convict a defendant of some particular crime, and sentence them to prison where they will not be able to do further harm to the public. We merely rely on evidence; and this is all I am suggesting we do, by extension. What I attempt to offer within these pages does seem to constitute meaningful evidence regarding the actual workings of our minds.

Of course, many of the ideas I will be discussing herein are simply my own imaginings regarding the human mind and its various thinking capabilities.

Certainly without having any definite proof, I lay out how I have come to find it dependable to consider the human mind to function in the manner that I will be describing.

Ideally, delving into this book will incline the reader to look at themselves in a different light, leading them toward a more in-depth understanding of all that generally tends to go on within the mind of perhaps the more-typical common man, in this day and age. This written material is designed to encourage healthy self- examination which culminates into a better understanding of yourself; including untangling some of the possible mysteries behind our conflicting thoughts and feelings, at times.

The fundamental principal involved in embracing this overall philosophy is the idea that our minds are actually made up of two separate thinking mechanisms, which, of course ideally may work together quite effectively; perhaps optimizing our creative problem- solving capability, as well as improving our sense of satisfaction, fulfillment, and contentment in life; particularly once we have come to better-understand the basis for my theories regarding the characteristic functions of each of these two thinking mechanisms that I consider are housed within each of us.

In a theoretical sense, and for practical purposes, I have come to view these two thinking mechanisms within, each as being a separate individual unto itself, psychologically-speaking; therefore, each having its own separate set of beliefs and values, which drive the various inclinations developing within each of these thinking mechanisms, throughout the day, given our changing present-moment circumstances, as we may perceive them.

However, regarding these two theoretical individuals housed in our head; which I will hereinafter refer to as the conscious and subconscious minds; I imagine that each of these two thinking mechanism's motivations, and the possible decisions and initiatives which will therefore be contemplated by each (of our two component-minds, so to speak), are destined to come about as a result of having embraced a separate and isolated set of beliefs and values; from that of its counterpart.

I can tell you, having personally begun to buy this idea, that thinking of myself in this light has naturally inclined me to continually wonder which of these two thinking mechanisms is generating just which of my thoughts and feelings, as I am sensing awareness of various thoughts and feelings being generated within me, from moment to moment.

At first, it could seem pretty hopeless that we might have any ability to identify and distinguish between conscious sources of thought, and subconscious ones; but I submit that, with some reasonable guidance, and with our sustained efforts at trying to better-sense what is going on in our mind, especially at key times, it will become more and more (usefully) probable to us, as to which of these two thinking mechanisms had originated any of various different "types" of trains of thought; (the result being the (conscious or subconscious) entity subsequently having inevitably developed, through a somewhat automatic calculation process, certain (conclusive) positive or negative feelings of inclination, and/or perhaps other various inclinations to engage in, or refrain from some activity, for example; the entity having developed an inclination to do, or not to do whatever it is you are thinking about at the moment.)

The final cog in the wheel of utility related to this philosophy, and in order to get the most out of this theoretical introspection process I have been describing, is to try and sense which, of these inclinations that have developed within, feel strongest within you in the heat of the moment, when the time is upon you to act, or react, or possibly to refrain from acting; as the case may be; and to then guide your behavior based upon what we can consider as this intelligently-computed initiative or solution.

Initially, pursuing the line of introspection I am recommending might seem pretty impossible; because for example, we may start out assuming that all mechanistic thinking is the same. However, personally I have come to realize that certain types, or categories, of thinking; or in other words, certain types of "trains of thought" which we can follow and observe as they are developing within our mind, can perhaps often be determined to have "likely" been the "brain-child" of the subconscious mind; and I see that certain other types of "trains of thought" could be thought to have probably become generated within the conscious mind.

For example, I talk later in the book about one type of train of thought which is basically, "I can get away with carrying out (some ill or injustice), and I can arrange it so that no one will be the wiser." I have earmarked this as a "(lesser-intelligent) conscious" type of train of thought; and in my own life experience, this brand of thinking will bite you in the ass, much more than it might help you. (However fortunately, we learn where we have been stupid from experience!)

By contrast, an example of a subconscious (or more intelligent) train of thought and its accompanying strong inclination, might be your becoming aware that a guitarist you have just heard play was so impressive that you feel strongly moved to go home and practice playing your guitar much more than you have, to date.

I say that this underlying idea to practice your instrument would be a subconscious inclination because perhaps, as of just after you had heard the inspiring performance, it hasn't even occurred to you yet, in your awake state (your conscious mind) that you have become inspired to practice more; perhaps initially, you are only consciously aware of your memory of enjoyment and excitement at having been privileged to hear such an inspiring performance. Consciously, you may merely be aware that you have a general sense of awe and excitement. At this stage, it may be that only within the mechanism of your subconscious mind has the plan to begin practicing more been newly hatched as a result of having heard this performance.

As you may have guessed, in my view, in general, what we can determine to "probably" be an "independently-subconscious" train of thought, and the accompanying strong inclinations which have developed as a result, are usually far better for us to act upon, and far more lasting than an "independently-conscious" train of thought leading us to inclinations, such as the idea of trying to get away with doing something shady, out of a sense of desiring immediate gratification; and of course, which might more-likely constitute a short-sighted strategy more prone to lead us to ultimate failings, rather than providing any more-consistent degree of overall success in the long run.

However, although I give these simplified examples for illustrative purposes, of course there are often quite a variety of factors and influences to take into account, when negotiating our own real-life situations; and I find that it takes time and effort, to identify probabilities as to the origin of conscious-versus-subconscious elements of our thinking. However, I suggest that once on the path to regularly engaging in this type of introspection, like me, you would probably get much better and faster at it, over time.

I'm thinking that readers will not even need to elect to utilize this philosophy; but rather that these ideas just naturally will become a growing part of our ongoing consideration in the future, having become oriented to the kinds of ideas I will be talking about.

I imagine that many of us could certainly conceive of their mind as having the ability to simultaneously embark on two independent trains of thought, (which, once separately-understood can also become much more intelligently integrated leading to our success, as well.)

Certainly, we need not always concentrate in this manner, but whenever it seems important enough to you, perhaps it usually just takes a bit more time and trouble to wade through your thoughts, memories, and other pertinent ideas and influences, as they relate to the subsequent development of your ultimate sense of strong inclination which would naturally lead each of us toward making related decisions; subsequently taking what we come to see as our best potential actions, or possibly having developed a strong inclination to refrain from actions we might have previously been considering going through with.

-And I consider that, for those of us who have learned how to harness their conscious thinking mechanism in this manner, and to put their conscious thinking mechanism to best use in objectively wading through the thoughts and feelings we consciously sense in the present moment, (prompted by feelings theoretically placed in our conscious mind by the subconscious division of us), the conscious and subconscious entities can become a powerfully good team.

I speak of this as teamwork, in the sense that first we become consciously aware of feelings we sense at the moment, then we might attempt to trace exactly what underlying thoughts have led us to form these particular emotions; and in having taken the time and effort to consciously think more about the subject, we become in better touch with that part of us which houses our more intelligent lines of thinking, namely our subconscious mind.

INTRODUCTION

You're singing this song in your head; a lick from the refrain; When your mind's made up.... When your mind's made up... (in this case it is a song written by Glen Hansard; and I like it because it speaks to me of all the frustration and distress it can cause, when someone you love so much, just doesn't love you back; and there doesn't seem to be anything you can do to change this; (and it also reminds me of other similarly strong frustrations, perhaps.) Anyway; suppose that you've been talking to a friend about this movie, and so this song comes to you later when you are home by yourself; and you eventually realize that without thinking about it, you've been singing this lick over and over in your head for several minutes maybe. Suddenly, a little voice in your head asserts, "Enough already! You're killing me with singing that phrase over and over again!"

We could view this as an example, or a little snippet of, the "inner dialogue" that goes on within each of us at some level, from time to time. But who's doing the singing? -and who's feeling like, "this is killing me!"

The simple answer is that we don't know; and we probably won't ever be able to know such things for certain, regarding the inner dialogue going on inside our minds. However, I assert that we really don't need to have proof of these things; we merely need to gather enough convincing evidence, in order to become inclined to find this type of introspection as a dependable aid, to wading through our various problems and issues of difficulty.

One and all, of course we do value arriving at certainty, and the quality of being "sure of ourselves." I have observed that many of us tend to value certainty so much, that we even imagine ourselves to feel entirely certain of various things we may try to tell ourselves or others, that in fact we really don't have any ability to know for a fact; and it seems we really may only do ourselves harm by taking this false position.

I call this unfortunate phenomenon a "belief become fact" within our mind. I see that many of us will all-too-often come to develop a <u>false</u> sense of certainty; and I'm thinking that this can't be too good for us, individually or collectively.

Yet, besides valuing certainty like everyone else, I have more newly also come to value "uncertainty." I apologize if that might sound a little nutty; but you see, if we don't know something, for absolute-sure, then we are naturally led down the path of "considering the possibilities;" and this truly seems to be good for us, one and all.

-And where the possibilities may not actually be "infinite," as it is sometimes said, I find it interesting, educating, and wise to consider the various possible alternative explanations for what has happened or developed. In other words, entertaining alternative possible explanations as to precisely how something has come to happen, or maybe to have developed over time; or perhaps we would do well to consider some greater number of alternative possible good choices we might choose from, given a certain situation that we seem to have found ourselves ending up in the middle of, for example.

Going back to my example about the movie, let's say you were having this conversation about this movie; and your friend, who had seen it with you a couple of years ago, says to you; "Is that the movie that starts out with a guy playing his guitar on the street; and then the woman comes up to him?"

And you say, "I think so, yeah…" but consciously at the moment when you said this, you honestly couldn't remember the beginning of the movie at all; you were just being polite and cooperative in the conversation.

But then, later, having been reminded of it by your friend, you do recall this beginning vividly; and you realize that on some level deeper within you, you <u>did</u> really know that this was how this movie starts out. Then we might ask ourselves, was this segment of the conversation with your friend, actually going on between the "subconscious you," and your friend's "subconscious entity?"

I mean, your friend didn't have it consciously in mind, the beginning of a movie they had seen a couple of years ago, right? They had to search themselves (i.e- query their subconscious mind), in order to bring this information to their conscious awareness.

These are some of the types of ways my mind works these days; in other words, I often spend some amount of time and energy pondering precisely where our various types of thoughts might originate, as well as the means by which our communications with another will just naturally become put into action, without my consciously even having thought about it; and I do consider this type of introspection to be an advanced form of thinking.

I'm guessing that probably, for most people, it has never really occurred to them that within their mind, they might house "two separate individuals," each existing as pretty-much a standalone entity with a personality all its own; and that it may be of good use to make ongoing attempts to try and determine which of those (apparently two) entities within us, that we might conceivably attempt to separately associate with each (mental voice within our head), so to speak, taking part in various internal conversations that go on between our ears.

In fact, I can only imagine that most of us have never even once considered that there is any other voice besides what they could consider as their "one personal individual voice," or thinking mechanism, as they perceive themselves.

Personally, I began developing a different sense than the rest of us starting about 40 years ago. In a very individual and personal manner, I began to sense various nuances regarding the workings of my mind, which I don't believe others were much aware of at all; and although you'd think that initially, I would have at least entertained these notions as purely theoretical in nature, I seem to have embraced them more as a true reality of the human condition, right from the get-go.

But more recently, after having written an earlier version of this work and distributed it to a few of my closest friends and relatives, and getting feedback that the way I had presented my arguments was not very considerable, I realized that, of <u>course</u>, this line of thinking is all simply theoretical in nature! -And that I had merely managed to present these ideas exactly in the manner that I seek most to discourage; namely I had tried to present my considerations regarding conscious and subconscious thought processes as a belief-become- fact!

I suppose the best you can do, once you come to realize that you have indeed developed a belief-become- fact (in other words, having thought about it further, you know you can't actually prove what you yet, appear to have embraced as a fact of existence), is to at least not be stubborn in arguing the point with others; instead making every attempt to keep an open mind by listening to, and entertaining the possibility that someone else's related ideas and impressions might also be valid to at least consider.

So, I suppose I have now embarked on a new initiative to try and present my ideas from a purely theoretical standpoint; as it seems quite obvious to me at this point, that this type of presentation would be the only manner in which these pretty unique ideas and concepts could possibly be meaningfully considered by anyone!

Regardless of my new realization, that I must relate my ideas in a purely theoretical manner, I still feel inclined to consider that my thought developments related to the concepts of consciousness and subconsciousness have led me toward increasingly- educational types of discoveries; and my persistent thinking along these lines appears to be of an ongoing cumulatively-developmental nature.

I also have come to believe quite strongly that my developing thinking along these lines has led me personally to a much more rewarding and more productive adult life, due to the formidable ongoing development of my further understanding regarding various aspects of human psychology, over many years.

I say this in light of the fact that I certainly seem to have a uniquely-individual sense of what is most just and constructive for me to pursue, regardless of anyone else's judgment of me; and I consider that I have justifiably taken license to operate beyond some of the restrictive bounds of conventional societal thinking, at points; I suppose because I see myself as having a rather unique capacity to make progressive strides in our common human evolutionary development, psychologically speaking; which the family of man quite obviously is sorely in need of, I might add.

Regardless of my possible standing within society at any moment, I do see myself as possessive of good integrity; and I would assert that I am only interested in pursuing human goodness; not that I am without potential to cause significant harm and damage acting out of ignorance sometimes, like anyone else.

It has long been occurring to me that many others could possibly make good use of the types of ideas that go through my mind; and that perhaps if enough of us could begin to embrace some of the different fundamentals I have found it more formidable to rely on, it seems quite possible that, as a people, we might be able to lead ourselves out of the great trouble we have quite evidently been making for ourselves and each other, over the generations; which I consider is probably mainly due to an off-base, disadvantageous manner that perhaps most of us more-typically have tended to think and act in terms of; perhaps often basing many of our ill actions upon some brand of shortsighted thinking, in this respect.

As I think about evolution, although we say it happens gradually; and in a more significant sense, I suppose this is true; but I think it is also important to look at how we personally evolve during our lifetime; some of us more than others, of course. As we keep learning more and more, and we keep being exposed to new and different things, we know that with each new experience, we can often at least gain some new kernel of knowledge, or maybe add further perspective to our knowledge on a given subject that we had previously known only a little about, for example.

While obtaining my degree in psychology, in school more recently, I learned of the tremendous impact that our cumulative life experience can have, on the psychological makeup of even the very next generation of that person's offspring. Things like, if you grow up in a starved atmosphere, like in Africa; your children may likely be born with an innately more-insatiable appetite; to compensate.

But it seems likely that other aspects of what we personally gain during our lifetime, in terms of mental advancement, will become passed on; at least in part; to our heirs, as well. And it is not as though we haven't been acting inhumanly to one another all along; as we can certainly glean from reading the old testament section of the Bible, for example; but along the way, we have certainly learned what constitutes a much better way of thinking and behaving toward each other; I think it's just that so many somewhat-mentally-sick, arrogant assholes feel as though they need not observe it; as they plunder away; and unfortunately, all too often perhaps, their bank accounts prove to them that they are right!

Yet, objectively speaking, it would seem to be much more fair and equitable, and best for everyone if the development of inclinations to plunder and otherwise take unfair advantage of others could somehow be eradicated from all of our minds.

But why talk of such impossible ideals?! Well I think it is important to at least keep <u>some</u> focus on what would be best for us, in terms of our mass socialization.

I had really not ever been aware of the phenomenon of sociology, the idea that as a young member of society, you would be subject to great influence to conform to the societal standards kept to, commonly by all other older family members in your midst, and by other authority figures presiding over you.

Personally, I suppose I have pretty uniquely resisted becoming psychologically programmed in this manner, so I had incorrectly assumed that we all think in our own individualistic ways. I never imagined that in general, we all become influenced to such an amazingly large extent, in terms of our values and the limits of what we will allow ourselves to give thought to, and possibly do.

I certainly now realize that, without possessing a good ability to take in and accept how we are told to think and conduct ourselves, by those guiding people in our lives, then consequentially in our own personal view, there would be almost nothing that we would embrace as taboo, for example.

On the other hand, if we are grounded in humanly- good qualities, regardless of some inability to utterly conform, a person who has not effectively become that socialized perhaps, such as myself, would also not have ever become inclined to plunder and take unfair advantage of others, for personal gain either.

It often appears that, regarding those who do become habitually inclined to gratify themselves at the expense of others, they have merely learned to embrace this attitude from observing and listening to elders before them. I find myself wondering whether there isn't some way we can stop this unfortunate transfer of ill-natured values systems, in a similar manner to the way we are working so hard these days to keep various other forms of abuse from perpetuating, generation to generation; such as sex offense and domestic violence. At least, it seems only positive for many of us to realize, in common, what some of our more healthy and constructive aims should probably be, as we look forward to spawning evolutionary progress in the next generation.

I start with the premise that, just like any other man-made machine, our human mental machinery could probably be pretty-well-understood by dissecting its component parts; but of course, not to make light of the potential greater assistance of a possibly-existent God, for example; it's just that, especially since I am concentrating here on theorizing about uncertain aspects of our apparent dual thinking mechanisms, I will want to limit my analysis here, to what can pretty-unquestionably be agreed upon by everybody, regarding some of the realities of our existence. Adding a possibly-existent outside source, such as God, into the mix of what I am trying to focus on about human thought processes, would seem to take us out of the realms of what we could more concretely come to depend on regarding the ways we might typically tend to think, in a more fundamental and pragmatic sense.

In general, I like to work more-exclusively within the confines of what we could all depend upon to be more tangibly real; as far as what the common man might more-typically observe to be going on within each of our minds; so I have tried to develop my theories and other concepts starting from this more-concrete basic starting point.

To begin, I'm sure that, generally all of us, have come to understand and acknowledge that we have a conscious mind, and a subconscious mind; although we may differ in our conception of what more-fully constitutes each of these thinking mechanisms. It is obvious that these two mechanisms work together; in that we can at times become in touch with thoughts and feelings "in the back of our mind," so to speak; this representing our consciously becoming aware of certain subconscious thoughts and ideas.

And moving in the opposite direction, we can "commit things to memory," as well, for example; this representing the conscious mind's ability to transfer some aspect of conscious awareness, to become learned and stored within the subconscious division of our mind.

However, for simplicity's sake, and also for more clarity of understanding, it would probably be more helpful initially to look at each of these two minds theoretically in terms of their separate, isolated functional characteristics.

The workings of our minds are certainly quite complex; and if we are to attempt a better understanding of our thinking processes, obviously we must indeed start with a simpler approach. As a starting point, I will lay out what I imagine as a separate set of basic characteristics associated with each of these two thinking mechanisms, of which I consider make up the entirety of a given individual's mind. If we begin with the premise that identifying two separate sets of characteristic thoughts; or in other words, trying to isolate certain types of thinking as of a conscious nature, versus types of thinking that we might categorize as of a subconscious nature, this would theoretically enable us to begin to distinguish between conscious and subconscious lines of thought.

For example, as one distinction we can make, between the conscious and subconscious thinking mechanisms, in terms of the limits of their thinking capabilities, I imagine that it is only within our conscious thinking mechanism, that we can think with intention; such as deciding to make choices. The other important major aspect of consciousness, is the ability to sense our various inclinations to do, or avoid doing things.

The conscious mind, of course, has the unique capability to gain awareness; of what is going on around us, as well as having some limited ability to sense various thoughts and feelings internally, deeper within us, at any moment.

I also imagine the conscious mind as having the exclusive capability to initiate our actions, as well; although probably in many cases, our subconscious mind appears to greatly influence the ultimate decisions which culminate into our consciously-determined actions.

In contrast, we could begin to define our subconscious thinking capabilities as independent of any ability we might have to intentionally think about something; and although we can try to exert control over our thoughts at times, I consider that the subconscious thinking mechanism has a "mind of its own," so to speak; and so therefore, I think that we might aptly view it as a separate, independent thinking mechanism, in many senses, from the thinking mechanism of our conscious mind.

Just to illustrate some further distinguishing characteristics between these two theoretical divisions of our minds; together making up the entirety of the human mind as I see it; I imagine the subconscious mind to house our universe of overall knowledge that we hold, including the many memories of our experiences and step-by-step processes we have learned to perform, for example; which appear to exist beyond the level of our conscious awareness; well that is, other than at those times when we may access relatively tiny portions of our vast subconscious human database; such as when we employ our conscious resources to "search our mind" with intention.

Therefore, I think we could reasonably theorize that; whatever it is in addition; the subconscious mind exists as a database of everything we know; perhaps eliminating the need to hold, within our conscious thinking mechanism, any of this greater pool of information, besides the specific information we may consider as necessary to hold within our awareness, as we apply our most-advisable conscious thought processes of the moment.

However, I also theorize that our conscious mind is not ever completely devoid of all superfluous knowledge held within the subconscious database, beyond what is necessarily pertaining to our immediate utility; and then too, we could be consciously thinking about more than one thing at a time; so of course, this makes it a bit more complicated to define the more-precise limits of our conscious thinking capability; but I think we could at least start with this simplistic idea, that theoretically, the conscious mind need not "hold" information, as far as establishing the bare essentials necessary for the minimal carrying out of our conscious thought-processing operations.

But in order to begin further-dissecting our conscious mind's various apparent mental operations, I consider it important to look first at the conscious mind's possible capability to "hold" various information, memories, and other ideas which it might work with, at a given moment; and then, next we could look more closely at our conscious "thought-processing" capabilities.

Of course, the "holding" of an idea involves a memory function. According to what I have recently learned in college, scientists have keyed in on three separate processes we all will employ, which are thought to make up our overall memory function; or in other words, the full extent of our memory mechanism.

The first of these is short-term memory, which surprisingly is said to only lasts for a few seconds. Of course, committing things to memory, or retrieving things from memory, both require conscious intention, as well as the conscious directing of our attention to what we want to remember, or to store in within our memory. Attention, and intention, are really requirements of all three of our memory functions, of course.

The second stage of our memory process is purported to be our "working memory;" and during this phase, we can hold things that we want to remember for little more than 10 seconds, perhaps. It is supposedly during this phase where we may begin applying conscious thought-processing operations; and then, once we have directed our attention and applied thought in this manner, some of what we have held in "working memory" will ultimately become committed to our long-term memory. It might seem pretty strange that something we were thinking 30 seconds ago could now exist in what we refer to as our "long-term memory;" but this is supposedly how our minds actually work. This is not my theory, but it is my current understanding.

Interestingly enough, what we hold in our long- term memory is said to remain there indefinitely. If this sounds a bit confusing, I should add that even though thousands of memories are said to remain stored within our mind, our ability to access any one of these is, of course, limited to the extent of the efficiency of our memory retrieval capabilities; and this may vary greatly, individual to individual.

Apparently, the main variable governing the effectiveness of our ultimate memory-retrieval abilities is the amount of time it will take us to locate and recall a specific memory; but at least theoretically, any and all of your long-term memories could potentially become recalled, at least eventually. Therefore, it can certainly be seen, that how we organize the information held within our mind can make a critical difference in how good of a memory we may have. We know that there are different possible ways of organizing, or different possible filing methods, for example. Hopefully, we have, just naturally, effectively tailored our own memory organizational structure to best meet our individual needs; but if we have not, maybe we could improve this, or perhaps other important aspects of our thinking abilities, by becoming more familiar with our basic mental structure; and it is my aim to point us in such directions.

Perhaps we could reasonably say, it would logically follow that short-term memory, and working memory functions would be the purview of the conscious mind; while long-term memory could perhaps aptly be categorized as existing within the domain of the subconscious mind; at least in a more simplified, overview sense.

But if this is the case, you may ask, then how do I explain our conscious sense that we can be aware of quite a lot at once, at times? I would suggest that this might actually be somewhat of an illusion; maybe our conscious thinking mechanism can simply be quite facile at accessing our subconscious-mind-database with lightning fast expedience; perhaps falsely giving us the impression that we are "holding" quite a lot of informational content in our conscious mind at once.

It does appear that we can often pass information back and forth between our conscious and subconscious thinking mechanisms in a split second; but this falls under thought processing capabilities, which we haven't gotten to yet, in our journey.

However, at this juncture, let me throw out some alternate possibilities, in terms of perhaps a more- expanded range of conscious-thinking-mechanism capability, which may alternately be a reality of its existence.

Let's start with the more-simple basics regarding my conception of conscious thought-mechanism capabilities. The scientific perspective I have more recently learned about while getting my degree; which, judging by the updated scientific explanation of our memory function, apparently assumes that the bare- bones conscious mind itself is nothing more than the combination of a moment-by-moment awareness, and an intentional-thought-processing mechanism.

In this sense, or on this level, we could view the conscious mind as a shell; and not even as an entity unto itself. Yet, of course, it seems quite apparent to me that, over thousands of generations, the conscious mind has certainly developed the capacity to do much more than serve, in a "shell" capacity; in other words where it might act solely as an assistant to its subconscious master, if you will.

This is where I consider that human evolution has gone astray; and at this point, it appears essential to reign-in our all-too-often-straying conscious thinking mechanism; confining it to more-primarily being much- more of a servant, to the subconscious thinking mechanism; for our advantageous further-evolutionary development; and maybe even for our continued existence; at the rate we are going! Things seem to have gotten exponentially worse in more recent decades.

In trying to further define my idea of consciousness in the sense that we might most-usefully consider it; if some fact that you could spout off is readily available, we could argue that anything we could quickly and easily remember and rattle off is something we are conscious of.

But did the conscious mind "hold" this thought? My point is that, conceivably, we would only become conscious of some fact being demanded we spout off, once it is called to our conscious mind, via our having been asked. And theoretically, it's quite possible that these readily-available facts are only being retrieved from our subconscious database; it could be that there is no information holding function at all, belonging to the conscious thinking mechanism. We could picture a chain reaction; a friend asks you what you had for lunch, this prompts your conscious mind to query the subconscious database, which in turn puts into your conscious mind that you had a bologna sandwich!

In any event, I tend to embrace the idea that; regardless of whatever the whole of the conscious mind might include; awareness, and immediate thought processing capability certainly could be seen to represent a huge part of all that is conscious; whereas, in contrast to this limited conscious scope, I sense that the sizable amount of data (in other words, all of our retained knowledge and memories), coupled with the subconscious mind's current-moment-related thought-processing capability, these together perhaps only make up a smaller part of the overall potential capability which the subconscious mind appears to possess.

I say this because I consider that the subconscious mind continues its automated mulling over of multiple ideas; contemplating, computing, and figuring things out incessantly; of its own volition. The subconscious mind, as I see it, is truly an awesome piece of mental machinery!

However, as we have continued to develop over the generations (in the modern day and age particularly), my observation is that the conscious mind's capacity for independent thought, of its own accord, is proving to have enabled it to become a formidable opponent of the subconscious mind, which, in my thinking, quite possibly may even have theoretically yet <u>created</u> this conscious division to serve its objectives. -And not that the conscious mind could necessarily match wits with its subconscious counterpart; but more because it is learning it has power, to disobey, counter, and otherwise ignore subconscious input; instead independently dictating our most prevalent thinking, and exclusively commandeering our behavior.

Thinking further about what we may associate with consciousness, we might ask, can you be conscious of something, while not being aware of it? This is yet another question it seems we could never answer with utter certainty; but these kinds of questions that pop up in me, I think are well-worth asking ourselves; as we unravel more of the mystery of how our minds might tend to operate.

Regardless of my thoughts on how much is held within the realms of consciousness, we certainly know that we can think on different levels. For example, we might say to our spouse, "In a way, I kind of hate your mother; but of course; as you know; I really love her, as well." We could say these are two "different levels" of our thinking. I imagine that most of us are well-aware of what a "love-hate" relationship is. Yet, to me it appears constructive for us to, at times, think more carefully about what is behind each of these mixed emotions towards someone like a mother-in-law, of whom you will probably be encountering regularly going forward; in other words, to think about what "makes me love them," and separately about what makes you hate this person as well; because this type of consciously-inclined search has potential to help you get to know your inner (subconscious) self better; and it is my impression that most of us don't tend to search themselves in this manner near enough; and therefore perhaps we don't know ourselves very well; and then in our ignorance, we don't know this either!

In any event, the possible complexities of the conscious mechanism notwithstanding, there are important differences we can key in on, between the value of acting solely based on conscious inclinations of the moment, versus attempting to abide more by our deeper sense of subconscious inclination, (undoubtedly to the contrary of conscious objectives at some points); to the extent we may become in touch with our thoughts and feelings on these deeper, more- complex subconscious levels.

At the outset, many of us may not be the least bit aware of anything but what their inclinations are at each moment, whenever they try to sense them. The idea that we might think, either alternately or simultaneously, in effect, separately utilizing one of two distinctively different (minds, so to speak); or "thinking process machinery" appearing to exist within each of us, may well have never occurred to you, up until this point.

I count having gotten in increasingly better touch with how I think and feel down deep, as having given me vast further potential to live a much better life, from the standpoint not only of happiness and fulfillment, but I find that, having gotten to know myself much better through searching my mind and becoming more sensitive to what is going on psychologically on deeper levels within me, has also greatly increased my ongoing potential to be further helpful and constructive in my dealings with others, and in the activities I take part in.

In my earlier version of this writing, I had falsely contended that, in order to get any appreciable value out of the subject matter I am discussing here, one must develop the capacity to conceptually imagine themselves to have two separate thinking mechanisms within them. If this is simply beyond you, it seems pretty certain that not much else written here will begin to make much sense to you; and consequentially, you may well be missing out on extremely important new understanding, of which more-evolved generations of the future will advantageously come to embrace and make much good use of.

However, I have since come to realize that probably anyone who is willing to entertain reading about this whole theoretical psychological world within my mind, that I have been dreaming up and further imagining about for a number of years now, could potentially get something significantly positive and useful to them; perhaps in a very real sense; out of simply having read through this material.

Some Basic Science Concerning Brain Function:

To touch on brain-function a bit, scientists have observed that brain neurons fire in successive chains of one "touching off" the next, sort of like dominoes each falling on the next, in a chain of dominoes set up on a table, for example. I would have to admit that this is really a vastly oversimplified depiction; the more-full nature of the functioning within neural pathways, and the many different types of signals involved in neural communication are quite numerous and complex.

However, what I wanted to get across is that our brain is made up entirely of neurons, each of which can affect other nearby neurons, as a result of the chemical and electrical activity going on within a given neuron.

When neurons do "fire", they often will "touch each other off," so to speak, in chainlike fashion, in effect carrying a signal from one part of the brain, to another brain area, as a communications system of sorts.

The many different types of electro-chemical processes typically going on between our ears can often involve extremely complex nuances. However, the simple principal I am getting at here, is that, again theoretically speaking, I wonder whether we could assume that additional perspective becomes added to our thoughts as they travel down these pathways; developmentally forming an increasingly-greater reflection of our ideas and impressions along the way; and I also imagine it might be somewhat likely that our conscious division perhaps intuits shortcuts, in order to more-quickly arrive at an end result that this thinking mechanism considers that an (alternative) subconsciously-led neural firing pattern would take us, in terms of attaining a computed psychological position on some issue; or in other words, in terms of an ultimate conclusion we might intelligently come to, at the subconscious level; or so the conscious mind may convince itself, in its shorthand process of achieving a more-immediate computational-related, and analysis-related goal. Theoretically, at this point, in other words, after the subconscious mechanism within us has thoroughly processed a related group of thoughts, I imagine that it would basically then send a message prompting the conscious division of something it wants us to proceed with, or to perhaps avoid doing, as the case may be.

It would make sense to me that the conscious mind can't help skipping over some amount of important considerations while hammering out its short-cut route, having falsely concluded that it is merely taking us more- quickly to a computational end product it assumes the subconscious process would eventually take us to anyway; and this is what I am guessing to be the true nature of the short-sightedness of the conscious thinking mechanism within us.

But perhaps it also seems that these consciously- developed shortcuts would be somewhat devoid of our greater perspective; which perhaps would have otherwise become involved; in a given subconscious decision- making process, for example; or had our minds instead utilized a subconscious route to run our thoughts (neural signals) along.

I wonder if the mind does actually "hold" thoughts?

Or are they perhaps only produced by the successive firing of various specific chains of neurons? Scientists certainly know the brain as basically a grapefruit-sized solid ball composed entirely of a network of neurons, through and through. If we could picture the brain, as likened to a city with a complex network of intertwining roads; perhaps we could start out with a goal of getting from where we are, to some destination of our choosing; and we would map out a route which might take us down a number of different roads before we get there.

However, suppose your traveling partner found a shortcut, which obviously looked like a more direct way to get where you are going; they may talk you, as the driver, into taking that route instead. And to draw a parallel, this could represent your subconsciously-versus- your consciously-perceived best ways to proceed, concerning some mental matter at hand.

But perhaps the map doesn't tell you what condition that each road is in; is it a dirt road? Is it full of a lot of curves, although it generally may head in a fairly straight direction as depicted on the map? Are there a lot of up-hills and downhills to this shortcut route, that will put more wear and tear on the car's brakes?

Now, let's say that on the longer route, there are signs all along the way which would help you avoid pitfalls, and that this longer route would also take you by places you have been before, that were enjoyable or otherwise meaningful to have experienced encountering; and that having been reminded of them would help you to more-enjoy, or otherwise add value and perspective, to what you are about to encounter once you have arrived at your planned destination.

And let's further say that the shortcut doesn't have very many signs; and one of them which is too small and not lit up, says that there is fresh tar up ahead; so perhaps if you had taken this shortcut route, you would have worn out your shocks because the roads were very bumpy; wore out you clutch and your brakes because there were a lot of hills and stop signs along this route; and you wouldn't even be aware that you had gotten all sorts of tar all over your fenders as well, until you had arrived at this destination and gotten out to look.

Let's even say that among the many helpful signs along the longer route, there was a very visible sign, warning against taking a stretch of the shortcut route's path that was being freshly tarred; as well as this longer route having rest stops, where the locals would likely advise you against taking routes to your destination which were deceptively seductive; in terms of appearing to be more direct, looking at a map; but were rife with different forms of setbacks, delays, and other possible difficulties.

We can see that in this case, it would have been much better all around, if we had taken the long route; and we would have gotten a lot more out of what we were to eventually experience once we had arrived, as well.

This example illustrates how we might symbolically view the nature of the type of differences that would perhaps exist, between a neural pathway route developed by the separate thinking-mechanism within the subconscious mind, versus a consciously-conceived shortcut neural pathway route, for example.

Of course, all of what I have been discussing in this section so far, is merely conjecture on my part; I mainly state it for the possible benefit to those who might be more up-to-speed in their orientation to the relationship between a person's thoughts and the corresponding neural activity which might produce these psychic thoughts. A novice need not pay any attention to this segment of this brain science explanation.

These are just far-flung theoretical ideas which I might explore more at some point in the future; but as for asserting my keenest, and most important sense, and the most major idea I would like to call our attention to, I see that, in some perhaps-less-identifiable manner, quite detrimentally, our conscious mind very effectively finds ways to compartmentalize itself, in terms of its having come to develop, evolutionarily-speaking, quite a number of isolated thinking capabilities; apparently cutting itself off from a much more intelligent potential-influence, when perhaps it could instead be more-well-connected to the person's infinitely-more-intelligent subconscious thinking mechanism.

So, as this illustrates, quite obviously, I do hold a conception of the conscious mind as possessive of much further capability, beyond present moment awareness, and intention-driven thought processing.

Just to further clue-in some possibly more- sophisticated thinkers along these lines, at this point, I consider the essence of the conscious mind's additional resources to probably exist as some sort of a segregation mechanism, which involves the creation of a subset of the overall resources of the subconscious mind; perhaps a shorthand version of the subconscious mind's overall understanding; but it occurs to me that this database subset, comprised of neural pathway shortcuts perhaps, significantly lacks important perspective; therefore inclining us, in a short-sighted sense, to, at times, act inhumanly toward each other; as well as toward ourselves.

I would also suggest that, as the commonly-used word "inhuman" indicates; a good many of us even know, on some level, that this perhaps somewhat-psychotic aspect of our conscious thinking mechanism keeps us from strictly acting in a manner which we could characterize as entirely human, at times; some of us more than others.

However, I also see that we apparently have the ability to correct this grievous "error of our ways," existing as a form of erroneous sensibility, that we have consequentially come to often-depend-on. Trying to correct this, is what this book is primarily about; more than anything else.

But I must add that this conscious mind "neural shortcut" idea actually isn't even really that important to my other ideas here; in fact, I really just dreamed it up pretty recently; and yet, I have been developing and embracing the vast portion of the "conscious-subconscious" theoretical ideas I will be talking about within this book, for quite a number of years. What *is* probably important for us to consider is that it is pretty evident to me that our conscious thinking mechanism has somehow developed a pretty complete mind of its own; although granted, it is by definition a lesser intelligent one; and therefore, I would estimate that there exists good potential to bring our conscious mind under the more-intelligent subconscious mind's control, at this point.

And yet, on the other hand, the subconscious mind; holding all the cards, as far as containing basically everything that makes up the major substance of our person; is actually incomplete, in that it needs a second thinking mechanism with the conscious mind's awareness and complimentary thought-processing capabilities, in order to effectively function. I consider that without this, the subconscious mind has no way of knowing what is going on in the outside world; and it also has no way of communicating its thoughts and feelings to others; therefore, having zero potential for having any kind of relationship with another, for example.

One problem with my trying to convey to others what I seem to have learned about human mental structure, perhaps which not many of us have yet become able to understand and utilize as leverage to our good purpose, such as I believe I have, is that although it might be much easier if I could concretely explain that I had started here, then I did such and such, and ended up where I am now.

Explaining the further perspective I seem to have gained regarding human nature, through having imagined a theoretical mental structure, as a means to "explore the possibilities," as it were, has been a bit challenging, to say the least, because arriving at my current level of understanding has not been a methodical, straight-line process of going from point A to point B; I have embarked on a very complex learning process, over decades, in order to arrive at the more-complete conception that I currently hold, concerning many of the apparently-counterintuitive workings of the human mind, as I see it.

Yet, as I recently went about, discussing the writing I had more recently completed, in the form of the literature I had created on the "AA for Agnostics" program I was previously trying to get off the ground, (within which I had attempted to explain myself on these levels), I inevitably found that most of the people I spoke to, who had made some attempt to read and understand what I was trying to get across, often seemed to be pretty mystified, or they just couldn't get a very good grasp on what I was trying to lay out otherwise, as being of any significance for us to consider.

I realize now, that what I was contending regarding the human condition was not based on what others could conceive of as tangible evidence. It has since become evident to me that the reason for this, was that I was missing a more-thorough explanation as to upon what exact basis anyone might come to reasonably assume that what I am contending exists, in terms of a group of distinct component functions which could pretty unquestionably be associated with each of these two separate thinking mechanisms making up the entirety of each modern-day human mind.

I realized, from hearing many skeptical remarks, that personally I have been operating based upon a set of assumptions which many others have indeed not arrived at, in their own quest to better understand various aspects of the realities of the human condition. I can see that I will have to trace further back, in order to take a closer look at where I appear to diverge from conventional understanding, in this respect.

I also seem to have been missing an effective entreaty to the reader. I think of the "Peter, Paul, and Mary" song I heard as a kid; where Johnny is going off to war; and his sweetheart wants to go with him. She keeps entreating him with various arguments, of which after each, Johnny says, "No, my love no." But after three verses of these entreaties, you get the sense that she finally realizes that she just isn't getting through to Johnny, in terms of impressing upon him the most important aspects of the way she feels about him, as he is planning to leave her side; so she steps up the emotional impact suddenly, to a whole 'nother level; and she tells him things like, "I love you far better than words can ever express!" -and he finally says that she can come with him, after all.

It occurs to me that I am challenged to do something similar, in order to get through to the more conventional reader, in ways which might help them to see some very disadvantageous ways of their thinking, and therefore acting, which as I have observed, generally, just about all of us seem to embrace, in common.

An effective entreaty seems more necessary in this case, as I find that there seems to be a natural resistance to the more-serious considering of the types of ideas I have come up with. Maybe this could even have something to do with the average person's conscious mind's possible ongoing vigilant attempts to hide its "subconscious master" from learning things about its aberrantly-developed capabilities; maybe trying to keep the subconscious entity in the dark, regarding the conscious mind's methodology it uses to command itself independent of the greater subconscious mind's more-full monitoring and influence; just a thought. I am just wading through a number of possible explanations that occur to me.

It does appear to me that far too often the conscious mind can find a basis to ignore the subconscious mind's suggestions and other input; perhaps involving some effective form of conscious rationalization being employed.

We know that at times, someone can give us advice, for example, that we could pretty-easily be inclined to ignore, consciously-speaking; but as far as the subconscious mind's potential monitoring, where it might be able to catch this false overriding influence, (i.e.- an internal emotional prompt of "can't you tell that it feels very dangerous to even consider this?!") I can only imagine that it is probably harder for one's separate subconscious thinking mechanism to be completely certain whether the conscious inclination to ignore the advice in question, had formed because in the view of the lesser-intelligent conscious thinking mechanism, the advice appeared to have no real and pertinent basis (i.e.- The head of the company assured me that no-one has ever gotten hurt bungee-jumping with his company's guidance), or if the conscious mind's rejection of the advice was merely due instead, to some form of what the smarter subconscious mechanism might know to constitute some baseless form of lesser-intelligent conscious rationalization; (i.e.- lots of people have bungee-jumped without getting hurt) which perhaps would have inspired the consciously-developed inclination to instead lead us into maybe what had subsequently proved to be a negatively consequential action we had taken, as a result. (I imagine that the subconscious mind's prompt of making you aware of its greatly-intense fear, that you could die taking this unnecessary risk, for example, would always be of paramount significance; probably any reasonably-intelligent person should acknowledge this within themselves, right?) Sorry, bungee jumpers!

Even though it probably never could be, if it could ever be proved that we did in fact have an independent conscious thinking capability from that of our subconscious thinking mechanism, we might easily imagine these two mechanisms to interact just naturally, at least to some degree, as well; and I will get to discussing how I imagine that to possibly be the case; but let's first talk about the separateness, in terms of the functional capacity of each; in more simplistic terms.

Of course, what follows is exclusively my own personal conception of the theoretical structure of the human mind. Following my line of thinking, in this respect, does not require the reader to buy into my personal conception; but I do ask readers to "consider the possibility" that reliance upon the following principals establishes a basis which may give us a more-useful sense of theoretical understanding, which could perhaps be of good value in helping us to improve our effectiveness at negotiating our problems, challenges, and difficulties.

To lay out one of the most basic fundamentals of my imaginings; of these two minds, the subconscious entity, or our "subconscious self" as I will term it, basically has a personality of its own. It is also perhaps the easier of our two selves to initially conceptualize as a separate entity; in that for starters, we could see it as a larger database of sorts, which contains everything we have learned, or have otherwise come to realize, including all of our memories, of course. Perhaps, the other most fundamental characteristic of our subconscious mind, as I have imagined it, is its isolated thought-processing capability. It appears to think, on its own, even while we are asleep.

Getting a good grasp on my imagined concept of the conscious thinking mechanism, or our "conscious self" as independently separate from our subconscious mind, appears to require a more complex understanding.

On a basic level, I imagine it to have two main components more-essential to its functioning; an awareness component, which in terms of its utility, is a "moment by moment sensing" aspect of our conscious self; and in addition, there is the conscious thinking mechanism, or our conscious "thought-processing capability" which might also be seen as our exclusive "intention-driven" thinking mechanism.

As I view it, the conscious mind uniquely has the exclusive capability to intentionally focus us on figuring something out; as well as being a mental mechanism which affords us the ability to take ourselves through some step-by-step process we are thinking about while we are awake, in some circumstance where we have chosen to direct our attention.

Of course, I imagine that we are all familiar with these aspects of consciousness; but most of us probably are not familiar with the idea that the conscious mind might appear to exist as a standalone entity, and that it may often have differing perceptions (i.e.- a subconscious one that bungee-jumping is dangerous-versus- the same person having a conscious perception that bungee- jumping is not dangerous), I see the conscious mind therefore, as often possibly having directly-opposing beliefs, values, and/or goals, from those of its subconscious counterpart.

I submit that viewing ourselves in this light grants us the ability to entertain a host of possibilities regarding the way we may well actually think; thereby potentially offering us a better understanding of ourselves.

CHAPTER ONE

WHAT WE MAY RELIABLY COME TO TRUST ABOUT OURSELVES

One of the problems of referring to a separate division of our overall mind as the "conscious mind," is that each of us may have any of a number of different ideas as to what the entirety of the conscious mind might include; in terms of the limits of its functional capacity.

Therefore, I will have to more-succinctly define consciousness, in the sense that would be of the greatest value, for the purposes of talking about my theories in a manner that I think we could make best use of, as far as potentially putting these conceptual ideas to good use, within our daily lives.

Certainly, I realize that some readers might tend to focus more on all of the ways that the tentativeness of these imaginings could seem pretty nebulous, perhaps thinking that all of our best attempts to analyze aspects of our psychological being, in this manner, could not possibly provide any more-concrete types of insights that could lead us toward indisputable levels of proof, which might then unquestionably be of good help to us in more effectively running our lives.

Well, of course, no one in their right mind could reasonably contend to offer us concrete explanations about the exact nature of our overall thinking mechanism, as human beings; alternately, there seems to be much about the human mind that we can only guess at, in terms of the actual nuts and bolts of its functional workings.

Certainly, all you will find offered within is a group of theories and concepts to possibly consider. However, we also can acknowledge that most aspects of scientific progress and development, of course, have been built upon the basis of considering mere theories, such as the ones I may reasonably present here.

I am hopeful that the mature reader will be thinking more about what we can possibly become a bit more certain of, regarding at least some aspects of the way our minds work; which could be of use; and therefore, possibly making concerted attempts to focus on what becomes, granted, perhaps a smaller set of probabilities that we could perhaps somewhat reliably assume are worth conducting ourselves based upon, at times.

Then too, where it may be quite disputable if I were to claim that what I have imagined here is truly the actual way our minds work, instead I merely ask others to read about what I have imagined, in this respect, claiming this to be of value, in itself.

To the extent it may be possible to determine probabilities regarding which of our two thinking mechanisms, as I have imagined them, might likely be the source of a particular train of thought or inclination that we have become aware exists within us, at a given moment, I suggest that given these probabilities we might arrive at, then theoretically, at times we might become much more apt to make the most advantageous choices, in terms of governing our behavior in accordance with our more-enlightened sensibilities.

I find that attempting to decipher which of your two minds is separately following some distinct train of thought, in different instances, using your conscious senses; and sometimes gambling a bit, where it seems more-necessary, that it seems more probable that certain of the types of thoughts and feelings present within you, at this given moment, have been generated within your subconscious mind, this can help aptly incline you to give these considerations more weight, as you weigh alternative possible decisions, or directions to move in, for example.

I have personally found much value in imagining this dual-thinking-mechanistic mental structure, and learning how to somewhat-reliably distinguish between some types of thoughts as coming from my subconscious, as versus my conscious self; and I will talk a lot about this throughout my writing efforts here; but it can't be emphasized enough, that there can be no all-knowing experts in this line of subject matter. The most anyone can do is to find somewhat-convincing evidence for oneself, that you have aptly characterized a specific "type" of thinking process or train of thought as either a conscious, or a subconscious one.

By "type" of thinking process, I mean in the sense of categorizing each specific thinking process you are trying to analyze, by what the apparent underlying motives of it would appear to be. If the motive obviously was immediate gratification, for example, with less regard for the interests of others, I would probably consider this to be a conscious train of thought; whereas, if what I was thinking about doing involved enduring some near-term inconvenience, with the prospect of a worthwhile reward a little farther into the future, this I would be apt to consider as a subconscious train of thought.

I imagine these two mechanisms to share their thoughts back and forth with each other just naturally, to some extent; but I find that I may achieve more effective results when working out my problems, by imagining which lines of thinking are being generated within my conscious mechanism, as opposed to the trains of thought more likely generated by my subconscious, and attempting, at times, to usher-along some additional thought sharing, as well.

I find that, not only does going through this mental exercise establish a hierarchy of which thoughts and feelings you might be best served in giving more weight to (this being what you may theoretically determine to have been generated by the much more intelligent subconscious thinking mechanism within you), but then too; in the next split-second, you might realize also that what you are consciously thinking at the moment, might be worth sharing with your subconscious self; or in other words, we may potentially gain additional value by applying our intention-driven conscious thought, analytically considering the specific reasons why there might be this difference of perception, opinion, or inclination; related to the conscious versus subconscious thinking mechanisms within you.

In other words, I imagine that, for those having embraced the possible validity of these theoretical constructs, these individuals would likely begin regularly entertaining the notion, from time to time, that their conscious mind is inclining them to move in one given direction toward goal A; while their subconscious mind is inclining them to take a completely different and opposing course of action, towards instead, accomplishing goal B, for example.

I find that what develops, once having become aware that I am currently harboring oppositional, or otherwise conflicting inclinations, my new discipline of consciously-searching to discover exactly what ideas and considerations lie behind each of these opposing inclinations, often leads to a healthy interchange of information, sort of a back-and-forth revelation and subsequent reciprocal understanding of each component mind's beliefs and motives, as I imagine it; of which I am exerting some control over, with conscious intention.

So, rather than simply having a power struggle as to who is going to win out, (the conscious mind's objective or the subconscious mind's objective becoming exclusively strived towards), in terms of making some arbitrary emotionally-charged snap-decision, as to how you will immediately act or respond, in the circumstance; at the times when you feel conflicted over what you should or shouldn't do; it may become more of a reciprocally-educating exchange. In other words, having turned my conscious attention to a focused searching of my mind in this manner, invariably, as I imagine, each of my two thinking mechanisms ends up with a greater opportunity to learn how "the other half" thinks, so to speak.

Of course, before I began thinking in these theoretical terms, I consider that I was merely in a state of "not even being aware" of "all (of importance) that I am yet, unaware of;" but once I began sensing an awareness of the possible existence of two entities within me, this had enabled me to begin making theoretically- driven discoveries of all sorts; things such as, attempting to gain a theoretical sense of what my conscious mind's confined personality characteristics appear to be, and a theoretical awareness of the beliefs and values it appears to hold most dearly.

-And by virtue of sensing mixed feelings about some of these conceptions as being my "exclusively being possessive of;" in terms of what I might consider to define my overall person; I found I could then attempt to contrast this conscious world-view of mine, with what we might think of as a subconscious personality that theoretically is perhaps largely-defined by my highest ideals; and my greatest sense of possible potential virtue and integrity that I might personally think, and act in terms of.

Perhaps even more importantly, once we begin theoretically-considering that we effectively have at our disposal, a separate subconscious database to search, and are especially receptive to its own good potential to educate and incline our conscious mind in various advantageous directions, as a benevolent psychological force inclusive of our greatest sense of intelligence; once having conceived of the mechanism it uses to enlighten our conscious self (specifically, through making us aware of different types and degrees of feelings that our subconscious mechanism can prompt us to consciously feel, which will then give us the ability to bring the most important considerations of the moment, to conscious; via our conducting a conscious searching of ourselves, to run down what is at the source of these feelings we are being made aware of; ultimately defining, or recounting to ourselves, the groups of thoughts that gave these specific feelings rise and magnitude). Perhaps, this may actually be the essence of human, higher-level intelligence.

I suppose that usually, someone with a college degree writing about their knowledge on some specific subject, would implicitly be contending to <u>be</u> some sort of expert. Yet, I would contend rather that it is quite impossible for any of us to ever become even close to becoming an expert at understanding the human mind.

Probably the best we can do is to gain some amount of theoretical understanding, regarding a smaller set of characteristic components of our thought-processing capabilities, and our memory formation and retrieval; among a much larger and more-complex overall set of brain processes and functions. -But it appears that we can <u>indeed</u> insightfully rely on some of what we can figure out, in this respect; at least, at key times; or so I would contend.

If it helps readers feel any better, actually I do tend to think that I am as much of an expert on the subject of how our minds work, as any of us could be, at this stage in our evolutionary development. However, I also realize that there is always more, of importance to learn about the mind, than I could possibly begin to figure out on my own; and of course, I aspire to learn more from other avid scientists dabbling in this area of theoretical understanding.

I would contend that, because this yet smaller set of probabilities which we might come to usefully rely upon, may still be extremely helpful to the individual; we must vigilantly seek to prevent ourselves from becoming fully-inclined to throw out the entirety of conscious- subconscious theory, simply because a full analysis regarding the complete nature of the mechanistic workings of the brain, is not a subject that we can learn all about, with any certainty.

Quite inescapably, we all live according to our own theories:

One thing that I think we <u>can</u> be certain of, is that we all do embrace a certain set of theories, each one of us; and our belief in these theories leads us to make certain assumptions; and then we work within this framework to plot our course in life; although of course, our life course will obviously change, as our conceptions grow and change; and of course, as our opportunities may change, with our changing circumstances, as well.

I will be discussing certain theories, of which I consider many of us to be holding in common; these theories, of course, therefore becoming the basis for many assumptions, in common, that these ideas would naturally lead us toward embracing; and at least in my own mind, I believe I have effectively poked holes through many of these misconceptions which I intend to point out; having come to look at the way we think and behave, perhaps pretty differently than most others.

Although some may dispute the degree of widespread-ness with which the public, in general, might be embracing these perhaps false ideas; but I would assert that, in order for readers to consider any possible validity to what I am suggesting, it would be important for us to keep in mind that the whole point of my communicating to the world-at-large in this manner, is to suggest that within the fabric of society, there is a sizable extent and degree of false thinking, which I see that many of us seem to have fallen prey to; so I would hope that readers might at least become willing to consider the possible existence of the problem that I am trying to address.

I would therefore encourage readers to avoid bringing any arrogance into this area of discussion. After all, arrogance is a degree of smug certainty which probably leaves little potential for the individual to honestly consider that there is any possibility that, at least some of what they are feeling so certain of, may not actually be quite as they have been believing, to date.

The book title reflects the idea that we can use our imagination to formulate a reasonable probability as to which of our two (theoretically-imagined) thinking mechanisms is more-probably the source of various specific thoughts and feelings, as we are sensing them; and the book title also reflects my firm conviction that, any of us, could find this type of mental exercise to be considerably helpful, at times.

Conversely, at present, most of us seem to consider that only the thinking mechanism that functions while we are awake, or our conscious entity as I will refer to it, represents our pretty full ability to manage ourselves, and to hammer out any success we might have as a person. Yet, we each certainly are also inescapably aware that we have another aspect to our thinking, which I will refer to as our subconscious entity, which quite- evidently processes thoughts independently of our awake, or conscious, thinking mechanism; and this component of our mind appears to be processing thoughts perhaps at all times, even when we are asleep.

I imagine that perhaps most of us would generally consider that, what I conceive of as merely making up the conscious division of ourselves, will yet exclusively manage virtually everything we do, (a notion I might dispute).

On the other hand, as I would contend, many of us may not be very aware of the significant level of influence over our conscious thoughts, which the subconscious component of our minds may often exert.

However, it seems we also appear to have developed a pretty extensive conscious ability to drum out much of this potential subconscious influence, at times. I tend to think that unfortunately, we probably got a bit off-the-track; in terms of the unfolding of a naturally-more-healthy evolutionary design; at some point. We seem to have turned human-thinking-ability on its ear, by having instead, naturally developed the conscious mind's ability to usurp its subconscious master, so to speak; in such an unfortunately-effective way.

I would imagine that, more-commonly, many of us tend to consider our subconscious mind to be little more than an assistant; as opposed to potentially having any greater ability to more-intelligently manage our day-to- day affairs; greater, in other words, than the ability of our conscious thinking mechanism, which it seems that just- about-all-of-us generally feel that we must solely rely upon.

Yet, perhaps many of us can probably conceptualize that, in the process of its functioning, our conscious mind would basically have to access something of a database within us, which we might more-commonly refer to as our long-term memory perhaps; and we feel comfortably assured that almost anything we have ever learned or experienced can usually be called to the forefront of our mind; which is to say that we can intentionally become conscious of it, when we wish to recall it.

Probably some of us, already can conceptualize this type of a structure, to quite possibly be a proper characterization of the way our overall minds work; at least in a theoretical sense; and after considering the ideas and concepts I discuss here, I imagine that perhaps many more of us could begin to consider that, at least in a theoretical sense, the subconscious component of our mind inevitably must exist as actually a far-more-powerful thinking mechanism than our conscious mind; given that, again at least theoretically, it evidently holds all of this vast store of information and memories, usually in an impressively organized manner; and then beyond this, the subconscious mind also appears to have a much more powerful computational thought-processing capability as well; far superior to that of our conscious thinking mechanism, as I imagine it. I will talk more about that later.

Another aspect of our mental machinery seems to be that we can sense inner turmoil over conflicts involving opposing values and perspective between these two theoretical thought mechanisms (consciousness and subconsciousness) which I imagine to make up the entirety of the human mind; yet I imagine that pretty- universally among us, we will more-exclusively consider our true beliefs and values to exist in that part of our thinking mechanism which is active while we are awake; or in other words, within our conscious mind.

Alternately, I would contend that our more- important beliefs and values would logically become formulated within the subconscious division of our mind; and I tie this conception to another primary theory of mine, which is that the subconscious mind possesses an independent thought processing mechanism, possessing by nature, a much-more-facile ability to access and work with its own complete, intelligently-stored collection of all our knowledge, and memories.

Of course, I also consider that we just naturally become consciously aware of some of our subconscious ideas and values, at various points; and this makes trying to look at these two somewhat separate thinking mechanisms within us from separate points of view, much more complicated. However, again, I am simply starting off by defining some basic characteristics of each of these two entities, or thought-mechanisms, if you will. A little later, I plan to get to some of the more-complicated theoretical nuances of the interaction between our two component-minds;

asserting that we would do well to use our conscious thinking capability to usher and manage further information exchange than would naturally go on within us otherwise.

Coming back to the subject of "values" conflicts, I have been thinking that it also becomes apparent to us, during the times we are struggling with a decision, or trying to determine which is the most important value to take into consideration, in a given circumstance, at these times we might sense that although we are feeling pretty certain of which is the more important consideration we should be taking into account, on a conscious level; at the same time, we may also become somewhat aware of reservations, or of different ideas, or perhaps alternate values, for example; existing and maybe haunting us, within the back of our mind; or in other words, emanating from what we may consider as our subconscious mind.

The dilemma is that if we theoretically posit our subconscious mind to be far more intelligent, by nature, than our conscious mind, yet the conscious mind takes precedence, theoretically possessing our full potential, as far as our ultimate decision-making and the initiation of any of our actions; then as such, to the extent that our conscious entity has developed the ability to have a mind of its own; considering itself independent of any need to access the subconscious mind as a separate, monitoring force of intelligence and further thought-processing aid at times; then perhaps all-too-commonly, we may actually be thwarting the valuable input of our greater selves; in effect overriding the alternate set of different beliefs and values that would seem to exist within our far-more-intelligent subconscious mind.

Further considering my theoretical model, assuming that our subconsciously-computed values and perspective would have been calculated utilizing far more intelligent mental resources, then I would ask, shouldn't we indeed be representing this greater personage within us? -instead of mainly tailoring our behavior consistent with values and beliefs that have more-exclusively been developed using a much-less-sophisticated conscious thinking mechanism? I would emphasize this idea as being theoretically, quite considerable.

It is clear that we are really struggling, all over the world, as a race; and many of us are continually making relatively poor choices and decisions, as we move about in the world; even some of our most powerful national leaders, perhaps; considering that there seem to be so many out-of-control conflicts, and unjust actions being taken against each other, all over the world.

I would attribute much of this trouble we cause for ourselves and each other, to be coming about as a result of so many of us leading our lives more-exclusively using their conscious thinking mechanism which may perhaps all too often be pretty ignorant of their greater person; or in other words, their conscious mind might often be thwarting their subconscious mind's more-intelligent considerations, and seemingly-much-better leadership potential.

Yet, I seem to have personally found a solution to my own disadvantageous level of conscious insubordination, in this respect; and I offer it up to those who would read and consider what I have apparently discovered, or otherwise developed; in terms of a conceptual understanding of the human mind. I would say that, if we are to improve the alarming state of our world affairs, we <u>all</u> really need to embrace similar ways of looking at ourselves, and governing our behavior; maybe even to save ourselves from soon obliterating ourselves from the face of the earth!

Although this book may serve many possible purposes, its main purpose is two-fold:

One, to show us that, pretty surprisingly, perhaps most of us really don't know themselves well at all, in some pretty important respects; or at least many of us don't seem to be very well-aware of our true internal essence, mentally speaking. In fact, by embracing my theoretical constructs here, the more-enlightened of us could probably observe that many individuals are out of touch with even the most paramount values which define the greater fabric of their own overall personal intelligence; and yet, apparently many of these people probably don't even know it!

-And Two, the even-greater purpose of this book ultimately is to help each of us to eventually come to understand themselves much better, and on deeper levels; becoming in greater touch with ourselves in ways which will greatly improve our potential for effective and fulfilling living; both as individuals, and as a collective people.

To be sure, this book is not just offering some alternate philosophy that we may or may not want to consider; in a fickle sense; as suits our individual fancy; I actually imagine the embracing the types of ideas I discuss here, to be a do-or-die proposition; and I am afraid that we just may not understand how utterly grave and dangerous it is to continue living the way we do; without giving any more-careful thought and deference to what I imagine to constitute the greater inner substance of our highest intelligence, until it is just too late to save ourselves.

I do hope that we won't just keep disregarding these kinds of ideas pertaining to the apparent realities surrounding human mental structure, until we are past the brink of global self-destruction; and I certainly do imagine that we seem to be well-along, on the path toward self-annihilation, these days. This is not a joke; this is for real; I am being <u>dead</u> <u>serious.</u> And we may well <u>all</u> be dead soon if the great majority of us cannot become much more serious about growing out of our long-standing personally-neglectful ways. By this, I mean that we are neglecting to pay respect to that greater part of us which perhaps, a great many of us could possibly imagine to theoretically exist, as their subconscious mind.

Although I warn of great potential doom if we cannot interrupt our highly-disadvantageous ways; on the other hand, the types of newer theoretical discoveries that I offer here, could be seen to represent a treasure trove of enlightenment for any of us; and perhaps we may instead, be equally on the verge of a potential proliferation of human goodness, and highly- advantageous levels of interaction between us; provided we can grow, and expand in our theoretical conception of human mentality.

Which way will we decide? Will most of us even wake up to the fact that we do have an alternate direction that we could move in? Historically, perhaps it has been our sociological programming which has inclined us to simply continue doing things, and thinking, as we always have. Could we ever break through the barrier of time- honored tradition, in terms of our finally turning our attention to, and growing to consider a new, more effective approach, to managing our lives?

As for my having any credentials which might identify me as any type of authority regarding the psychology-related ideas I will be discussing, not only have I read many different kinds of psychology books and maintained an interest in psychology over the 43 years of my adulthood; but in terms of formal schooling, I have also more-recently received a degree in psychology; which means that I have had the benefit of becoming familiar with some of the most recent brain-related discoveries, and some newer theories which have been developed, as a result of these newer ideas and discoveries. Had I instead received my degree in psychology in 1976, when I was first of college graduation age, I would have missed out on being schooled on a great many advances which have been made in the field of psychology over the past 40 years.

During the past five years, prior to my starting to write this book, I had taken roughly two dozen psychology and brain-physiology-related college courses, covering some of the most updated areas of psychology- related knowledge we have gained in more recent decades.

Another main purpose in writing this book is to open the reader's mind to a variety of suggestions; not in a hypnotic sense, but more in the sense of our potential greater ability to "consider the possibilities."

Although my contentions here are merely theoretical in nature, this doesn't mean we can't begin to feel almost completely certain that this "two minds" idea may define what is actually true about our human thinking capability; utilizing some conceptual ideas that may be of great benefit for us to think in terms of.

To point out one universally-understood aspect in evidence of this "two minds" phenomenon, at least we <u>do</u> know for certain that virtually all of us will become aware, initially as young children, that we have a subconscious mind; in the sense that we each certainly come to realize we will commonly have dreams while we are asleep, which are created in a different division of our mind, if you will; than the conscious mind which, of course, only functions while we are awake.

Throughout this book, I will be using certain terminology, the connotations of which I assume will probably need to be defined better, so that the reader might suffer a minimum of possible confusion; hopefully gaining a better sense of clarity regarding the ideas that I will be trying to get across, from my having made this defining effort.

I plan to introduce these "word connotation" clarifications, in the general sense that I would like readers to think in terms of; as far as the meanings I wish to attach for my purposes here; as I use each term for the first time; and I also plan to list this set of the most-important and often-used words, in alphabetical order in the glossary at the back of the book; so that readers may refer to these perceptions (or conceptions) of mine again, when desired; while reading further into the book. Additionally, whenever

I use one of these terms in a different sense at any point in this writing, I will clarify the alternate meaning, at the time I am using the term.

Having defined my perception of the conscious versus the subconscious mind; in the sense I will mostly be referring to these somewhat-separate thinking processes, as I suggest we might begin to consider them; I suppose I should acknowledge that we are all probably well-aware of how our "subconscious" bears connection to our "conscious." (i.e.- these two divisions of our mind have obvious connection.) -And just to clarify, when I use "conscious" and "subconscious" to function as nouns within a sentence, as I just have; this is just "shorthand" for the "conscious thinking mechanism," or the "subconscious thinking mechanism."

Of course, some readers will have little idea of what these concepts might clearly mean as I intend, at first; but ultimately, coming to better-understand my theoretical conceptions of the conscious and subconscious minds will be a very important tenet, toward coming meaningful grasp the subject-matter I will be discussing, throughout this book. Therefore, I will begin by talking further regarding these two concepts, in the hopes that readers might more-quickly gain a good sense of how I have imagined that our mental structure appears to exist.

Before I begin defining a somewhat-larger group of terms that I will be using throughout, while attempting to get across the major tenets of this somewhat- revolutionary new philosophy, let me first define the few most-important terms which I will be using quite frequently. When I am talking about "perception," unless otherwise stated, I mean this more in the sense of "conception." (For example, my perception of religion is that it is based on considering God a reality of being; therefore, for example, I think it would be reasonable to consider the AA program as a form of "religion," even though AA members say it is not.

Instead, AA is commonly said by its members to be a "spiritual" program. (For some reason, it seems they intend to mask the apparent fact that AA is ostensibly a religion; I suppose this idea is spread to try and keep from turning off so many nonreligious problem drinkers who, nonetheless, need help.) - But in terms of my connotation of the word perception; more importantly, I am usually <u>not</u> referring to a perceptual process of the moment, such as a visual perceiving of something in front of our eyes, for example. Our perceptions of what is happening at the moment may differ of course, from individual to individual; but as in the AA example above, my intended connotation of perception describes how some particular idea might be more-universally understood by most. Throughout this book, I attempt to establish "common ground" ideas and concepts, that we could more-or-less all universally embrace, and use to good purpose.

Here within this writing, I will talk in terms of our potential to expose to ourselves, fallacies in our prior thinking; and of how coming to new realizations can sometimes be exponentially helpful to us. As an example, for years I have thought I was a decent writer; and I suppose that when the story naturally and chronologically has an inherent order to it; such as the storyline of a novel I might write; I think I probably do a decent job of this kind of creative writing; but in terms of laying out to others exactly what my cumulative theoretical thought developments have culminated into; in terms of providing the framework for a revolutionary philosophy I have come to live by much of the time; I see that I am merely a creative thinker; and very recently a good friend of mine, who is also a writer, helped me to realize that I am actually sorely lacking in my skills and organizational competence, in some senses; as far as being able to effectively layout the fundamentals of my cumulative thought developments along these lines.

And now, six months later, I have just come to realize that, in my earlier effort to present my ideas in the former version of this book, there appears to have been a great chasm of misconnection, in terms of any ability I might have had to state a convincing case regarding the significance of these ideas; all because I had actually done exactly what I most advocate that we avoid; which is to have made certain beliefs become facts within my mind; then trying to express these mere beliefs as facts of our existence, to others.

Reflecting on a meeting I recently had with my good friend helping me with presenting this material, I am reminded of how we can hear the same person express something repeatedly many times; such as at a mutually-attended weekly AA meeting over the years; perhaps not even realizing the more-full meaning, until we suddenly hear this expression from a different perspective; or in other words, once this expression is stated in a different context.

For example, I never knew quite what Chris was talking about when he talked of a "matrix moment" as being that nothing in the world had necessarily changed, but suddenly his perception had changed in some enlightened way in this moment; and, in a way, everything seemed suddenly different.

Up until this recent meeting, I seem to have thought to myself, who could argue that I am anything but a good writer; I have written half a dozen or more books, for Christ's sake! However, our meeting the other day was truly a "matrix moment" for me; my suddenly coming to understand just how short-of-the-mark my somewhat-laborious writing efforts had actually fallen; even given many hours of effort, over three years of continued effort at further-developing and writing about these theoretical ideas!

While having my first meeting to discuss the content of this book at this meeting with Chris, I began to realize that what I had written had only scratched the surface, in terms of more-clearly laying out the entirety of my thinking, on the subject of the significance of what I have discovered or otherwise figured out, regarding the way our minds seem to work; which, in fact maybe <u>should</u> ideally give everyone in the world a matrix moment; once they truly come to understand that we have been operating on the wrong assumption that the subconscious mind is simply to be tamed and controlled by our conscious resources.

Of course, to some extent, this is actually true; we certainly must maintain the ability to consciously manage our behavior pretty consistently. However, in addition, I imagine that we are usually best off looking to the subconscious entity within us, in order to have the benefit of garnering the most intelligent guidance we are capable of personally receiving.

This could seem confusing, because of course, in our initial attempts at doing anything new to us, or where we feel pretty-certain that we are faced with having to deal with a challenge we are not equipped to competently negotiate yet, it becomes most sensible to consult more of an authority in this area; but when it comes to feeling as though we are in familiar territory, in dealing with some present circumstance upon us, for example, I imagine that we are best-off merely consulting ourselves, or in other words, attempting to better-utilize our own subconscious mind's informational and memory-related resources.

I imagine that each of us has the ability to better- tap-into this greater subconscious personal resource, simply by turning their conscious attention toward "more keenly sensing" the nature and magnitude of their current feelings and inclinations of the moment, related to whatever situation or problem that they may be grappling with.

If we are able to focus our "conscious thinking-of- the-moment" on analyzing our (strongest and/or stronger) related-emotions and our sense of current inclination, to the best of our ability, we will probably develop good potential to realize many different considerations which are pertinent to helping us figure out the best ways to proceed in a given situation.

Actually, it seems that, not choosing to acting in this manner could be seen as ignorance in motion! In other words, it would seem that what many of us are doing, in this respect, constitutes ignoring your inner self's prompts, (theoretically in terms of its wanting you to keenly give thought to the nature and magnitude of emotions and inclinations related to the subject at hand), therefore dashing your good potential to consciously search yourself more-intensely than has been historically usual for you, in this manner.

The contended conscious competence we have all been embracing, that so many of us have been basing our communications and actions towards each other upon, is probably just a foolish bravado, I think. Perhaps, it is far better to try not to feel as though you need to impress upon others that you know exactly what to do, in all of your various ongoing situational circumstances.

It seems to me that it would undoubtedly be better for everyone, if each of us would instead, make our best attempts to effectively communicate whatever more- constructive thoughts and feelings we might feel naturally inclined to express, while moving through our fears and apprehensions to do so, to a greater extent; trying harder to work things out with the parties involved, wherever significant conflict or difficulty persists; as opposed to easily allowing ourselves to build anger and resentment, and ill feelings toward others.

Maybe our reservations about becoming more kindly expressive, as a means to resolve conflict may often have to do with a childish "not wanting to be at all friendly with someone who thinks like <u>that</u>!" (even though there could be many other areas where your thinking is in accord, perhaps). Maybe there is a general fear that if you <u>were</u> to become more calm and cooperative, ultimately, discussion may lead to your having to concede that certain aspects of your adversary's understanding are more grounded in truth and accuracy than your own, to some degree, coming into the argument; or maybe, even though your upset may not actually be due to anyone else's fault or cause, as Tolstoy writes, "it is hard for anyone who is dissatisfied <u>not</u> to blame someone else."

Yet, it seems truly evident that just about any two human beings have plenty of common ground; in that, in many ways, we all think and feel, in a manner that is consistent with our convictions, we are dealing with the same blessings and hardships related to our shared environment, and we all just want to feel, at least okay, if not supremely happy! Why don't we resolve, going forward, to foster negotiating and working things out in a respectful, cooperative spirit?

I find that this kind of communication usually not- only resolves a current conflict; it can also be further-educating; I'm thinking we should be educating each other more; not just declaring "gloves off" wars with each other. Yet, this often seems to be the way so many of us act and react; apparently even the leaders of the largest countries in the world, in some cases.

Again, I consider the essence of this simplemindedness to be our personal thwarting of taking any direction from our subconscious self; a greater entity within each of us, of which currently perhaps many of us might barely even have a nodding acquaintance with; instead obstinately doubting that any other possible consultation in the matter, with any other mental force besides their own conscious thinking mechanism, might be of any importance to pay any attention to, perhaps.

For example, so many of us seem to laugh off any possible significance of the dreams they have, while sleeping. I suppose it is easy enough to just think they are completely nonsensical, and not to be given any further thought to. -And yet, as I consider it, this dream- mechanism-form of communication, going on between our conscious and subconscious selves, which we can later consciously remember and think about, once we have awakened, just may provide us with the most paramount insight (into our true inner essence perhaps), that we have the ongoing potential to intuit for ourselves; at least, to the extent we might better-learn how to interpret the symbolic meaning within our dreams; in the context of our personal mental makeup, and our current position in life at the time of the dream.

Anyway, now that I have realized that I still have further good potential to try and introduce my ideas to others more effectively, with Chris's assistance, I seem to have become truly inspired to work even harder at getting across my points to the world at large; anticipating that I may well be able to garner ample assistance, perhaps for us, working together, to be able to paint a more-full picture of these important new ideas and principles, which I believe could perhaps vastly change the way we conduct ourselves, in ways that just may constitute a huge improvement in the state of humanity, in general; in time.

At this point, in the mind of an apt reader, perhaps this assertion could only seem to have come from one who is quite nuts! Of course, I might well have hesitated to speak in terms of such lofty ideals. However, then I got to thinking that maybe after reading about what I seem to have to offer here, to the world at large, many readers might possibly come to realize the great potential goodness that could come about, as a result of virtually all of us coming to understand and embrace this newer theoretical consideration process of viewing the workings of our minds, and conducting ourselves consistent with newly-developed convictions; as I seem to have, personally.

I have been developing and writing about this philosophy for almost 40 years now; and I have also been talking about different aspects of it to many of the people I've gotten to know better; and with not a lot of luck either. So, I do realize that quite obviously, it is not very easy to grasp this philosophy; and I suspect that the major reason why this is so, is that perhaps embracing it requires a type of faith which is not easy to Summon.

You see, all throughout the country, and really all over the world, religious leaders and the many religious services and publications collectively portray a very vivid image for people to grab onto, as far as making it easier for them to embrace not just a mild belief, but a firm conviction that God exists; as well as vivid impressions leading to firm convictions of precisely how He is said to interject involvement in the lives of each of us.

Now, personally I have a hard time believing this; but also, I am the first person I know, to vividly lay out an equally-sound image of contended reality concerning where our sense of enjoying valuable outside assistance has its true origins; I imagine it to actually be a second voice within our own head; the voice of our subconscious. Yet, in all honesty, I cannot contend this with any factual certainty; it's just that theoretically, my idea makes a lot more sense, if you think about it more carefully!

The philosophy described herein is moreover a broader general philosophy, which can newly be used as a basis for a different method of intentional employment of your conscious thought processes, potentially providing greater insight; and inclining you to remain more open to a greater variety of alternate (what may newly be considered as being truly possible) explanations for how things have come to be as they are; as well as a greater variety of (truly considerable) alternative possible behaviors to choose from, than you previously had the ability to conceive of yourself as being possibly willing to entertain; having limited yourself to a single strong conviction that there are no possibilities necessary to consider, you already know the true explanation; it's as God has arranged, right?

Well, personally, I wouldn't be so quick to utterly depend on this notion; yet, I can begin to understand how it is that so many of us may develop a sense of conviction, as to the existence of God.

But besides being seemingly as easy for me, to embrace conscious-subconscious theory as an apparent reality of our human mental workings, as for anyone else to embrace the contended existence of God; as well as my having become consistently-inclined to act; based upon this alternate notion; with strong conviction; I also consider that my inclination to live by the guiding light of my imagined human mental structure has led me toward making many personal improvements; and I imagine that embracing my ideas could help you too, to make improvements in how you might newly tend to conduct yourself, perhaps more effectively, as well as possibly helping you to perhaps, otherwise newly-become- overwhelmingly-inclined to (overtly) react to, and respond to others.

As the author of this book, I live by these principles myself; but regardless of my own track record, I suppose we must each gain a sense for ourselves, as to how much stock we might put into employing these suggested methods of viewing ourselves personally.

Although I have long conceived of the human mind as having a conscious and a subconscious division, I had not actually put together the concept of each of these two divisions of mind as having two separate personalities, until a few years ago; and at about the same time I also began to realize, at least in my imaginings, that our two somewhat-separate minds could be working against each other, to some extent, as well; this felt like a surprising revelation, but I explain this later.

These imaginings have not only piqued my curiosity, and led me to further expand my imagination in these directions; but I consider that they have also formed the basis to move in good directions, having embraced what I could only consider as a sound philosophy. I assure you that I remain quite sold on utilizing this philosophy to augment my thinking capacity, and behave to good purpose.

I would entreat any of us to try trusting that the prompts and ideas which will commonly come to you, that you can sense are probably coming from your subconscious thinking mechanism as a source, are pretty-consistently well-worth paying much attention to; and I would contend that trying to become in better touch with this conception of an alternate (inner) self, forms a basis for the beginning of a much more productively-interactive interchange between your own conscious and subconscious entities, if you will.

The true added value of this potentially-much- greater interchange lies in your establishing much greater contact with the mental component of you which is actually more the <u>real</u> you; in other words, you will perhaps be getting in much greater touch with the vast store of everything you know, of which the conscious thinking mechanism within you may only access a few tidbits of this larger human database of sorts, at any moment; you will, perhaps likely, just be spending a lot more moments, working on gaining this further access!

You may-well get to know a different "you" than you ever imagined was actually inside you; I know I have been surprised at what I further discovered about myself, much more often than I would have ever thought!

Perhaps somewhat unfortunately however, many of us have developed a conscious entity, or thinking mechanism, which may, in itself, have become pretty formidable in ability and scope; and this seems to be another reason why the people who I have discussed this philosophy with, over the years, have been so hesitant to believe it might be better to think in terms of operating by any other means, than sticking with the compartmentalized conscious thinking process they are so familiar with.

But, to be honest, I imagine that others just haven't yet bought what I am contending because they have already "bought" a different set of "beliefs-that- have-become-facts" within their own mind. It also seems impossibly hard, I imagine, for most, to face the fact that we can know almost nothing for certain in this world.

Smart people doubt everything and question everything because they have realized the folly in buying any idea or contention of any consequence, hook, line, and sinker.

I suppose I have been thinking in a uniquely- individual manner for many years now. To allude to a bit of the evidence of this, I've written several times in my books that I sort of feel like Galileo, in that I recognize that we are embracing and living by some fairly backwards false premises; and I have come to feel quite sure that I see something about humanity which seems to elude the common man, in general; apparently even some pretty intelligent souls.

Of course, I wouldn't wish to have a similar result, to how people reacted to Galileo! I am hopeful that instead, by attaining some much- needed help in figuring out how to lay out these ideas so that they will more- effectively reach the reader, I might be able to bring a valuable new body of knowledge, actually a fairly large set of newer knowledge, at that, to bear; hopefully, without having to suffer Galileo's type of fate!

CHAPTER 2

THE CONCEPTUAL CONSCIOUS AND SUBCONSCIOUS

Concerning the conscious and the subconscious; at the outset of course, I am offering that these two conceptual thinking processes which we might consider appear to exist within us, are possibly quite separate in many of the most important ways that we think of separateness, perhaps.

When it comes to a more-in-depth figuring out of ourselves on these theoretical levels, we could possibly be subject to much confusion at times; because it seems we may often have no idea which of our thoughts, are what we could classify as necessarily of a conscious, versus a subconscious nature; and yet, I imagine that once we have delved further into our understanding of this particular theoretical model of the human mind, we will begin to sense that, beyond the portion of our present-moment thinking that we could clearly sense as exclusively of a purely-conscious nature in the forefront of our present-moment thinking, I imagine that many of us also could begin to sense that there also appears to be some additional thinking going on within us, on perhaps a more-distant or removed level, from those thoughts in the forefront of our mind; which we could, at least somewhat-clearly define, as occurring beyond the scope of our purely- conscious thinking of the moment.

Once having read about this idea, and having then consciously directed ourselves to focus on an example of this "more-removed" sense of our thinking; which sort-of-automatically goes on churning, in the back of our mind; of which I'm pretty-certain that all of us gain a sense of this phenomena within at times; I imagine that many of us could see this as their first glimpse of, what we might newly begin to conceptualize as, our own individual subconscious thinking mechanism in action.

However, when beginning to entertain, a bit more regularly, the idea that we may have two different thinking mechanisms operating within us at the same time, and newly trying to gain a sense of which thinking mechanism is thinking which of our thoughts, these more-than-occasional aspects of uncertainty would seem to be a significant problem, in itself. Perhaps, this form of perplexing uncertainty could continue to plague us at times, indefinitely, unless we could better-learn how to establish some, more-reasonable form of sensible order; in terms of <u>which</u> of our thoughts and feelings to give most importance to guiding ourselves by, whenever we may have doubts, or conflicted thinking, for example, surrounding some issue of any importance to us.

We might be well-advised to strive toward potentially developing a more-useful theoretical understanding on these levels; or in other words, developing a greater ability to determine a level of considerable probability, as to which of these two entities within us, that any particularly-important feeling (or group of thoughts) seems to have been generated within, at the given moment.

Once having begun on this journey; of attempting to develop a more complex theoretical awareness in this respect; at this point, we may be well on the way to a world of self-driven-education, hopefully beginning to shed light on some of the more plaguing and confusing personal dilemmas within; such as our apparent compulsion to drink or drug, perhaps.

We have long understood that it is of great value to "know thyself," as it is said.

Wise philosophers may have interesting questions for us, such as, "Which is it, Might makes Right? –or Right makes Might?" Yet, it seems pretty clear that in our real-world setting, it is that Might Makes Right! Idealistically though, it should really be the other way around, shouldn't it? If we are incorrect, but so mighty that we can force our brand of understanding to be accepted, and our rules to be followed, or perhaps severe punishment will be the consequence for those who refuse, this is nothing less than oppression, is it not?

Looking at it from the opposite direction, if we correctly understand something important which seems to elude others; perhaps even a whole mass of people living with the less-enlightened ideas of the past, our pointing out to others that this is chiefly what is causing a big problem for us, perhaps should aptly turn all eyes toward those reasonably offering such observations and contentions; and perhaps, at least theoretically, these individuals <u>should</u> become mighty, in terms of becoming a force of intelligence to be recognized as more formidable, whom perhaps all of humanity might listen to more intently.

I imagine that, once having begun to believe that we seem to be newly developing some ability to see ourselves perhaps more as we really are; theoretically conceptualizing of ourselves as being of a dual psychological nature, as I have; we may potentially begin to analyze our thoughts and feelings in ways which, I have found, can help us to achieve greater personal effectiveness; and having been able to at least theoretically solve more of the mysteries, concerning the essence of our mental and emotional makeup in this respect, I imagine that accordingly, a great many of us might likely begin working more constructively, and enjoying greater peace of mind, as well as getting the chance to experience greater happiness more often, and more deeply as well, theoretically-speaking.

But some might ask, isn't it important to rely <u>only</u> on what we can be sure actually exists, as a reality of being, especially when deciding what to base coming to our important personal conceptions and decisions upon?

Yes; probably in most instances; but with regard to our sometimes feeling it necessary to develop plausible conjecture, related to various aspects of what indeed we could not possibly become entirely certain of, (for example, related to the precise (unknown) happenings leading to the development of a situation we are grappling with); and also, perhaps having more-newly become oriented to conscious- subconscious theory, I imagine that we would yet, come to feel as though "we probably owe it to ourselves" to at least make our best guess; in terms of determining related probabilities to bank on; perhaps, often ultimately becoming inclined to act based on these greater probabilities, as we consider them

Of course; as it is said; the truth is ever elusive; so in fact, how can we ever really be sure that what we think to be real and factual, is in fact a reflection of true reality? Personally, I imagine that we probably should not allow ourselves to feel quite so certain in these matters; and yet, I imagine that countless people all over the world to have been quite-effectively socialized (or in other words, societally programmed) consistent with cultural standards, to develop a firm sense of utter faith, as far as having accepted as factual, the contended reality that "God truly exists; of which there is no proof, of course; only evidence that supports each of our varying degrees of conviction on the matter.

Yet, in the Constitution, it says that we hold certain truths to be "self-evident;" like that we should see everyone as our equal; nothing less, nothing more; and such other mentally-healthy and reasonable principals. I imagine that, in time, our sensing, in common, of our psychological selves as actually being comprised of two individuals, will become as self- evident as our inalienable rights to freedom are to the average American. In my mind, the only question is in how long a time? Will it be ten years from now, or will it be many hundreds of years from now?

Certainly, it could seem like the blind leading the blind, while first attempting to consider looking at the individual in this theoretical light. However, as I begin grounding these newer imaginings, in ideas and concepts that many of us are already familiar with; perhaps the reader could begin to better-understand some fairly simple theoretical principles, that we all might usefully hang onto.

In the modern world of psychology, it is well known that, among the most effective ways that we learn something new, we "learn by association;" or in other words, by associating something we already know and are familiar with; as it is thought to apply to our understanding, as to the essence of some new idea or product we are becoming newly introduced to; contended to be of value to learn about, and to utilize; from this point, on.

For example, let's say that we grew up playing ping-pong; and using a thick rubber paddle, we learned how to put good "over-spin" and "backspin" on the ping- pong ball, quite well, over the years. Then, as an adult, if we take up tennis; the concept of putting an "over-spin" on the tennis ball will be very easy to associate with the similar wrist-movement we have well-developed, over our years of playing ping-pong; and it becomes more-likely that we will develop a good over-spin on the ball, on the tennis court, as well.

Concerning our general perception of reality, I imagine that most of us may probably rest assured that much of what we see as "real" may well be a constant that never changes, in our mind's eye; such as that when we are out in the wilderness there is surely ground under our feet. However, I also would imagine that perhaps at least some of our personal perceptions may be apt to change, in a somewhat fluid fashion, for those working toward becoming more theoretically-enlightened, in the directions that I am suggesting here.

Personally, I find that my picture of reality tends to continually evolve; in that I imagine myself to have been gaining an ever-expanding ongoing sense, of having (at least theoretically) solved some of the many mysteries regarding my own thinking processes; the more I am reasonably able to newly-imagine, in this respect.

More specifically, as I make continual attempts to get to know myself better, working within the framework of my imagined theoretical perspective, I enjoy an ongoing sense of becoming continually more-enlightened, as to various further nuances regarding the essence of my apparent inner nature; and by extension, I find I am also achieving an ongoing greater sense of enlightenment regarding the nature of what we all appear to share, in common; in terms of the many apparent basic functions of our human psychological thought mechanisms.

I see all sorts of indicators that I am making continual strides in my psychological development along these lines. For instance, some of the ideas I was inclined to express in my last go-around with writing this book almost kind of turn my stomach as I re-read them, at this point. I can see now that expressing my thoughts in the light that I had, could only be a turn-off to anyone who doesn't already share my convictions regarding my having attained a sense of near-certainty that our minds do work, in the manner that I have been theorizing about.

However, I have recently come to realize that I am probably much better off simply asking others to read of, and merely to consider, what I have personally been imagining, in this light; without insisting that we all must come to think in these terms.

Having gathered further perspective in recent months; as an example of how my ongoing developmental theorizing has helped me to grow in my understanding, learning ever more about the human condition; I leave in the following paragraph; that (I now can more-clearly see) would only make it seem to some, like I am full of myself, in some nutty way:

"If we could truly get a glimpse of stark reality, it might actually be pretty unusual looking, and quite strangely unique; as we begin to better glimpse it at various moments; at least I have found it so, upon developing these new ways of thinking about myself. I also suspect that many of those reading through this material will find my contentions and expressions to seem a bit odd, as a result."

If this, or any other passage I have written, does turn your stomach to read, I would ask you to try and disregard the particular passage in question, and read on anyway, unless this might happen too often for your taste!

Continuing on; as we go along in our lives, I can only imagine that for many of us, our perceptions of various aspects of what we see as the realities of life may change, as we view things from various different angles in the future. In other words, some of those aspects of life that we see today as a true reflection of reality, may not continue to appear as quite so unquestionably true, in the future; due to our experiences, or our future learning, otherwise.

One example of this might be in how it is common for any of us to "Jump to conclusions" at times; meaning that, for example, we may witness someone being nasty to another, apparently for no good reason as far as we can tell; and we might begin to feel as though the person saying these nasty things is just being an out-of-control jerk; or in other words, we have jumped to this conclusion; meaning this occurs to us as pretty-undoubtedly being the true reality of the situation.

But then, later we may learn that the person being yelled at had earlier spread a damaging rumor, or acted in some other unjustly-offensive manner; and at this point, your belief about the incident you saw indicating "nastiness for no good reason," and the conclusion you had earlier come to, that this person was "just being a jerk," might-well change, to considering that perhaps, they were somewhat justified in being a-bit- uncontrollably-angry, under the circumstances.

It is my understanding that scientists have more recently come to discover that it is the nature of our perception, to be subject to illusion or alteration from actual reality, within our minds, much more often than we might ever have imagined; and that, for example, some of the events we have experienced, that we will later retrieve from our memory, will sometimes be disputed by others who were also present, as to what really happened. Our perception is not always a snap- shop of reality, in every case; yet it seems that many of us behave as though it was; and of course, this can be problematic, for all concerned.

I imagine that we are all much-more aware, that we are subject to various <u>visual</u> illusions in common; for example, as a sculpture on the Southern Connecticut University campus in New Haven reveals, a large ball located at a distance from us, will look the same size to us as a smaller ball which is also in our line of vision, but nearer to us. Once we have walked toward the larger ball in this case, it becomes plain for us to see a big difference between the sizes of the two balls; which at first appeared to look the same size.

Many of us probably consider our eyes to be merely a window to our mind, giving us an accurate picture of what is <u>in front</u> of our eyes. However, scientists have discovered that our eyes themselves are merely sensors; and what they sense is carried into our brain as signals. From there, the brain processes these signals in order that it may interpret the signals as a picture. When we become subject to a visual illusion such as the ball sculpture just described, this illustrates an example of how the mental processes at work to give us a picture in our mind, our eyes are actually not truly able to provide us with an accurate reflection of reality, in a visual sense; yet we may well consider that as we look at the world, our eyes are providing us with a completely-accurate picture of visual reality.

In other words, visual illusions themselves, actually involve flawed mental processes, of sorts, which at times, can be pretty misleading; such as when we fall for a magic trick, and we can't see how we could possibly have been fooled.

So, although we might have been thinking all along, that a visual illusion is different from a possible mental illusion; of which I imagine, most of us don't really believe we ever experience, to any significant degree; in other words we might say to ourselves or anyone, "Mentally-speaking, I always see reality pretty clearly;" and this being the case, therefore perhaps we could have previously considered visual illusions as something different from a "false mental perception" one might have; but as we can see, this would really be an incorrect assumption.

Perhaps we might newly begin keeping in mind, that whatever we see visually, is basically just a mental process in motion within our brain; and not necessarily an accurate picture of what truly exists in front of our eyes; at least, not in every instance. Our vision is merely a mental perception which at times could deceive us; and likewise, it is also pretty inevitable that, at times, we will have a tendency to develop other types of false ideas, (that we may yet consider as realities), related to some of our (other-than-visual) perceptions as well; probably more often than we would like to think, perhaps.

Possibly as our further awareness develops, as a result of our new learning along the lines of the subject matter being discussed within this book, certain other aspects of our personal perception will expose themselves to us as illusions which we have previously been falling for; but perhaps not anymore; once we have become more theoretically-enlightened.

–And this is key to our progress and eventual recovery on many different levels; to discover where we are being tricked, and tricking ourselves. Some of us may discover that we are being tricked all over the place! –And by ourselves at least as much as by others; and perhaps, some of the illusions we have fallen prey to, may not have even been intentionally designed for us to stumble over; we have merely fooled ourselves, all on our own!

All the same, it seems that if we are to evolve at a more optimum rate, this is our charge: Wherever it is important, discover the nature of the trick, and don't get fooled again!

In terms of routing out aspects of our self- deception, from what we have been discussing in this respect, I imagine that many of us can see how it is of great importance, to continually work at improving our ongoing perceptive capabilities; and I also imagine it becomes more evident that the subconscious division of us; at least theoretically, could be conceived of as probably being much more intelligent, than the conscious element of our thinking capability.

-And to the extent that we might find these ideas and contentions to appear somewhat plausible, I believe we could also imagine our "subconscious self" as perhaps having much greater potential to become "hip to our tricks."

Therefore, if we can try to be especially sensitive to related subconscious prompts, in the form of "feelings of skepticism," theoretically we can improve our ability to steer clear of being tricked, more often; via running down exactly what is behind, or at the source of, our feelings of skepticism, in the heat of the moment.

Before we leave the subject, let's talk just a little further about beliefs. Although it is not as prevalent of a belief as in ages past, many of us contend to others that they believe in the existence of a perfect God as if he were indeed perfectly real. There certainly has never been any tangible proof of this, although we have all certainly heard the testaments of plenty of souls, to this effect.

On the opposite end of the belief spectrum, perhaps many of those who contend to be agnostics don't really believe that the true existence of God is even possibly real, in any way, shape, or form. They may merely pay it lip service.

In thinking further about this phenomenon, it occurs to me that; just as nonbelievers would be inclined to claim that God's existence may be a true reality, in order to relate to others more universally, and especially to avoid alienating others as much as possible; it probably follows that many of those who overtly characterize themselves "knowing in their heart" that God does truly exist, perhaps often speaking of their perceived evidence of this, and of how they intuit various signs of His presence and intended guidance, may sometimes be merely contended for the same basic reasons.

If so, wouldn't it be ironic, if people who were speaking to each other all the time, in terms of the reality of God and His perceived workings in their lives, merely were falsely expressing themselves, just in case more-than-a-few religious nut-jobs truly held these unwavering convictions; this perpetuating a chain of communications which were based on ideas that no one really believes?!

Of course, this may actually seem pretty doubtful; but personally, I tend to view it that, people immersed in religiosity in this fashion may simply be misinterpreting that these signs and interactions, sensed as coming from a higher power; or in other words, their sense of "another soul's aiding existence" within them, probably in fact, would have, as their true source, the individual's subconscious thinking mechanism; and they just haven't ever become oriented to thinking in terms of this theoretical possibility, to date.

Our entertaining of this, as possibly being the ultimate true reality of our human condition, would be given more ground yet, if we could begin to imagine this subconscious mechanism within, to exist as an individual, with a personality different from that of our "awake state" personage (that we are well-aware of; and indeed have always considered "our conscious being," in this respect, to be all there is, to our person). But I, for one, certainly have developed a strong sense that there is much more to me than who I am as an "awake state" personage; and my ideal of "conscious contact" (which is often spoken of, as an ideal to work at improving), is not being sought with an external God; but rather with this more-than-theoretical subconscious individual within me, as I see it.

Speaking a little further regarding false contentions and deception; we know that, at times, others may falsely contend to us that they "agree there is some possibility that what they are considering to exist as the realities of a particular situation," in the matter you are discussing, "could actually be different, than they seem to them at the moment," as though they believed there was at least some really miniscule possibility; within their mind; that they may actually have the wrong impression.

However, later it may become quite obvious that making this assertion conveniently at the moment, really amounted to the telling of an out-and-out lie.

People may simply use this strategy as a convenient tool, in an attempt to avoid remaining completely at odds with another whom they may be trying to manipulate in one direction or the other.

In the mind of such an individual, lying and hiding their real feelings of utter and doubtless certainty contrary to your own strong convictions, concerning their apparent perceptions surrounding a particular issue, perhaps is indeed often being employed as a good strategy on their part. Then too, quite possibly, if someone we are dealing with can avoid contending that they wholeheartedly see things differently, they may have embarked on this strategy so that they wouldn't have to listen to all of our own reasons, for believing differently than they did on the matter. -And if you think about it, what an effective way to hold onto whatever conceptions you had developed, and conclusions you had earlier-arrived at; by arranging it so that you don't even have to hear any arguments to the contrary! -But of course, this strategy is not very conducive to our becoming educated, as to what possible information or perspective we may be disadvantageously in the dark, regarding.

It can be a real eye-opener, to realize how mere beliefs can apparently pretty easily become utter certainties within someone's mind, at times. –And sometimes these impressions seem to remain permanently so, regardless of any number of sensible suggestions to the contrary. Sadly, it also seems that we may have no hope of straightening out these kinds of distorted and twisted perceptions, either in our own mind, or in the minds of others; unless we resolve to open our own minds to the possibility that any important aspect of what we see as real, should probably not be held unquestionably as such; and even our firmest beliefs probably should cease to become substituted as facts within our minds, unless some supposed reality, as we are inclined to feel certain of it as, were to somehow become utterly proven, beyond a shadow of a doubt; of which I imagine in most cases, (or in other words, regarding almost anything we could possibly come to believe), it would be pretty impossible to find this level of proof.

Yet, unfortunately it seems all too evident that, in quite a number of situations where there can be no firm proof, many of us have the false presence of mind to instead feel utterly certain of what, at least perhaps on some deeper level, they may actually sense to be at least a bit uncertain within them.

This perhaps constitutes further (theoretical) evidence; when considering the possible validity of the "two minds" idea; that apparently, the lesser-intelligent conscious (component entity) tries, and sometimes succeeds in selling our subconscious entity on, as well; that something that it (the conscious entity) is inclined to believe so strongly that it (unintelligently) considers it a "fact of reality," can be thought of, and depended upon as such.

I imagine that the only way that our being (as a whole) can avoid being bulldozed into believing various uncertainties in this manner, is to do our best to always try to raise a little doubt, even when contending something within ourselves; especially when we are entreated that it is only reasonable and best to have blind faith in something that we know there is no absolute proof of.

I would even encourage anyone to doubt that my theoretical perspective on human thinking, necessarily represents the true reality of our mental existence. Otherwise; if we were to consider it an utter reality of our mental structure; then perhaps others could all-too-easily stumble into the same pitfall I just did, in my last go-around at having presented "conscious-subconscious" theory (in the earlier version of this book), as an utter fact of our existence; thereby, having lost any good ability to sell my audience, on the idea that conscious-subconscious theory might be of significance to consider basing some of your future behavior and actions upon, at times.

However, having said this, I must confess that personally, I do stand strongly convicted that, in order to bring ourselves out of the deep hole we seem to have dug for ourselves, often perhaps really acting based upon masked false certainty; I suggest that we look to this framework of theoretical structure regarding our human thinking mechanisms; and to strive toward <u>getting</u> to, or rather "getting to know" ourselves better, on deeper levels of our person; and thereby, we would, theoretically, also be making more use of our highest sense of intelligence from within, in this respect.

-And how might we know when we are possibly embracing false certainty? Well, personally, I just ask myself whether there is any definitive proof, that what I am assuming to be an utter reality, that I am about to base taking some significant action based upon, really is an undeniable fact of life.

I imagine that, once we begin to start unwinding our "beliefs-become-facts;" through the conscious practice of "interjecting at least some shred of doubt;" any of us could more plainly see just how much we base quite a bit of our overall conception of reality, not only regarding our position in life; but we even base many of our important values perhaps, upon assumptions affirmed merely by our (pretty-blind) convictions; perhaps usually for which there is, quite honestly, no definitive proof to support, in any absolute informative sense; and accordingly, many of us may perhaps intelligently-develop the sense that there is almost nothing, in the realm of the many alternate beliefs we could possibly hold, (of which, nonetheless, we will pretty-inevitably still have to decide, between choosing to embrace either one, or another belief; as a "lesser-of-evils" proposition, at points), but concerning almost anything we could believe, almost none of our beliefs can actually be seen to have an indisputably- factual basis.

-And I say that our false certainty is masked, in that we are not consciously aware that we have chosen to rely on uncertainties; instead we have come to see some vastly unprovable ideas (i.e.- God exists?) as utter certainties.

However, in order to begin to unwind this dependence on, what we would objectively have to admit, are really not, known, indisputable facts; I imagine that we would have to challenge the very essence of our sociological programming, as youngsters growing up; and I also imagine that, most of us don't even consider that they actually have been quite strongly steered, (i.e.-sort of effectively hypnotized as to the realms and limits of what they will allow themselves to think and believe).

Really, the only way I see, (to undo some of the most detrimental aspects of what we have perhaps been effectively-programmed to falsely accept as undeniable truths), is for each of us to look to our one and only true, (yet of course, merely theoretical), individual (moral and directional) compass, of which I imagine that we can sense via searching our inner self. (In other words, ask away: i.e.- for example, do I feel entirely comfortable, through and through, with stating privately to myself, that God is most definitely real and present, and interactive, within my life? -or, maybe now that I have heard the suggestion that the inner voice, that I do certainly have a true sense "is real," of which I have sensed as "a different individual besides myself," which has been interacting with the awake "me," may simply be the subconscious division of my own mind? Am I maybe starting to feel as though this may be a bit more-likely-the-reality?

-And, for anyone who did privately answer themselves in like manner, their next rational thought might be, maybe I should begin considering this alternate possibility, as well…

I imagine that unless your inner self has become hopelessly contaminated by hypnotic false programming, you have become hopelessly brainwashed somehow, or have otherwise had the true autonomous individual completely socialized out of you, you are going to sense at least a little shred of doubt. (Personally, I have a huge amount of doubt about this).

But don't stop there; maybe try asking yourself (one question at a time per day perhaps) if working where you are working, living where you are living, being with who you are loving, etc… feels, with complete certainty, to be entirely comfortable to you, through and through; no reservations.

I imagine that anyone who is being completely honest with themselves is going to become in touch with at least some doubts. I would suggest that the nature and magnitude of those feelings of doubt are nothing less than prompts put into your conscious mind by your subconscious mind. Okay, this is only a theoretical supposition; but then if this is not a true reality, then how come thinking on these terms feels so valuable and rewarding, and as though it has helped me in so many meaningful ways?

I posit that querying your inner self is the very best way to become guided, in terms of a moral compass and bullshit detector, because theoretically speaking, our subconscious mind is where our greatest intelligence resides. Objectivity seems to be its middle name. For anyone who can't be entirely objective at this level, I pity both of us; you, for your lack of ability to judge; and me, for your lack of ability to judge!

But even if we can sense that what we have been buying as "really being the absolute truth," isn't really what we could consider, through and through, with every fiber of our person, the entirely and only truthful reality, in our estimation; well, if our conscious mind has been "buying it" for such a long time; and let's face it; I imagine that for most people reading this, up until now, in your own interpretation, your conscious mind has always historically been considered as the one true and only whole you; so it is not going to be easy to fight this.

In order to grasp at a fighting chance of getting out of your own way, in this respect; as I have imagined it; your conscious mind must train itself to follow its subconscious master's lead, from this point on. Again of course; this is all theoretical; but I can only imagine that you too will find great value in having begun to gain the sense that it is probably a good idea for you to take direction from your subconscious mind to some extent, through directing your conscious resources toward thinking further about, and paying heed to, various strong inclinations that emerge within you. I would advise us to "go with it," and don't be afraid to abandon hanging onto, and basing so much of what you have historically been utterly depending upon, (as the group of "solid realities" you have always pretty-much accepted on blind faith, really), stemming from your acceptance of old portended truths and realities, as they had perhaps been impressed upon you in your unformed youth, for example.

As I understand it, focusing on and thinking about what is "behind the formation of" our stronger inclinations, appears to have much potential to serve us in quite a variety of functional capacities. Although we may first come to rely on our newfound ability, (to "more-keenly focus" on what we are sensing, at the moment, to exist as our strongest inclinations), to provide us with a new and improved basis for considering what we may probably "owe it to ourselves" to go forward with, or to avoid doing any further, I imagine that, becoming more sensitive and attentive to examining our various inclinations, will not only have the potential to serve as a pretty-dependable moral compass; but I imagine this to be merely one component of the overall potential usefulness of sensing and considering what has caused your various stronger inclinations to form within you.

I imagine that making ongoing attempts to take direction from what we might sense as the separate and more-intelligent ideas being generated within the subconscious division of ourselves, to be moreover a <u>directional compass</u>, that will lead us, if we dare to follow, (it may feel risky at times), to an overall greater sense of human goodness; perhaps, often in more of a "delayed gratification" context; in other words, taking the initial steps in the plan may often require enduring some degree of challenge or discomfort, at first.

However, if things generally turn out like they seem-to-have for me, you may perhaps discover yourself to be engaging in some of the most rewarding and important activities, as well as forming more meaningful and rewarding developmental- relationships; of course, which also would seemingly have the potential to bring you an ongoing greater sense of love, joy, happiness, and fulfillment. (at least, I find that guiding myself via what I can imagine to be my own subconscious thoughts; and the feelings of inclination that will naturally develop within me once these groups of thoughts become intelligently processed within me, has typically worked out well for me.)

Alternately, as I think back on how I have historically often felt the need to squelch doing what I might <u>really</u> feel inclined to do or say, in so many instances; out of a sense of pragmatically having to force myself to move in more-acceptable, conventional directions; (in general, attempting to utterly conform to what others around me see as some narrower scope of supposedly-reasonable choices I might be relegated to choose from, under the circumstances); and formerly having always assumed that I must force myself to work within this dictated historical framework (which granted, provides comfort for the people I am living around); my breaking free from this bondage in some situations, often adds to my sense of independence;

even though going against the grain, in terms of having to endure of others' resulting displays of discomfort and disapproval, may sometimes constitute a considerable near-term disadvantage; but I find that sometimes it's worth it!

Yet, this is different from going on a consciously- planned willful bent; instead, it constitutes having the strength of character to put your trust in what you sense within you as a strongly desired aim; and accordingly working towards a valued goal, in this respect.

If newly making decisions and taking action based on the idea of listening to, and serving this strong and intelligent inner voice of competing direction (to the idea of conjuring up pragmatic consciously-developed strategies), is quite different from the way you have typically behaved historically in the past, it may seem a bit fearful at first; in terms of considering how others around you will react; but I have found that usually, others don't really much care which endeavors I really would like most to pursue, just as long as what I seem to be aiming at accomplishing is not potentially harmful, or bothersome to any extent.

In order to start making these types of potentially-positive changes, to the way we might more-typically conduct ourselves, it seems that we must begin effectively disarming our strong sense of conscious acceptance regarding the many contended truths that we may have always felt entirely certain "do hold true;" you know, just those accepted truths that; as of the next time you are about to predicate some decision or action on; you remember that some shadow of doubt has more-newly crossed your mind, as to whether you really have all-that-much unshakably-convincing evidence, to keep assuming a given truth, with such certainty. We could call it the willful practice of "suspending our disbelief," or in other words, refraining from "locking ourselves into" a firm sense of serious doubt, that any alternate idea or explanation could possibly be the true reality of the matter. This "suspending of our disbelief" concept seems to be a good way to augment our ability to "consider the possibilities."

Even if we are not comfortable in these realms, perhaps we would be well-advised to, at least, discontinue allowing this most serious overstepping of our conscious mind's power, as to fall prey to basically the surface-inclination, to close our minds, refusing to consider any other imaginable significant real possibility, other than what we have been more-blindly accepting all along, as the indisputable facts of life, (that we have always made our decisions, and taken our actions based-upon). It is my firm conviction that each of us should fight this denial, as much as is humanly possible for us.

With this goal in mind, we might do our best to honestly reconsider such possibilities as whether God may indeed exist; or whether maybe not?

Yet, on the other end of the spectrum of possible beliefs, in the case of an unbeliever, attempting to really try and open your mind up to consider that (what many others contend to definitely exist as a true reality of being), might be thought of, as having at least some miniscule possibility of being the true reality of the matter; even though we might have never really even once considered this before; this could be seen as having made a relatively healthy choice, both mentally and emotionally. In other words, rather than just accepting one "contended truth" of the matter, or one "utterly-believable explanation" for what has resulted, for example; making the choice to further entertain a wider number of possibilities; I imagine; is almost always a step in the right direction.

-And even if you can't conceive of the possibility that God may exist, for example, it seems that outwardly paying our respects to others who have come to believe something important to them, that we do not, could only help us to get along better with each other; and this we certainly might find well worth striving for.

Yet, we must keep in mind that there is a vast difference between behaving respectfully by not consistently disputing the alternative beliefs of others at every turn, and purposely deceiving them by giving them the false impression you believe as they do. This would rarely be helpful in the long run. I imagine many would agree that honest communication and a sense of respect for the beliefs and considerations of others is pretty essential to any meaningful ongoing relationship.

Here within this book, I present merely a group of theories and concepts I have dreamed up, which decidedly have inclined me to guide myself in a different manner than most, perhaps; but then again, it seems pretty-inevitable everyone else must also guide themselves consistent with their own group of theories which they hold, representing their own conception of reality.

-And whereas, in effect, concepts may be considered as certainties; theories, or rather the proof of them; by the definition of a theory, <u>cannot possibly</u> become a certainty. However, hopefully not to become too confusing; it is quite possible to prove certain theories to be incorrect; if a given theory indeed emerges as such, upon further investigation.

In fact, the eventual discovery that an earlier scientific theory doesn't hold water, may often actually lead to the development of a better and more-dependable theory in its place. In other words, coming to discover that you had the wrong impression earlier; realizing that maybe you were previously thinking stupidly to some extent; could have been just what you needed in order to more-constructively adjust your earlier apparent misconception; or in other words, mistakes and false impressions along the way seem to be a somewhat necessary part of any further good development; they are certainly nothing to be afraid of, within the realms of our honest ongoing attempts to uncover the truth.

However, "feeling-pretty-certain" that some important theory you have been considering is indeed a true reflection of reality, also has potential to incline you to depend on this, as you move forward with possibly developing various theoretical lines of thinking, such as I have here; which may even lead to the creation of a new useful product, or idea.

For example, Einstein apparently relied on the perceived correctness of some of the theories he had dreamed up, which led him to create the atom bomb; however accidentally. As many of us might consider, this single development changed everything about the way the world approaches war; also leading to our sudden paralyzing level of great fear of another country's offense potential. Our various "country-to-country" provocations seem to have become a lot more limited in scope ever since, in terms of the number of war casualties; and the leaders of many countries have since become much more careful and less unbridled, in their reactions to other countries they become in conflict with.

But the important point to consider here is that it was Einstein's dependence on what he felt certain he could bank on, in terms of the correctness of certain theories, which led to an amazing development.

It is also notable that in the years since, we have discovered that some of these theories were actually quite off-base! So, this illustrates how feeling "pretty certain," even of things which are not necessarily actually true, can still potentially help us to make important constructive developments. Yet, there is a <u>huge</u> difference between "feeling-pretty-certain," and harboring a "belief-become-fact" within your mind. The latter may erase all gains, perhaps.

Our ability to imagine concepts is arguably the most useful aspect of our imagination; as beyond opening our own minds up to important considerations, this may greatly help others to grasp some understanding of newly-considerable ideas, and sometimes hugely-beneficial principals.

Many of the most ingenious concepts that any single person will grasp, and make much useful sense of, can also be just as illuminating to many others, as well. Our ability to communicate to each other in such intelligent terms holds potential for the perpetual making of great advances; certainly in a technological sense; but I imagine that perhaps our most important potential is for further personal, and interpersonal development.

Many great minds have suggested in common, that as human beings, we are each a unique, fascinating wonder of nature, mentally-speaking. Even the simplest of could be considered somewhat mentally-complex, in that within the cauliflower-looking brain of each one of us, there are dozens of brain structures; it has been determined that theoretically, we all will have the same brain structures, which are little sections within our brain.

Speaking in more simplistic terms, basically, each one of these brain structures is located next to another brain structure which is also involved in completing certain more-common types of mental tasks which will require the working together of the two; as well as possibly other more-distant brain structures, to which neuronal signals can be sent back and forth to, as well.

It is understood that various ongoing chemical and electrical processes are carried out within each brain neuron, which can be stimulated or otherwise affected by another neuron situated next to it.

However, again in simple terms, we could consider these chain-like, sequentially-influencing interactive processes, apparently constituting various types of communication signals, will for example, effectively become generated within one brain structure; next traveling to other brain structures via these chains of neuronal signaling influence.

Given that we have established that the brain is entirely composed of neurons; wall-to-wall, including throughout every brain structure, in simple principle, the basic nature of neural communication often consists of one neuron after the other firing and setting off the next neuron in the chain; much like one domino falling on the next, in a chain of dominoes set up on a table. Theoretically, there are thousands of these chains firing throughout our brain at every moment; working together to form our thoughts, which will ultimately lead us to carry out our many different possible behaviors. As we consider the great complexity inherent in the mental workings of even the most simpleminded person, it is easy to see how anyone's mind could be aptly regarded as being of an extremely complex nature.

Yet physically-speaking, we all have basically the same attributes and body parts; and we all share the same physical world of material goods and machines, for example. I imagine that this should probably tell us something about where we should be heading, in our further research regarding ourselves, and our world.

Attempting to gain further insight into each person's uniqueness of mind, on a personal level, appears to have incredible potential to lead us toward richer lives.

Perhaps, having newly become somewhat intrigued as a result of considering the ideas and arguments I have presented thus far; while continually trying to remain flexible as to what we <u>may</u> more-objectively become inclined to "come to believe," may certainly have the potential to expand our thinking in relatively healthy ways; whereas, it may even likely be a kind of mental <u>sickness</u>, to close our minds so often, to the possibilities that might come to mind otherwise.

Had we not apparently sold ourselves certainty, at least on a conscious level; convincing ourselves, perhaps in a false knowing sense, of what the one true explanation is, for something that has happened, or come into existence, for example; I imagine we may begin to consider a much greater number of possible explanations for what is happening within us, and around us.

Perhaps, we have been accepting various explanations as absolute certainties, across a myriad of different aspects of life; having apparently accepted only one; of perhaps many possible alternate explanations we might otherwise have been inclined to consider, then perhaps we have merely relegated ourselves to thinking in terms of a very limited number of possible reasons for why we might be best off moving merely in one "exclusively-considerable" direction all the time; and I suppose we have also relegated ourselves to believing in the certainty of it being best to think in terms of one "singly-considerable" solution, as to how to deal with each of our problems; necessarily resulting in our becoming "exclusively-inclined" to undergo only a "singly-considerable" process; such as working to embrace a certain program of recovery that was recommended to us.

We learn, even as children, that there is more than one way to skin a cat.

CHAPTER 3

THEORIZING, TO A MORE EXPANSIVE DEGREE

I find that theorizing is very important to my well- being. Obviously, you can't tell yourself to sit down and come up with a theory, at will. What I mean is that, as you are contemplating whether to take one action, or another, for instance, it can make an important difference to the outcome of this decision, if you look at the simple basics of probability regarding the situation, in the context of conscious-subconscious theory.

For example, often I find that one of the options I am considering points me away from danger and risk; while the other option I am considering may be offering me a degree of excitement or immediate gratification; and I may-well find myself trying to rationalize that the riskier option is still better for me to choose, because it promises me a much greater probable level of excitement and fun.

Let's take my earlier example, of bungee-jumping. You could rationalize that it is safe enough; thousands of people do it every year, and you never really hear of people dying from it (even though this may only be because you never come into contact with reports on this aspect of it, for various reasons). However, you probably don't have to be standing looking over a high bridge with one tied around you, to imagine how fearful you would be at jumping off and plunging hundreds of feet straight down! This should tell a reasonably intelligent person that they are intrinsically aware of a real danger attached to engaging in this activity; regardless of any suppose-ed convincing arguments to the contrary!

I ask you, isn't life exciting and stressful enough without taking such foolish risks, just for a cheap thrill?! Even speculating on a volatile stock would be a better option, in order to try and experience the thrill of having taken a bold risk that paid off handsomely, in some instances. At least there is probably no possibility that you would die from this!

My point is that you would be wise to bet on the theoretical probability that this voice within your head telling you to avoid bungee-jumping, is the more intelligent inner you; the subconscious component of your overall thinking mechanism. It is evident to me that playing these kinds of sensible probabilities is the only way to go, for the most part. I find that life will still be plenty exciting and risky, quite enough of the time.

Of course, we are not perfect, and we can all-too- easily be seduced by the part of the mind that throws caution to the wind; in fact, I even doubt that the idea of throwing caution to the wind is what ultimately moves us to do foolishly-risky things. Rather, our making of these types of decisions is perhaps mainly due to our imaginative ability to convince ourselves that nothing bad will happen to us, because we will be careful enough, and smart enough, to manage controlling the perceived possible risks. Yet, of course, sometimes we will fall short of the mark, and fail miserably; in terms of our ultimately not having had the ability to avert these potential detriments and consequences; therefore causing ourselves and/or others significant harm.

This form of wishful thinking illustrates one example of how we tend to sabotage ourselves, without any clue of how unwise our consciously-conjured best-laid plans may often be. Yet, in my mind, it seems we have only to listen to the right voice inside our head in order to avoid great tragedy and atrocity, in connection with our misguided following of the wrong inclinations, in a given situation.

So, this is what this writing is all about: the forces of inclination. – And the big question is: How might we effectively examine our senses of inclination and disinclination; and thus, keep ourselves on a trouble-free path, to the extent this is possible for any of us.

We must resign ourselves to the fact that we are going to make mistakes; and for starters, we must forgive ourselves, resign ourselves to suffer any necessary consequences which may be upon us; as a result of having made a foolish decision, or given-in to an unfortunate whim; and

I imagine that we probably must also strive to do this with a minimum of self-deprecation; moving on in a spirit of the humble plotting of progress.

This would seem to give us the ability to learn, and to often benefit from past stupidity on our part. It occurs to me that the smartest among us is still pretty stupid about some things, at times; but if we truly have redeeming qualities to our person, there would seem to be some probability of our forging a level of overall success, over the long haul; at least if we can go much farther to straighten out our false thinking, in the heat of the moment.

I tend to find that the good life is all about spirit; the spirit with which we go about our day; and this could potentially change, day-to-day; even minute-to-minute sometimes. Our happy state could be dashed by a single piece of new information; our depression could lift, even with one kiss from the right person, perhaps.

Of course, it seems impossibly difficult to stay aware of all important aspects of your situation, always making the best decisions in response to this overview, on a minute-to-minute basis. Personally, I have to settle for coming to periodic epiphanies, where I suddenly realize that one simple corrective move on my part can effectively free my clouded spirit, and allow me to go forth with a renewed sense of balance, comfort, and the pleasant sense of excitement and optimism that often accompanies this.

-And sometimes it takes so long for me to see how I have been punishing myself; meaning that I imagine my brighter inner-intelligent self will, at times, purposely sabotage the effective execution so my consciously-

devised plan, in order to prevent me from attaining the satisfaction I might otherwise bring about for myself. I imagine that this subconscious strategy might occasionally be put into effect in circumstances where my underlying motive constituted an immediate-gratification- related plan, which my baser conscious-self has been trying to bend the rules to provide an unjust benefit for myself.

At these times, I will end up suffering a downtrodden spirit, theoretically by subconscious design; and it also seems that my greater (subconscious) self won't allow my overall spirits to be lifted (i.e.- returning me to my previous level of having fun, satisfaction and comfort) until I comply with its wishes, that I have been thwarting with unknowing stupidity, masquerading as a clever plan within my beady little conscious thinking mechanism; although this idea may be hard for readers to swallow, at this point in my explanation.

It seems all too easy, for any of us, to forget that our conscious mind, at least theoretically, really doesn't fully run the show; the way I see it. Personally, I have come to realize this, more and more these days.

Yet, I'd have to guess that virtually everyone I know, views it that they do very-much, completely run the show, solely with their conscious efforts, in terms of managing the present, and the future of their lives. I sense that this conception appears to be quite common; even rampant, in my view!

However, I have learned to live differently in this respect; I say instead, sit back and relax, and let your smart inner-intelligent self communicate its inclinations to you. Then, play the smart probabilities.

I have actually found that, with the help of reliance on this complementary set of theories I have developed, of which I imagine others could also learn to employ. I find that it is often pretty simple to determine, in all probability, which of the two theoretical voices in my head is the rational, sensible one.

Although in general I would advocate that we employ liberal strategies most often, this is one conservative strategy I do recommend. In other words, at a time when the potential indulgence or excitement of something you are contemplating doing seems to be beckoning you, if there you can sense that another voice within you; or train of thought, or however you might picture your alternate entity to exist, is providing you with a sense of fear over the risks at hand; I would recommend that you listen to that voice, as the voice of reason you should guide yourself by, at this moment; and to let go of your propensity to do otherwise.

I imagine that just about any of us would still consider that life is quite eventful, and thrillingly dangerous enough, even if you start to play it this safe (betting on the relative intelligence of making one in particular, of your possible alternative decisions and actions; via pretty-strictly utilizing a conservative strategy grounded in the principal of making theoretical determinations regarding the greater probabilities, as you might begin to imagine them). I offer that life will still be plenty exciting because, for example, there seems to be plenty of times when you will have little choice but to take a risk, in order to avoid certain detriment or setbacks otherwise; and there's also bound to be various other situations where taking some sort of risk seems to be the most reasonable option for you, in certain situations.

Although it would probably seem a little dubious for me to contend pretty-much having utter certainty that, not arguing with yourself on this level, and not falsely trying to rationalize the purported safety and benefits of allowing yourself to be operate outside of what you can sense as your inner self's "comfort zone," in this respect; but I actually do feel pretty certain that this is the best way to manage a continuing good life, for any and all of us. This is actually the major theory that this whole book will revolve around.

I would be the first to admit, that I have not consistently behaved in this manner; certainly not in my own more-distant past; and in some senses, I have paid a dear price for this. Here I am, now at retirement age, finally arriving at a strong sense of realization regarding what has been at the center of my previous propensity to act all-too-often based upon errant inclinations; (not that we don't all have errant inclinations, to some extent); but for the most part, ever since I have gotten hip to my consciously-planned strategies that perhaps tend to be disregarding of my greater self's concerns; for at least the past several years, I seem to have instead been taking action, mainly based on honoring my strongest inclinations; that is, after having more-carefully thought through my situational position, with an eye toward achieving what I can sense as being my subconscious mind's aims, as well as toward protecting my relatively- healthy interests, as I am able to discern them. In addition, I seem to have become much more acutely- aware that it is very important to "give ear" to <u>all</u> seemingly-significant inner messages and feedback, going on between my ears, at the moment; and trying to avoid allowing myself to feel <u>so</u> sure of myself, as to charge ahead with taking actions to attain my immediate desirable end, without a second thought.

Of course, these behavioral ideals constitute merely the most basic concepts and principals, of which I am trying to suggest that others could benefit from embracing for themselves. I have also been looking pretty closely at various types of more-complex influences over our thinking, and particularly those factors having greater influence on the natural formation of our feelings of inclination, and disinclination. Here, I am often looking at thoughts almost as equations with a logical answer; often involving several larger groups of related thoughts of some importance; which will often culminate into particularly strong feelings within us; and even into somewhat-automatically-planned strategies occurring to us, at times. This type of "automatic" thought-processing function I am of course theoretically attributing to the subconscious element within our minds.

Although distinguishing between internal "voices," so to speak, is indeed my greater aim, I am certainly also well-aware that it is not always that simple to determine for yourself, who's the smart inner person perhaps trying to reason intelligently, within you; when faced with a significant number and degree of conflicting thoughts and feelings, for example. -And indeed, to complicate matters further, the conscious self also brings much valuable awareness and integral thinking capability into the mix; not to be ignored or discounted.

No, it seems that the greater challenge is in figuring out how to integrate the two somewhat-separate thinking mechanisms in the most successful ways. —But first, we must begin to see them as at least partially separate. However, of course, this is where things can seem to get confusingly-complex; given that vastly expanded consideration of new, perhaps even more- obscure possibilities, can become so mentally and emotionally taxing at times, that it may even border on causing us some form of insanity!

I suppose it isn't safe to go too far beyond more- conventional realms of reasonable imagination, in this respect. Yet, I can understand how it might seem confusing, to first be advised to try and expand the number of possibilities we might consider; and then to be given the opposite suggestion, that we will want to try and limit the number of possibilities we will allow ourselves to consider, at any moment.

-But you see, although it can sometimes be exhilarating (the idea that the possibilities are infinite,) the smartest of us also know, (as we begin to embrace the idea that almost anything, perhaps quite unlikely even, could unexpectedly happen anyway), that we can't afford to go very far down that rabbit hole, without going pretty nuts!

On the other hand, as seductive as it can be to fully invest ourselves exclusively in only playing the probabilities; in terms of basing all our decisions and actions upon these narrow guidelines; we also owe it to ourselves not to rule out somewhat-less-probable possibilities which may yet, seem more-reasonable for the intelligent individual to consider might happen, or be the case. For example, let's say a single guy goes to a social event, and there are two very attractive ladies that catch his eye, and a couple of other reasonably-attractive ladies who would yet be more comfortable for him to approach, because they are not so "tongue-tieingly pretty and more-likely out of his league," he still may sense that he is inclined to first approach one of the pretty ones, if he has managed to keep his mind opened to the possibility that she might find him interesting and alluring; even though he may consider that he would probably have a better chance of successfully approaching one of the ladies that were more of what he would consider are more "in his league," so to speak.

Also, in terms of occasionally considering taking "a long shot" at something, some people might almost never consider such ideas as being the least bit sensible; but I have found that, in situations where the stakes are not high, in terms of what I might lose if the long-shot doesn't come in as I had hoped, it can be fun and exciting to gamble a pittance on a long-shot.

I typically look at it as an indicator, of an overbearing "consciously-self-controlling" disposition, when I encounter people who more-consistently snuff out any consideration of such frivolities. I also consider them to be sacrificing some amount of potential fulfillment and excitement, by not being the least bit open to considering, that it may not be that foolish to sometimes "bet on the unexpected" to possibly happen; because I imagine that it is within our (relatively-healthy) nature, to yearn to be a bit carefree and adventurous at times, and to want to give ourselves a break from always being completely sensible and pragmatic in our approach to everything we do.

Always maintaining a dismissive attitude toward gambling on, or otherwise investing any of your time and energy, in terms of betting on anything to develop or occur, other than based-upon what you can determine to be the probabilities related to the matter, appears perhaps to be another rampant shortcoming among those who consider themselves most pragmatically logical and sensible.

However, perhaps most of us just naturally will have competing inclinations to sometimes do something unlikely; something fondly mischievous maybe; or just something frivolous and fun. If you can't ever submit yourself to any such urges, I see this as possible evidence that you are snuffing out the significance of the input and ideas of your inner self, perhaps.

This humbug attitude which may often lead to argument with others, that will at times see value in stepping a little outside the purely-logical; and this resistance and disapproval, of course, can be so maddening to anyone trying to keep alive the exciting possibility of an "unlikely dream that might come true," by planning to make a relatively small, hopeful investment on a "longer-odds" proposition, or potential opportunity, for example.

In other words, we might occasionally buy a lottery ticket, or invest a pittance on a long-shot otherwise; especially where a good-sized reward of some kind is at least remotely possible for us to attain, in so doing. It's not that this is necessarily so important, from the standpoint of what we might more-likely gain by our unlikely-successful speculation; but it can sometimes raise our spirits and our sense of hopeful and exciting optimism; and I imagine that engaging in this activity every-so-often would also be a helpful reminder, that we do ourselves a great favor by doing our best to break out of our otherwise-never-ending pattern of perpetually assuming and tending to believe only that which we have always assumed and believed. What's that Porgy and Bess song, "It ain't necessarily so!" -and then too, continually endeavoring to be responsible and sensible all the time doesn't have to mean that we can't have a little fun along the way, as well!

CHAPTER 4

MENTALITY IS PHYSIOLOGY

I've learned from my recent college courses that, at least regarding every "psychological event" of any impact, it has been established that there is a corresponding "physiological event" occurring within the brain, which of course, theoretically is the true origin of any specific thought or emotion we might sense or become aware of. Although I have historically given much consideration to the mentality behind emotion (i.e.- the development of an emotion you sense, appears to be the intelligently-computed conclusion you have come to, after a certain group of related thoughts you are considering, have been "mentally processed," related to the given subject at hand), but I had never imagined such a significant association between our mentality, and our physical bodily functions (in this case, specific physiological brain "electro-chemical activity," corresponding to our every thought and emotion).

It's kind of mind-blowing that every mental thought is a neural event, in terms of a chemical and electrical phenomenon theoretically associated with the formation of every last one of our thoughts and feelings.

That statement has me thinking; if each separate thought is represented by a certain electro-chemical action within a certain brain region; then, my theoretically positing this to be the case; and also that a group of associated thoughts are, at first being considered, or processed; and it is only the completed task of, for example, drawing together, or drawing from these thoughts a conclusion, that has taken the form of an inclination we can sense within us; then I ask myself, does the manufacture of that feeling simply involve, or is it perhaps made up of, the electro-chemical fingerprint, so to speak, of how someday we might be able to identify each thought considered in the process?

Thinking further about this automatic "drawing- together" mental process of considering the ramifications of each thought, within a related group of thoughts; (that I suppose each reminds us of the next thought that becomes a part of this particular cumulative group of thoughts); culminating in the ultimate development of an (end-product) inclination that we will sense awareness of; (i.e.- the eventual finite collective of thoughts we are drawing together in order to reach an intelligent conclusion); the question I ask myself is, does the brain physiology occurring simultaneously while the more- impactful feeling of inclination is developing, merely consist of the combined electro-chemical thought action collectively-generated in order to come to this intelligent conclusion? I tend to suspect this, because inclinations feel "as if a light has gone off in your head," we say; or at least we could probably all relate to an effective surge of energy and excitement that we can sense, at the moment we have figured something out; and also, when considering the degree of strength of an inclination we are sensing, this mental sense, might physiologically correspond with "the combined electro-chemical thought action collectively-generated in order to come to this intelligent conclusion," as well?

-But I digress; going back to the idea, that every thought theoretically is a neural event, involving electro- chemical action; it's interesting how, as far as I am aware, even many smart people perhaps, often have no conception of this. A "Brain event," like a stroke for instance, is thought of as something that just happens, independent of any mental cause; Yet, I can only imagine that many scientists in this day and age would consider, as I do, that all brain events, at least by theoretical definition, are mental events at the same time.

Could it be that if we take utmost care of ourselves, in terms of ongoing management of our mental and emotional condition, we may be able to avoid ever having a stroke? (This is one example of the type of interesting possibilities we might begin to consider, having opened up our minds a bit more due to these revolutionary theoretical imaginings, regarding human mental structure.)

Well, perhaps even many of the smartest people I know, would not tend to think in these terms; and this sets me to wondering, how smart (really), is a person who we generally consider, is really smart?!

I actually imagine that perhaps, each of us may indeed have much potential to grow, in our personal level of intelligence, due to having newly-embraced conscious- subconscious theory. -And assuming that the vast majority of us eventually might grow to depend, as I have, upon what we can theoretically determine exists as the specific structural nature of the mental forces at work within our minds; each of us working out various useful probabilities that help us to make more-intelligent and beneficial decisions, which we may then base our actions upon, then it would seem pretty inevitable that the society of mankind, as a whole, would achieve our greater potential to become exponentially-more intelligent.

Societally-speaking, perhaps our more-typical conception of superior intelligence; or how we might define the generally-accepted attributes, or the level of apparent adeptness and capability that will lead to the general public's widespread observance of a "smart person," these conventional measures are certainly of great worth to consider.

Yet, even though a small percentage of the people we know, or have heard of or read about, are clearly much smarter than we are, it could be that maybe even these people couldn't really be that smart, compared to how much more-intelligent they may become, by having augmented their degree of effective internal communication, perhaps having more-newly considered themselves possessive of a mental structure comprised of two, somewhat-independent thought mechanisms, of which our challenge is to mediate their effective teamwork.

We know that there are many brilliant people in the world; yet, as I can only imagine, so many of us appear to have missed grasping the most important conceptual feature of the workings of the human mind; namely that it appears to be of a dual nature, in my estimation.

As I also can only imagine, many of us appear quite convinced that only a few of us are much smarter than all of the rest of us; and yet, on the other hand, many of us also tend to think we are a lot more intelligent than we actually are!

Since thinking this way could only constitute the embracing of a paradoxical idea; that many of us yet may typically be holding onto; I consider this to be a further indication of our heavy reliance on independently- conscious plans and ideas, that we perhaps foolishly rely upon all too often; considering that many of us apparently believe that their strong conscious conceptions and perceptions seem pretty infallible. I am, more and more, coming to realize that they most certainly are not!

However, I find that there do appear to be ways to more-objectively evaluate your relative level of intelligence; and your absolute level of intelligence as well, perhaps; but I imagine this can only be reasonably self-assessed via our ultimate sense that the "consciousness of thought" we all typically have solely relied on to guide ourselves by, theoretically has a (subconscious) partner it can communicate much more frequently and effectively with, to much greater benefit.

However, it occurs to me that you won't ever develop the ability to more-objectively evaluate yourself if, for example, you are one of those who can't ever really feel it was "fair enough," when someone has done something against you. I conceptualize that, in order to see more clearly and objectively, you will have to effectively grow (pretty much all the way) up, first; in terms of your basic overall grasp of the importance of honesty-with-self; as well as having achieved greater maturity of character. -And as far as I can see, it seems that many of us just haven't been able to accomplish this, no matter how many years of age they may have eventually attained!

It seems obvious that a great many of us see themselves as being pretty mature; yet it appears to me, as I interact with others on a variety of different levels, that so many of us are not!

The way I see it, maturity cannot be assumed to accompany intelligence, for example; it seems you could be very intelligent, yet quite immature.

You could be commanding; be able to come down hard on people; maybe you have a 327 hemi under the hood; but that's actually the opposite of being assertive; perhaps it just amounts to having an overly-aggressive "parent" ego state, technically speaking; and as I have observed, this could often lead to a degree of disadvantageous thinking and acting.

Oddly enough, I would consider that real assertiveness looks more-mild in nature. Perhaps, the epitome of assertiveness is basically explaining what you want, while trying to help others explain to you what they want. Given its somewhat-counterintuitive nature, I suppose it isn't any wonder why real maturity and assertiveness could be so elusive!

As I imagine it, in order to act with reasonable maturity and assertiveness, it seems you must effectively achieve the combination of acting in milder ways, yet without allowing yourself to be taken advantage of, to any degree.

It seems reasonable to assume that each of us has a great pool of knowledge and experience, held within their subconscious mind; and yet most of us, so far, just haven't seemed to learn much about how to more-effectively tap into these worthy personal resources, in the much-more-effective manner that I am describing. In other words, I believe that we're all pretty intelligent, in terms of the holdings within our subconscious self; but perhaps we're too busy, more-exclusively using our somewhat-stupid conscious self to make our decisions and base our actions upon; and we lose out big, as far as having the more exponential levels of success that we would seem otherwise capable of, in my view.

Of course, I cannot reasonably contend this "two individuals within" idea to be any more than a theoretical imagining of mine; and therefore you would think I have reservations, as to the definitiveness of my convictions to this effect. However, after having spent many years basically "trying on" this belief for size, I suppose that at some point, just naturally, I eventually came to believe in this apparent reality, more and more firmly; while continually testing this theory using my own lines of thinking; and as I have been going through my own personal life experiences. At this point, I seem to have become quite certain of our dual nature in this respect; so, even though others might remain skeptical at this point, I don't want to leave you with the impression that I personally have any doubts!

-But of course, objectively speaking, I'd also have to admit that I have been kind of a screw-up all my life, as I have wrestled with this completely independent- minded lifetime exploratory expedition, from which I feel I have ultimately somewhat-mastered a solid theoretical understanding of many of the workings of the human mind. More typically in my more-distant past, I was prone to feel as though I didn't possess much social capability, in terms of knowing what to say in order to fit in well with the popular crowd; I suppose that I had not been clever or socially-inclined enough to surround myself with conventionally-smart people; which I suppose just begot more obscure ways of looking at things, and thinking, in general.

Perhaps, my only redeeming value would be my awareness that, beyond the awake person that is the "me" others may come to know, I have an inner intelligence; that I had come to imagine as of about three years ago; like it was a revelation to me; is really a separate individual unto itself; unto himself, of course, because I'm a guy. It's me. But it's not me, really. I'm just the putz that represents him; somewhat stupidly at times, I might add. But he seems to be as smart as anyone; and he is trying to make me smart too; perhaps, he just has a huge challenge on that front!

Well, how about that- It may not be so crazy after all, to talk about yourself using the third person! –But this can be socially confusing, of course. How do you explain that you are you; but you are not really you; you are only part of you. This sounds pretty ridiculous! But you see, I have also come to realize that I don't really have to be more than I really am, in this respect; instead I must intelligently come to accept whatever outer level of intelligence I seem to possess; remembering that the smart person inside is pulling the puppet strings, to the extent I can attain the wisdom, and the capacity to allow it.

The way I see it, I just have to listen to him, and take direction; be the eyes and ears, and the quintessential servant to him. –And yes, obviously, at this point in time, people would think you were nuts, if you tried to portray yourself socially as consisting of two individuals. I imagine that presently, this represents a huge stumbling block, for any of us, to making optimum personal progress through embracing these ideas; and unfortunately, perhaps it will continue to be a formidable stumbling block, for quite some time into the future.

As far as coming to accept my having taken the actions I am most strongly inclined to go through with at any moment (after first, hesitating; for further, more- thorough analysis of my person, and my situation); I don't find it that emotionally difficult; not nearly as much as I fretted whether I was doing the best thing, before coming to understand myself in this theoretical light.

However, sometimes I tend to wonder, and to doubt myself a bit, even while I see myself as somewhat- safely "acting in a servant capacity," (to my subconscious self, at least in my imagining). For example, I have felt, at times during my initial stages of writing this manuscript, that perhaps this whole book is kind of stupid so far; but at least, by this point in my developmental theorizing and descriptive writing endeavors, I feel I have learned that it's not really my job to judge; as I see it.

I hope it doesn't sound too ridiculous to express it this way; but conceptually-speaking, I'm just supposed to sit here and move my fingers for him, in effect. -And of course, I follow inclinations to do much editing! –But we could certainly ask, does this kind of apparent absurdity really amount to a much better way of life for us all?!

I suppose you will have to judge this for yourself; but beyond considering how "attempting to embrace" these concepts might make your character and personality appear a little nutty to others at times, perhaps; it may follow that, to the extent you might develop some amount of conviction, due to the significant improvements you sense, in managing to intuit further understanding of yourself, through positing the existence of a second psychological entity separately adding its own input to your conscious thoughts; (in other words, I sense a more-powerfully-intelligent individual sharing and adding perspective to my awake-state conscious thoughts within my head); maybe like me, you might also find this theoretical insight worth compromising some of your vanity for, in this respect.

Then, there is the idea that some of the most influential people in my life are going to think that, since I am writing about hearing voices in my head, this is simply an indication that my medication needs to be adjusted!

But of course, I use this "voices" concept simply as a figure of speech. I suppose I should more accurately characterize what I am talking about as "trains of thought," rather than voices in my head. It's just that many times, I've heard people say that they heard a little voice inside their head telling them something like, just forget it; or let's not do this again; or don't bother; or maybe it's time to quit, etc…

But I like the idea of thinking of each of these trains of thought to be representing the voice of one (of two possible particular thinking sources), because then it makes it easier to imagine ourselves as two individuals housed together within one body; a bit like Siamese twins!

You might think that although at first, I probably would have had to take the conscious position that this is all merely theoretical; and that I would have had to start with the premise that the "two individuals" idea might only be a figment of my imagination. But to be honest, it had pretty suddenly struck me at once, that each of us exists as two individuals; and soon after, it suddenly made sense that many of us may often be fighting it out for dominance; the certainty became pretty real to me, very quickly, once I got on to this idea.

At close to this "aha" moment of revelation, I was thinking about the movie, "2001," where Hal, the on- board computer for the space ship upon which this movie takes place, slowly develops a mind of its own devoid of any greater perspective; and it methodically carries out calculated malfunctions that eventually kill off the entire crew; thinking this would ensure its best potential future. It suddenly struck me that powerful leaders think and act this way, too; sending their countries into war, for example.

-And I do consider this to represent at least one advanced aspect of my conscious self; I had developed the ability to strongly sense consciously, as though resounding within every fiber of my whole being, that my inner self has made an important discovery about human nature, that perhaps would go way over the heads of almost everyone. I find some truths, possibly like this one, to be amazingly counter-intuitive!

But the idea of a dual identity has been an extremely useful concept for me to embrace; and the further I have developed along these lines of thinking, as a basis for making continual attempts to objectively evaluate my current point of view related to some matter at hand; ultimately helping me to develop further perspective on various matters of relative importance; it seems the better I have come to understand my more basic motivations; and therefore the relative forces of strength behind the inclinations that develop within me, from moment to moment; which I hold is very important to anyone's ongoing well-being and progress.

You may have noticed that I have begun to transition into talking about my theories as if they were a reality, regarding the proposed structure of our minds, relative to our thought-processing capabilities. I suppose this somewhat-gradual transition is a bit like that of the format of the AA step book; in that, in the beginning steps, it first suggests that it is not important to feel a sense of conviction as to the contended actual existence of God; but then at some point in the middle of the book, it begins to portray how it is pretty-essential to view God as a reality, and not merely to consider that a "higher power concept" is minimally all that is necessary in order to make dependable use of the suggestions of the AA program.

In like fashion, I too had started out presenting my ideas about the structure of our human mentality in an entirely theoretical manner; and then somewhere along the way, I began to portray this theoretical mental-processing-structure also as a reality of being. I suppose this amounts to attempting a form of seduction, as AA literature certainly is designed, of course.

However, even though reasonably, I would always have to admit that my ideas are purely theoretical in nature, I seem to find it most useful to think of them as if they were a reality of being. I suppose that I have taken on a definitive conception of the existence of the conscious and subconscious minds due to my impression that it has never really hurt me to adopt this stance, and to consider everything from this viewpoint. I consider that trying to intuit distinctions as to the origin of my thoughts and feelings has pretty-much always been relatively harmless; while I seem to have developed a strong conviction that it almost always has been helpful to see myself and my circumstances in this light.

When I compare the basis for my own convictions on this level, with that of the believer in God, I also consider that the basis for my way of thinking and believing makes much more sense, than merely believing in something so nebulous, dubious and nonspecific. If a benevolent loving external God is at the helm, there can be no reasonable explanation for why people inflict horribly-painful, and vastly-destructive atrocities upon each other relentlessly; and why there is so much injustice happening to us, and all around us. What a crock that this is necessary by his design; and that ours is not to question, but to accept what the infinitely-wise God has seen fit to do! At some point, a great number of us are going to have to wise up to this, if we are ever to avert our ultimate mass-self-destruction; as in World War 3 maybe.

Alternately, I simply consider that it is our unregulated conscious minds; at least those of a great many of us perhaps; that is causing and perpetuating this great trouble for us; I think that any half-way mature, reasonable person reading of what I am laying out here within this book, should be able to follow the evidence I have gathered which supports this idea.

I imagine that the main reason why thinking in these terms has always seemed valuable to me, is that I believe this to provide me with a way of gaining valid perspective on almost any matter at hand; and the gaining of perspective regarding whatever we are dealing with at the moment would seem consistently helpful to us.

I have also found that I can depend on certain principals to universally-apply, such as that when I say to myself that "no one will be the wiser" if I do something out of favor secretly, for example, or any of a whole host of other bright ideas I can delude myself into thinking, through various rationalizations and wishful thinking; I can be certain that these are not thoughts representative of the smart person from within. Of course, I certainly realize that there are times when my situation demands that I try to finesse getting away with trying something secret and shady perhaps; but only when it appears I am totally screwed, if I don't at-least try to help myself out of a bad situation, utilizing some more-calculated minimally-risky strategy.

However, I should disclose that in my past, there have been many times where my trying to get away with something, was being attempted more as a potential enhancement to my enjoyment, or my standard of living; and not as any kind of necessary last resort, to save me from calamity or anything.

By now I've learned that, with very little exception, I owe it to myself generally to throw out any possible validity to my considering of certain types of ideas, such as "no one will be the wiser," when contemplating sensible alternative strategies, one of which I may ultimately feel most strongly moved to put into effect.

Although taking certain types of "otherwise considerable" strategies "off the table," within my universe of considerable options, involves sacrificing certain benefits I would gain by getting away with cheating when nobody is looking, for example, I find it exceedingly advantageous to remain ready to make this sacrifice willingly; especially when the potential consequences are more-grave, in the case where someone does find out that I have done something secretly sinister (foiling what I thought I could probably effectively-hide, in this respect.) I have learned to see taking the position of "simply refusing to risk employing short-sighted conscious strategies" as being a dependable "blanket policy," in terms of it pretty-consistently constituting the lesser of evils for me.

I consider that these kinds of realizations are helping me to avoid pitfalls, and perhaps saving me from many of the types of troublesome dilemmas I managed to bring upon myself in the past.

Of course, my careful self-examination becomes an increasingly more-complex task; the longer I stay at it; as I find that my ongoing search toward getting to know myself better reveals deeper aspects of my person, which I slowly and gradually am able to digest, and then try to make sense of, over time.

Making sense of human emotional developments, in terms of understanding the factors leading to the formation and development of an inclination, and communicating my imagined insights into the nature of human mental and emotional complexities, these are the kinds of helpful things I intend to write about.

In order to illustrate what I mean by saying it is important to trace emotional developments, and look for the essence of the "good sense" that our emotions become formed on the basis of, let me throw out a "for instance."

For example, I could initially develop an inclination to confront someone I suspect has deceived me; and then when I approach this person, he could contend that my thinking is way off, trying to belittle me in front of his friends; but if it continues to become increasingly more- evident to me, from all he says in the next few minutes of our bantering conversation, that he is just trying to throw me off the trail of suspicion that I seem to have latched onto; and yet, if it follows that every time I think I have effectively cornered him into admitting his ill deed, he craftily thinks up some further fabricated story, or deceptive ploy; all the while trying to insinuate that I am being daft and ridiculous, in front of his friends; then my inclination to really try to catch this slippery bastard in a lie, and nail him for the nasty shit he has pulled against me; you could see the good sense behind the idea that the strength of this inclination would be apt to naturally grow in intensity.

Not that the above example points out anything significant in itself; I state this example merely to orient the reader to the type of trains of thought and emotion I am studying and writing about; looking more-closely at the complexities of thought and emotion which drive inclinations that seem to have many influences, in terms of related thoughts and feelings the individual will become in touch with, during the formation of a stronger inclination.

Much of what I have been able to explain in this regard, stems mainly from looking back on my own personal past, and recalling examples of past bouts of my own inner dialogue; that I can perhaps examine with greater perspective, now that I have more-recently become better-enabled to determine precisely how, and why, I was seductively tempted to lead myself astray, through some consciously-perceived shortcut to success that turned into a disaster instead; and yet, as a result of my more-newly developed perspective, I have since become able to stop myself from making foolish, troublesome choices and decisions, more-consistently in recent years.

CHAPTER 5

WITHIN US EACH, THERE APPEAR TO BE TWO SETS OF INCLINATIONS

Again, I must reiterate that all of my personal contentions here, are purely theoretical; but I hope that many of you will become curious to try "acting as if" my theoretical perspective were a true reality, in terms of existing as the actual structure of human thinking capability. "Act as if," as an arguably-useful concept, is actually one of the suggestions you will commonly hear at an AA meeting, even though I don't believe this is written anywhere in AA literature. But I think there's a lot of common recognition that embracing this concept can very effectively empower us, perhaps to a surprising extent.

But for our purposes here, I am making a strong recommendation that readers "try on for size" the notion of acting as if our minds <u>are</u> truly structured with a conscious division, and a subconscious division.

At the end of the last chapter, I explained how I believe that viewing ourselves from this standpoint can often be very beneficial; and it appears to be a rarity that this is the least bit detrimental; at least in my own experience; as I remember.

Assuming that you have come to a decision to try out analyzing your thoughts, with the "two selves within" concept in mind, if we at least theoretically assume that there are indeed two separate minds within, this would mean there also must be two separate sets of inclinations; or in other words, two distinct sources of inclination.

Whereas, identifying which inclinations are coming from the conscious (versus the subconscious) mind can sometimes be difficult and a little uncertain; I find that making reasonable assumptions, as to the isolated origin, of conscious versus subconscious trains of thought, can bring about good ability to discover valuable information about ourselves, while also deepening our perspective in other ways, too.

I will start us off by contending that if we think more carefully about it, it seems pretty clear that; other than purely physical pain, or other physical sensitivities such as hunger and muscle fatigue; (certainly all of our feelings of inclination, at least), are made up of groups of thoughts which lead us to some reasonable conclusion or judgment.

I find that if I think about one of my feelings of inclination in the moment, I can almost always trace it back to the thoughts that led to the development of this inclination; and I'm pretty sure that almost anyone would be able to analyze their mental operations in this fashion. (i.e.- I'm happy right now (a feeling) because (three thoughts) I am standing in an ice cream shop, I just ordered a chocolate ice cream cone, and I love chocolate!)

-Or when it comes to feelings of disinclination, an example might be; I'm not inclined to go back to that auto repair shop because I tend to believe the owner is a bit of a crooked double-talker; and I have not had good experience with getting timely repairs at a reasonable dollar value at this shop, in the past.

I state the obvious here, because I find that people don't usually think of their feelings of inclination as being determined like an arithmetic problem (I have two, I add two; so now I have four.)

Another way that we can use an "arithmetic" concept, to make some sense of "the strength" of one of our emotions, in terms of what we feel more strongly inclined to do in a certain situation; versus perhaps other inclinations we may be aware of at the same time, that are not as strong; is to conceptually "add-up" the impactful factors that come to mind as we are assessing a given situation.

For example, let me dream up a simplistic scenario, that you have been invited by three different friends to spend the afternoon together; and each friend has invited you to join them in a different activity; and let's also say that you are similarly close with each of these friends.

Let's give your friends names: Bob invites you to go bowling, Joe invites you to a movie that you are interested in seeing; and Tom invites you to his house to go swimming in his pool.

Let's say that all three had texted you while you are out shopping and you had left your phone on the front seat of your car; so you just got home, and you see the three texts; and the scenario is that you have to decide who's invitation you're going to accept, over the other two.

So you think about Bob's invite to go bowling, and it comes to mind that although Bob lives near the bowling alley, it's a 20 minute drive for you to meet him there; and although Bob is a really good buddy, in the past he has often brought his little brother who likes to tag along; but he can be a bit obnoxious; then you remember that your shoulder's still a little sore; even though it's not too sore to bowl, necessarily.

So then you start thinking about Joe's invite; you've heard that this movie is really good, from a few other friends; and you've been looking forward to finding a time to go see it; but the movie doesn't start until 3:00, so he has invited you to join him for a late lunch at a nearby restaurant; but then you remember that you just spent a bunch of money shopping, and it will use up almost all your cash, to pay for your ticket and lunch; but you could stop at the ATM on the way, if you didn't mind breaking into your savings a little.

So then you think about Tom's invite to come over and go swimming in his pool. You consider that you haven't seen Tom much in the last few weeks; and that when you've been over to his house before his wife always makes good hors d'oeuvres, like nacho's, or guacamole, and she's pretty attractive to look at; plus she has a fun personality; and you recollect that often tom's sister often hangs out around the pool on hot days like this; and she can add to the fun usually; and then in addition, you could conserve your cash, after your shopping spree.

So let's add the pluses and minuses; Bob's invite has three minuses; it's a long drive; he is apt to have his obnoxious little brother come along; and your shoulder's a bit sore.

Thinking about Joe's invite, the (3) pluses are that the movie is good, you were looking forward to seeing it, and now you have an immediate opportunity to. However, the (2) minuses are that you have three hours to kill until the movie starts, and you would really rather avoid spending the money you would have to for the movie ticket and lunch; as you are a bit cash-poor at the moment.

But in considering Tom's invite, the (4) pluses are that you'd really like to catch up with Tom, as you hadn't seen him as much recently; you like the idea of Tom's wife possibly being around, you're likely to get good eats while conserving your cash today; and it is somewhat likely that Tom sister will be around too.

Of course, there could be many other subtle factors that would influence the strength of your inclinations in such matters; but in some senses, just the mere number of significant positive factors – versus- negative factors related to each possible choice, often make it pretty quickly evident which is the best choice.

I was thinking about conscious strategies versus what we could consider as subconscious strategies, concerning the same problem that we are faced with solving. If I'm experiencing a problem that whenever my cat jumps up on my lap while I am having my coffee and cigar out on the back deck, she needs her claws into my lap for several seconds, as her natural habit of preparing a place to lie down; but those little needle claws are sharp!

So let's say I go out and get a book on how to train your cat; and it has a very pragmatic strategy that it recommends for just such a situation; which is to lightly slap the cat, and say "no," gently, but emphatically.

Now this could make sense to someone looking for direction and having a problem such as this; and of course, you don't need to get a book on training your cat, to come up with this idea of how to solve the problem.

But this is my point; this "giving the cat a light slap" was a consciously devised strategy;(oh what's the problem? Okay, I can think of a way to solve this.)

Well, after having done this several times; it didn't seem to have any good effect, at getting the cat to stop prickling me when she jumped up on my lap. The only way it helped the problem was that it inclined her to jump in my lap less often; but I don't want to upset the cat, and I like it when she lays in my lap while I'm having my cigar and coffee.

So one day, I'm sitting out there with my coffee and my cigar, and I'm not really focusing on anything, my mind was just wandering; and the cat jumped up in my lap and began to needle her little claws into me as usual; but I was lost in thought; so instead of consciously reacting, I noticed that just naturally I became inclined to move my hand with the coffee cup and it, slowly towards her nose.

First of all, this action distracted her, and demanded her attention, so she pulled her head back a little, and she stopped scratching. I noticed that this was having a good effect; but then a couple of seconds later she would start needling me again; so I just repeated it, slowly moving the cup back toward her nose again, and after doing this two or three times, she just laid down in my lap without doing the needling!

I would say this is a good example of how much more effective it is for us to guide ourselves by subconscious input, rather than consciously conjured plans and strategies.

But there was even a much nicer benefit that came about as a result of my remembering to move the coffee cup toward her when she started scratching me, immediately after jumping in my lap, over the next several days; because now she often jumps up in my lap and lies down without doing the needling. In short, I effectively taught her something important instantly, through an automatic subconscious strategy I carried through with, without even thinking about it; yet I had tried several consciously-conjured ideas and strategies literally for years, before I figured this out.

And as soon as I did figure this out, it came to me that, what a stupid idea, to even very lightly slap a cat; or even to raise your voice to a cat; cats are so skittish; all this does is alarm the cat, and in an excited state like that, how could a cat learn anything?!!

But you see, I couldn't tell that it was a very stupid strategy, until I had easily solved the problem through other-than-conscious means; and another reason why this never occurred to me before perhaps, is that this is a very widely used conscious strategy to deal with an unruly cat; give it a little slap and yell at it!

You see, we are all doing stupid things, and advising others to do the same stupid things; through writing "how to" books, for example; all because devising conscious strategies has always been the best we think we could do, in terms of trying to deal with our problems.

But the good news is that we could certainly change that relatively ineffective (or at least much less effective) approach to solving the bulk of our problems, perhaps; simply by merely getting in better touch with the superior resources of our subconscious selves.

So, going back to my above example of getting these three invites from Bob, Joe, and Tom; let us explore what we could consider as the consciously intuited factors involved with coming to a decision about which activity you might ultimately decide to do; contrasting this with some (imagined, for illustrative purposes) subconscious input that would interject itself as you are carrying through with your decided plan.

So when we last left off, you had decided to head over to Tom's house to spend the afternoon socializing and swimming in Tom's pool. But suppose you had gotten your car and were driving along, with the conscious intention to head straight over to Tom's house; but your mind was wandering and you were thinking of something not even having anything to do with these three invites, and then you suddenly realize that without thinking about it, you had made a turn, and you realize that you were instead right on course toward heading to Bob's house instead. Now you certainly could cuss, and immediately turn around and get back on course to head over to Tom's.

However, if we were to put conscious-subconscious theory into action regarding the situation instead, it may have occurred to you that there was something important that you really wanted to talk to Bob about; which had slipped your mind during the time you were making this decision to go to Tom's and swim in his pool instead.

And then in addition, you suddenly remembered that Bob had told you last week, that his little brother would be going off to camp for three weeks, so he would not be around to tag along if you were to instead go bowling with Bob.

You might then consider the possibility that your more-intelligent subconscious mind was in the process of altering your decision as you were driving along; and you now start to believe that maybe going bowling with Bob was a better decision, after all.

But then you sense this feeling that it might be upsetting to Tom, if he was really looking forward to you coming over to spend the afternoon with him around his pool. Then suddenly you feel an overwhelming inclination to pull over, and you decide that you will call Tom to see if this is the case.

So you call Tom, and you tell them that you had also received an invite from Bob to go bowling this afternoon, and you ask Tom if he would mind, if you did that instead of coming over to his house. So if Tom tells you that that's not a problem; because as it turns out, a couple of other friends were coming over as well; and he reminds you that he would be seeing you at the baseball game tomorrow anyway; you come to realize that your concern over upsetting Tom by changing your plans doesn't really seem to be of any object.

So at this point, you call Bob back, and tell him that you decided that you'd rather go bowling with him, if he hadn't made plans to do something else instead, by that point. And then you end up meeting Bob at the bowling alley.

So if we attempt to analyze what has altogether happened in the course of the previous hour, we might first realize that the most we could do, of course, is to identify various possibilities and probabilities regarding the situation, related to your initial plans, and your ultimate change in plans; but I think we can see that this could still be of some value.

First off, we might note that it is pretty impossible to completely isolate the thinking that goes on within our mind related to some specific situation, as being of an entirely conscious, or an entirely subconscious nature; and of course this is all theoretical anyway; because of course, even if we were to assume that we do in fact have two separate thinking mechanisms, it would also seem pretty evident that these two thinking mechanisms pretty clearly would pass thoughts, feelings, and ideas back and forth, as we move through our considerations of the moment.

However, I find it most useful to identify certain thinking processes involved, which would appear to primarily exist as a conscious idea or strategy perhaps, as being an "entirely" conscious-thinking-mechanism-generated phenomena, just for simplicity's sake.

Certainly, it would seem that any time we might be able to effectively "simplify" aspects of the complexity of our overall thinking capacity, for purposes of our analysis, this could be seen as most helpful.

-And in like manner, it would appear to be similarly useful to identify thinking processes which appear to be mainly of a subconscious nature perhaps, as conceptually being of an "entirely" subconscious nature; or in other words, labeling it simply as being a subconsciously- generated thinking process.

So with this in mind, let us start by identifying all of the initial considerations that I had first listed regarding Bob, Joe, and Tom's invites, as consciously- generated considerations. In other words, for simplicity's sake, we will divorce any subconscious input that (theoretically, in all probability) did contribute to your having come to these realizations of the various significant factors which immediately came to mind; or rather that you had become consciously aware of; in your first go-around of considering which way we might decide.

And then further, let us identify your loss of conscious focus while you were first driving to Tom's to go swimming, (and your sudden new consideration that maybe it would be better to go bowling with Bob, after all); for simplicity sake, let's call the (theoretically- deliberate) distraction that caused you to lose focus while driving to Tom's, and the subsequent inclination to keep heading toward Bob's instead; let's identify these as being subconsciously-generated.

Of course, we could also add (as being subconsciously-generated prompts to your conscious mind) the sudden memory-recalls, that Bob's little brother would be at camp, and that there was something significant you had been meaning to talk to Bob about; both of which were not in your conscious awareness of the moment, when you were first considering the most significant factors in determining your decision whether to go to Bob's, Joe's, or Tom's.

This being the case, we could see the sharp contrast between the conscious strategy, that would perhaps normally entail cussing and turning around to get back on course to go to Tom's and go swimming (also thinking to yourself, I'm so stupid for having taken a wrong turn, and now I have wasted time and gas, too); contrasted with what allowing your subconscious mind to put into effect for you has pointed you in a better direction, or in other words, this had caused you to actually have made a more advantageous choice, in terms inclining you to instead continue driving to meet Bob at the bowling alley; after calling Tom to see if this would be okay with him (of which ultimately it was found to be not of any upset to Tom, to change your mind); and you were ultimately able to talk to Bob right away about a matter of some importance that had been weighing on your mind; although maybe it was initially in the back of your mind, at the time you had first directed your conscious attention toward looking at the factors surrounding which activity you might decide to do that afternoon.

This is the kind of thing I'm talking about; that it is often a lot better for us to try and stay in tune with what would appear to be our subconsciously-generated ideas and inclinations; and to be receptive to various possibilities and probabilities that our subconscious mind is influencing us to consider; often "going-with" what we have automatically seemed to be doing differently than what we had consciously planned.

And while we are thinking about this particular scenario, let me also add in something further about the significance of dreams, related to my having devised the previous passage, giving further thought to last night's initial dreaming-up of the three invitations scenarios.

I remember having a long dream last night, and of course it was a little strange, perhaps as dreams usually are; but in the dream, I had boarded a plane, on my way to a vacation; at first I was on my way with a partner; and then later in the dream I was merely by myself; which may have been a reminder that, within my mind after I had gotten married in 1994, I had initially thought I would be spending my whole life with my wife; but then we unexpectedly hit a bad snag, got divorced, and now I'm on my own. But I suppose this is not that pertinent to the larger message to myself, that I later was able to theoretically-glean related to this particular dream I had.

But anyway, just before the plane was about to take off, and I was thinking that they would be left behind, my parents quickly came through the door; and I felt relieved that they had made it, and had not missed going on this vacation with me. But I never had any conversation with either of my parents; which maybe is reminding me that although I'm very close with both of my parents, that we don't really seem to connect on some very important levels; and to that end, I feel very much alone in seeing all these mental-process-related ideas and suppositions I have been coming up with.

Anyway, that's also in the background perhaps; and the most impactful parts of my dream started after we had arrived. After I got off the plane, I went to go pick up my baggage. I had brought a guitar, my golf clubs, and a suitcase; and I was having trouble locating them in the baggage claim area. I remember having found my suitcase and my golf clubs, but I couldn't find my instrument; and then I suddenly saw my cello, there by itself without its case; and next I remember approaching someone who had a cheap soft case for sale, and also a stronger padded chipboard case; and I figured that one of these was just what I needed; as the instrument I had brought was now actually a bass guitar, and this was the instrument

I had seen the case for, nearby; not a cello. - And you have to take into account that whereas, I don't play the bass guitar, as one of my principal instruments, I can play the bass guitar, and I had even played bass guitar in a rock band for a couple of months, once.

But again, this is still background, although all of these screwy details bore some symbolic meaning to me; which I had gradually figured out, by hours later; but again, these weren't the most important point.

The next thing I remember I had bought the more protective case, a used case for $35 from this guy in the baggage claim area (I tend to be a good value shopper, I am pleased to be reminded of), and the resort hotel that I was staying at, was just upstairs; something like having arrived at Grand Central Station, and then walking upstairs and checking in at the grand Hyatt Hotel; as I had done many times before; yet, I have never stayed at the Grand Hyatt since about 20 years ago; I don't know what significance this might have had. (But the point is to believe that each of these details probably does bear some significance; and that it is probably worth my while to think more about the events of the dream that seem most interesting; or that haunt me to figure out, maybe.)

But anyway, I remember that I'm walking up the stairs toward the front desk of the hotel, and I suddenly realize that I have my golf clubs and my guitar, but that I didn't have my suitcase with me; I had left it behind somewhere in the baggage claim area. At that moment I was pretty pissed with myself; how could I have so stupidly left my unattended suitcase; which would've obviously been the most important item I should have remembered, at a minimum, that I would essentially need on this vacation?

I suppose that like a drunk dream, this was my fear in the back of my mind, that I would slip back into being irresponsible and forgetful; even though after I woke up, instead, I was relieved that I had not been.

Next thing I remember was being in a hotel room with a woman near my age, who at first seemed somewhat attractive, and I was considering that I may want to get to know her more during this vacation; I remember that I had done something for her to help her get settled into her room; perhaps something small like carrying in one of her suitcases, or something; and I suggested that maybe I might see her out around the pool over the next several days, perhaps.

Her response was to give me a bit of a sour look, and to indicate that she wasn't crazy about meeting men on her vacation, and I sort of completed her sentence, saying because all men want is to get in your pants! -And she smiled and agreed.

So, as I was walking toward the door, to leave her room, I told her that it might interest her to know that I hadn't had sex with anyone in over five years (and actually it's been over 10 now, so I don't know why I would've said five; but again, that's not so important here); so that she wouldn't have to worry about me trying to do what she was afraid of men typically doing when she had allowed herself to be with them.

So, this is what stood out to me that I remembered once I had awoken this morning; and then shortly thereafter, while having my coffee on the back deck, these new ideas of how I could use the example about Bob, Joe, and Tom, to illustrate further aspects of the usefulness of conscious subconscious theory; in that I began to think of various ways that I could use the example to illustrate further aspects of possibility and probability regarding an interpersonal situation such as this.

I also see some strong connections perhaps, between my last night's dream, and what occurred to me in connection with this little scenario I had created last night. Let me try to explain some of these; and let me also attempt to explain how I believe that dreams, such as this one, can be very helpful for me to think about, on the following day. (Well, I suppose that I am not moved to do a lot of explaining of the specifics; suffice it to say that reflecting on the dream correlated to my having come up with some additional ideas I could interject into my dreamed-up scenario of the night before.)

My dreams do appear to offer me insight; and help steer me toward, or away from embracing various ideas in connection; and thinking further about a specific dream may often incline me, or disincline me, in terms of my possibly-engaging in various activities I might be considering; and I think that dreams could be potentially helpful, in these respects, for almost anyone, once they have developed a reasonable ability to constructively analyze them.

My point, in this case, is that I imagine there is a good possibility that the dream I had, although it didn't seem to make much sense to me yet; as of when I first awoke; had been of good help to me in thinking up these new twists to the scenario that I could lay out, in order to make some additional good points regarding our potential apt consideration of various possibilities and probabilities.

I imagine that when followers look back, they would "remember it was the case" that, before we had begun considering conscious-subconscious theory, when faced with a situation of any importance, where we were aware that we possessed strong feelings of inclination regarding some issue at hand, historically we might have usually thought to ourselves that, "there is no need to think about my point of view any further; I should just act accordingly with these strong inclinations that I am sensing." –But with our newfound perspective, in considering the "two individuals within" idea; of course, that would be skipping an important new step.

In order to update ourselves at this point, and utilize our new added potential, we would probably do well to ask ourselves if this strong inclination we are tempted to act upon might be a conscious inclination, or a subconscious one? –And perhaps at the same time, we should also ask ourselves what other related, maybe weaker inclinations, also appear to currently exist within at the moment? I find that studying my various related inclinations can often help me to become aware of important and useful information and helpful perspective, that I had possibly overlooked.

Of course, we wouldn't go through such a thorough and painstaking process at every turn; but where you sense you are dealing with an issue of any importance, in terms of possible consequences, (should you take the wrong action, for example), searching yourself further can result in some very beneficial effects and protections, in many instances, I have found.

Then again, inclinations can change, of course, with new information you might become aware of; or from coming to a new realization, for example. Once you have become more well-versed in theoretically discerning between your conscious-versus-subconscious inclinations; if you're like me; you will also develop some facility to subordinate a conscious inclination. In other words, a predominantly strong conscious inclination could also potentially be made to take a back seat perhaps, at times; but of course, this could only happen provided that you have first gained a sense of more-necessary priority, for your own good; to more-usually subordinate the importance of the conscious thinking mechanism's immediate plans, goals, and inclinations otherwise; in favor of becoming more sensitive to an alternate, subconsciously-generated point of view, and plan of action.

For many of us, it seems, this has never been possible; and perhaps unfortunately for many, developing this psychological position may-well never be in the cards. For these people, any possible struggles, (between what the rest of us might imagine as the conscious and subconscious thinking mechanisms), have always (and undoubtedly <u>will</u> always) be won by the conscious mind. – And in fact this, I believe, is actually our biggest obstacle to a better world.

Of course, a valid reason must be seen, in order to think on any other terms, than consistently relying indefinitely on our plans to act solely based upon consciously-determined ideas, and consciously-reached conclusions related to our problems, and our potential opportunities.

However, I can attest that personally, I have certainly found good reason to think twice about possibly carrying through with even my strongest inclinations to proceed in a manner, of which I can also sense could be of any potentially serious negative consequence, unless I give additional careful thought to these considerations. – And of course, in my estimation, if I am to be more thorough, and ultimately less-uncertain as I move forward, what I consider to be my subconscious mind's considerations, must amply be involved!

More and more these days, I find myself interrupting, or at least postponing my sudden impulses, to take an action or deliver a message, or to embark on a consciously-conjured strategic course of action; pending more careful consideration. I didn't used to think so much about what could be at stake; should I charge ahead, based upon my first notion.

Instead, I often prefer to take the time and trouble to break my stronger feelings down into their "thought components" in a pretty thorough manner. As my level of maturity continually develops further, I find that I am more often inclined to work toward coming to understand, more-comprehensively, my true underlying motives, before overtly reacting, or taking any further action; to the extent this is possible for me in the heat of the moment.

I also find that; by more-closely examining what I imagine to be the main contributing factors in the development of my related strong feelings of the moment; I often tend to uncover considerations that I was not-at-all consciously aware of, during my earlier development of my initial inclinations, that I had first considered acting upon.

-And often, the stronger my feelings are, related to the matter at hand, the greater my opportunity will usually be to more-effectively search out all important considerations; provided I will just take the time, and exert the energy, to run down (take an inventory of) my thoughts surrounding an issue that my mind is currently consumed with.

Related to my possible consideration of carrying through with an opportunistically-offensive strategy, at times; of course I can potentially be as manipulative as the next guy; but I try to take into account that any "taking-advantage-type" of offensive action I might take, may often engender an equal and opposite reaction, coming back at me a little later; so I will want to be careful not to unnecessarily trigger consequential reactions against me, in the course of seeking any potential I may have, in terms of attaining immediate gratification in the situation. I think we can assume that taking advantage of someone is pretty- much always an immediate-gratification strategy.

Far too often, I find that others will usually grasp opportunities to take advantage of others they are dealing with, simply because they realize, in an instant, that they have become in a position of power to do just that; and they don't seem to respect that their powerful action taken against the object of their ruthlessness, may well bring the potential to incline a powerfully-troubling or hurtful reaction against them back, in retaliation.

-And unfortunately, I also find that usually, people who tend to blithely take strong actions against others will not heed any warnings of this nature either. It becomes necessary for them to become embattled, and for (at least metaphoric) bloodshed to result; I mean the perpetrator having become perhaps badly wounded, later, in an act of retaliation. Rather than developing a tendency towards more hesitation in the future, they instead try to become more steeled to the retaliatory blows which could perhaps be more-typically expected to come back; and of course, once having suffered from these at all, this only distorts their sense of fairness further. (Now, there is <u>really</u> no "fair enough" action that could have been taken against them.) Immaturity can become a well-trodden emotional path.

However, I submit that we do seem to have the capacity to stop ourselves from living blow by blow, provided our own inner sense of rationality and reasonability becomes more-well-recognized by many-more of us. This might be realistically possible, to the extent that we might stop persisting in paying exclusive homage to our less-sophisticated conscious entity, lurking more on the shallower surface of our sensibilities.

Commanding your own respectful, constructive thinking seems to be a give-and-take proposition; there are times when you will want to carefully continue to run down your strong feelings, to look at the specific groups of thoughts that seem to be behind them; or in other words, to have made these strong feelings come into being. However, there will also be times when you are lying in bed awake into the wee hours of the morning, ruminating through circles of thought; for example, "trying on" different alternative postures you could take in an anticipated upcoming confrontation, for example.

If this becomes torturous, and you just wish your mind would stop churning, and sparking different emotions which are mentally exhausting you, this is a time when it would probably be most helpful to realize that this is really mainly the conscious mind's fault. In fact, I would contend that whenever you have almost any persistent and lingering unpleasant emotion, the conscious mind is usually going to be the culprit, keeping this tormenting process going.

However, as I have said previously, in many ways, the conscious mind mainly becomes prompted, by the subconscious entity within, to think about much of what we will end up ruminating about, perhaps. So, if you can try to stay aware that there is a <u>teamwork</u> consisting of the two minds within you, potentially churning the entire time you are awake, you will probably have a better ability to interrupt the process whenever you are pretty- exhausted due to this natural inclination, to exchange various thoughts and feelings, back and forth, between your conscious and subconscious thinking mechanisms.

Of course, the natural cycle is to become consciously aware of internal feelings and the thoughts that make them up; and in this manner, a useful computation process can take place, ideally which eventually helps us better understand, and be at peace with, our internal perspective. But when the churning won't stop, I probably help myself most-frequently by telling myself that this is the fault of the conscious mind; and that it needs to be largely shut off from thinking about what is troubling me any further; to the extent I can force myself to stop focusing on aspects of my disturbance; until I sleep off my fatigue, for instance.

I accomplish this by asking myself the question, in this present moment, what is wrong with me?! –And the answer I tell myself repeatedly for a while is that it is the conscious mind's flaw, or fault. It's just my weaker mind not being able to control itself. It obviously needs some help from my greater subconscious self, if I am to relieve myself of this burden, and get some sleep. I find that this is often enough, in and of itself, to calm myself enough to fall asleep; or to at least move on, to consciously think about something else entirely, if it isn't time for me to sleep, for example.

Regarding our conscious preoccupations; as I was saying earlier; to some extent, we may realize that the conscious thinks purely about what the subconscious puts on its plate; so it could be confusing how the conscious mind may act at all independently. However, it appears that in many instances, the subconscious simply triggers conscious thought processes into motion, regarding some subject or problem vexing us or stressing us out, on a deeper internal level.

Yet, pursuant to this triggering, it seems the conscious mind then does very much have the capacity to take the ball and run with it, from this point; in terms of its then having potential to think pretty-independently, unto itself, in many respects.

However, another way we can look at this, is that when we can't seem to shut our conscious mechanism off from churning, with endless concentration on a subject it has been harping on persistently for hours, for example, this is one clear sign that things have (at least temporarily) gone beyond control of what we might best consider as the proper controller of our overall thinking activities (the subconscious mind).

It occurs to me that the conscious thinking mechanism takes over, certainly at times like what I have just been describing; and it is only those who have become aware that, theoretically, there is another separate and more powerful thinking mechanism within, which does apparently have some capacity to shut down the monotony of conscious churning; but perhaps it is only those who have embraced such an understanding, who may be enabled to more-consistently bring themselves relief from this torment; well, except for the relief that could possibly be obtained by ingesting a drug of some sort, alternatively of course!

But it seems that otherwise, mental dis-ease is imminent; and a long-enough time-period of this, becomes what we call a just plain mental disease, or a mental disorder of some kind.

This could be thought of to serve as just one very minor example of how merely thinking in terms of your having two minds; as I have been suggesting; may greatly improve your potential to avoid developing a mental disorder; but this is only the slightest clue of our exponentially-greater potential to avoid trouble, and manage ourselves in ways which will enable us to have a significantly better life, all around; once you have come to understand more about the dual-natured theoretical workings of the human mind.

CHAPTER 6

ALSO, TWO DIFFERENT SOURCES OF DISTURBANCE WITHIN

As we are all probably well-aware, our inclinations can be powerfully influenced by psychological disturbance. As many of us know, it appears that the two chief manifestations of disturbance are the emotions of anger and fear; and these can be extremely influential on our reactions and behavior, when they are strong within us. My theory on this aspect of our humanity is that greater levels of fear and anger appear to be conscious creations.

I say this because I see the workings of the subconscious thinking mechanism as pretty objective in nature. I consider the subconscious to be a desire-based system of thought, rather than any other emotion; but I imagine that its considerations appear to have the potential to be overridden by a significantly fearful or angry state of consciousness.

I ask myself how probable is it that the subconscious mind, or thinking mechanism can be poisoned by conscious fear or anger; and I rather sense that it is pretty compartmentalized unto itself, and it goes on churning with thought as usual, whether we feel consciously paralyzed by fear, or antagonized by anger at times, for example.

In dreams, which we could consider as a hybrid of consciousness and subconscious-ness, I imagine that the subconscious mind sets up a scenario, of which the conscious mind will perceive as a real situation; then dealing with this dream scenario as effectively as possible using conscious resources. Only after we wake, can we realize that the dream situation was not really a real situation; and then we may attempt to consider exactly why, and of what value it may be for us to have "tried on" an adjusted perception or conception during our dream state.

I conceptualize that our emotional reactions to the impact of finding ourselves in the middle of a dream scenario have good potential to later lead us to break down these emotions into the thoughts that seem to have made them up; and this often seems to provide helpful insight, potentially adding meaningful perspective to our consideration of the real situations we are presently dealing with, at the time.

Creating dream scenarios for us, seems to be a very important mechanism for the subconscious to educate and clue-in the conscious mind, as to some of the more-complex aspects of a given situation we are currently grappling with, that the lone thinking capacity of the conscious mind would not have had the mental resources to realize and think through, of its lone capacity. It seems that dreams can have the effect of getting us to consider a wider variety of somewhat real possibilities; perhaps, including some that we foolishly have rationalized away; instead considering that, with regard to this given scenario that our conscious mechanism had imagined on its own, would be highly improbable to actually come to pass, given the circumstances.

Of course, we may well have falsely come to this conclusion, in terms of having exclusively utilized our conscious thinking mechanism purely under its own steam.

Further, I have observed that dreams are almost always emotionally charged in some fashion; ranging, for example, from extreme fear or anger, to extreme happiness or enjoyment. This would constitute further evidence that emotions represent our highest sense of intelligence, in that basically each of our feelings can theoretically be traced back, as to the group of related thoughts that had culminated into this single strong emotional feeling that we are sensing within.

Curiously, based on this theoretical perspective, it would seem that those experiencing the strongest emotions, as evidenced by the individual's comparatively volatile expressions perhaps, could also be considered as being the most intelligent of us. Yet strangely in a way, I imagine that most of us will generally tend to consider a highly emotional person as disadvantaged, due to their apparent negatively-disturbed emotional state; in our view, constituting handicapping levels of hindrance to clear thinking; therefore seemingly rendering this individual as a less-than-capable person intellectually.

Yet, upon closer inspection; perhaps, once we have begun regularly considering our emotions as an intelligent subconscious prompt, leading us to consciously search ourselves for what thoughts have apparently led them to form; theoretically speaking, we might certainly acknowledge that, at times, our own stronger emotional reactions can potentially provide us with greater assistance, in terms of aptly having pointed us toward effectively searching ourselves within, to achieve greater understanding of all pertinent considerations that we should perhaps be taking into account.

Likewise, it should follow that, as we help others to break down their (apparently stronger emotional reactions than our own), this might also have good potential to enable us to consider additional relevant thoughts, beyond our lone capacity; related to an issue or a situation, of which we share involvement with this other person whom we are communicating with, in a given situation.

-But I observe alternatively, that most of us usually don't seem to see much value in engaging in extensive interchanges with a highly emotional person; instead, more usually we discount their potential to possibly be any sort of good resource for us. We say to ourselves, and to each other, that this person is crazed, and their ideas should probably be more-or-less disregarded.

I also see this as further evidence that the conscious mechanism within us seeks to short-circuit the subconscious thinking mechanism; leading us astray with its seemingly-clever sense of quick-thinking, perhaps often based on various rationalizations. The conscious mechanism can take considerations right out of the equation, in situations where it has more-exclusively taken over control of our thoughts and actions, for the time-being.

However, although the conscious mechanism can incline us to act as though a certain important consideration isn't really that important in the matter; of course, it won't make (the important consideration being discounted), any less potentially-consequential, in reality.

It would seem that a short-sighted consciously- computed course of action of this nature may lead to devastating consequences, in some instances; and then, to compound the problem, the resulting ramifications we have brought about could be either consciously-denied, or perhaps rationalized away, as having been the lesser-of- evils, as well.

So I think we would all do well to try and "wake up" to the competition, and the "dirty pool" that our conscious mechanism can sometimes play, in order to prevail as the leader of our mentality and actions. I hope you are getting my vision of how we sabotage ourselves and each other through more-purely-conscious strategizing and carrying through with simpleminded plans.

Getting back to dreams, and to how we can better become consciously in touch with our subconscious mind, theoretically speaking, let's take a closer look at the mechanism of how I imagine that emotions, especially powerful emotions, come into play.

As one option, we could assume that at times, we have great subconscious fears, just as we know we have great fears on a conscious level; or alternatively, perhaps we could consider that it is only when we become in touch consciously with what our subconscious mechanism is thinking about, that fear of any greater magnitude can develop within us. I have been thinking that quite possibly, it is only due to our sense of consciousness that greater fears can really develop within us.

I find myself toying with the idea that the subconscious mind limits its sense of fear to what we could consider as healthy fear. When fear helps us to stay on our toes, to be vigilant, and seek to avoid more serious forms of trouble, for example, this is what I mean by healthy fear.

We can be sure that the conscious mind seems pretty-easily able to magnify our sense of fear, to immobilizing proportions. It occurs to me that, as we consciously ruminate further about a fearful situation we have found ourselves in the middle of, our sense of fear will often grow exponentially. Of course, great fear can make us freeze up; it can disconnect us from our good ability to "think on our feet," more pragmatically; given that when we are not immobilized, we appear to have good ability to successfully "fly by the seat of our pants," as I've heard it said, using our creative means and our sense of intuition; sometimes even in situations that we have had no experience with.

At times, we may become in touch with an overwhelming sense of fear, so strong that it appears to be resounding throughout our entire being; yet, it would seem that any time we are not devastated to these proportions, perhaps even the worst of our fears can be calmed most effectively by coming into touch with our subconscious self's objective assessments, and the resulting inclinations we can later associate with this calmer, more-in-depth assessment, as we might sense it.

So, the potential value of starting with the theoretical premise that more-intense fear doesn't reside within the subconscious thinking mechanism, would perhaps lead many of us to spend a good deal more time studying exactly how it is that our greater subconscious self finds ways to circumvent falling into a greatly fearful state somehow, for one thing!

In my estimation, we don't seem to be able to become in touch with a sense of great fear without first consciously considering a fearful situation; and even when we develop intense fear while dreaming, perhaps it is only due to the conscious component of the hybrid (conscious combined with subconscious) dream state.

Delving further, we might consider that more- automatic body functions, such as hunger, sleep, or feeling like we need to go to the bathroom, can become disrupted when we are in a state of deep fear; so why wouldn't this suggest that, for example, at times when we know we haven't eaten for a long time, yet we are not hungry; shouldn't we conclude that we are experiencing great fear subconsciously?

Well, not necessarily; if we think further, the feelings of having to go to the bathroom, feeling hungry, or sleepy, these are all conscious perceptions. Normally, the conscious mind must cooperate with what we know as subconsciously-governed bodily processes, in order to feel hungry enough to eat, for example. Perhaps, hunger is more purely a conscious thought, an awareness given to us by our more-objective subconscious self that the body needs nourishment. At least on a theoretical level, couldn't we consider the pangs of hunger strictly as a conscious invention?

So, why might it be of any importance, whether we are more-highly emotionally charged in our subconscious realm of thought, or not? Well, if we could grow to depend on the idea that the subconscious mind is more-well-contained, in terms of its emotional balance, then theoretically, this is one further defining point helping us to separate out conscious thoughts from subconscious ones, perhaps.

Again, to the extent we can theoretically isolate which types of thoughts are developed within each of our two minds, I imagine that this could be helpful to us, in our continuing quest toward coming to know ourselves better.

Even though these types of ideas may all continue to be quite theoretical, I can offer that personally, I have been able to become increasingly comfortable depending on such theoretical aspects of our mental makeup; and I find thinking in these terms to have been quite useful and advantageous. I suppose this is why it has become my main purpose within this writing effort, to potentially help others to embrace these types of theoretical concepts.

So, regarding the gaining of greater emotional stability, it certainly seems helpful to me, to think in terms of having a mind that is never overly fearful, at my constant disposal, deep within. It provides me with a certain additional sense of grounding. I have become inclined to reason that unless and until I come to realize otherwise, I might be well-advised to operate based on this theoretical premise.

You see, I continue to assemble a vaster set of intertwining theories, such as this one, that I may develop a sense of dependence on, as I move forward; and although I certainly have proved myself wrong, at times, having falsely assumed that some of these ideas held true, (later coming to realize that I had the wrong impression), if most of these mini theories of sorts do seem to continue to hold true, on an ongoing basis, then I imagine that I can potentially come much further along in my understanding of human nature in general; perhaps while having good success in my day-to-day life much of the time, as well. –And I must report that I have been having much overall success, both in terms of progressing in my understanding of the human mind, and keeping myself happy and fulfilled, to a large extent; although I have certainly suffered some dismal failings at points in my past; I can't deny. None-the-less, I continue to forge on with a positive spirit!

I find that my earlier-conceived theories, (the ones that have not become disproved, that is), often give way to new ones, in a developmental manner. For example, based on what I have theorized so far, here's another theory that comes to mind; when you are very upset, there must be a lot of reasons; as opposed to just one big one.

As it is said, we find (more exclusively) what we are looking for. If consciously, you come to attribute your upset merely to one event, or one new piece of information, then you probably won't be inclined to look any further, and this idea theoretically cuts you off from searching for greater subconscious assistance; and also, if the upset is overwhelming enough, your conscious thinking mechanism will probably be on "tilt" anyway; greatly hindering your thinking ability to deal effectively with a crisis, or a stressful situation demanding good decisions and problem-solving action.

However, from our previous insights, perhaps we could newly become inclined to realize that this is a time to search as deeply as possible, tediously and carefully breaking down your feelings of the moment, into the thoughts making them up; in order potentially to derive the greatest number and magnitude of positive benefits, of having enabled yourself to become consciously aware of your subconscious mind's more-intelligent perspective.

When I reflect on the way that so many around me are always anticipating the worst to happen, and taking extreme measures to prevent this possibility; and also that so many around me seem to cling to the way they have always done things; apparently for fear of the unknown; (I think we should really try living in the spirit of adventure more); but it occurs to me that the conscious mind is such a fraidy-cat! It really needs lots of coddling, reassurance, and coaxing, it seems. The worst part is that collectively, we tend to feed each other's conscious fears and insecurities.

I can only imagine that the conscious mechanism tends to be pretty pessimistic; in that perhaps over the past week, for example, maybe you had been given to some serious fears that your situation appeared to have much potential to turn into a confrontational mess, involving law suits and long-standing expensive legal battles, fierce family squabbles, and other serious un- pleasantries. Yet, as it turned out, the potentially problematic mental and emotional positions you feared would develop, or otherwise persist within the minds of certain key people involved, either never actually developed as you had feared, or perhaps troublesome earlier positions held by a pivotal person in the mix, had simply dissipated, by some stroke of minor miracle; and the resistance that you had feared, had actually melted away, out of the mix. (My father ended up agreeing that assisted living was best, under the circumstances.)

However, if now, despite all these turns of good fortune, (brought on perhaps due to some careful thought and strategic wording or actions either solely on your part, or additionally on the part of some ally in the situation), the conscious mechanism within you has managed to grow another huge set of concerns over how potentially bad things could still become, at worst; even though in actuality, things had just gone better than your wildest dreams, as far as fortunate changes of heart and mind which had transformed the negative potentials into a favorable outcome; is this serial negativity really any way to live?! -slipping from one emotional crisis to the next, without stopping to acknowledge your most recent fortunate success, this certainly doesn't seem like a very healthy way to live!

To me, it just figures that if we keep falling for these kinds of self-devised mental and emotional pitfalls, we will obviously continue to bring upon ourselves a continuously-stressful state of mind, no matter how many favorable things might actually happen for us!

One of the great benefits of things having fallen nicely into place, and having averted potential adversity, is that it affords you the potential to get that "wind in the sails" feeling, which can perhaps greatly help to positively propel you into the next chapter, namely of trying to deal most effectively with the ongoing challenges of your moment-to-moment life situation, as it continues to unfold.

At least at the theoretical level, if you allow your conscious mechanism to effectively maintain a mental stronghold over your being, to the point where all prior gains are taken for granted, and your main mental focus is always to remain-on, vigilantly guarding whatever financial fortune you have attained, for example; it seems this fear-based form of vigilance of spirit will rob you of all excitement and enjoyment!

True, if on the other extreme, you were to become so elated at having experienced good fortune, or success otherwise, that in your elation, you threw caution to the wind, and celebrated your good fortune by perhaps spending a wad of money foolishly or frivolously, in the honor of your recent success; this certainly would have great potential to erase the gains you have made, and then some!

But like I was saying, if you allow your conscious mechanism to constantly employ this type of ongoing pessimistic rationalization, in order to defend such a level of fear-based conservatism that it takes the joy and excitement out of living, this certainly seems unnecessarily defeating; especially taking into account that one of the great benefits of being alive is that you might experience as much relief, joy, excitement, fun, and happiness as possible!

Managing yourself in a manner, so as to continually feel uncomfortable, just so that you will be on your toes, to guard against careless loss, this cheats you out of the comfortability that you may well deserve to embrace, due to your successful manner of conducting yourself in many situations. It could even give you a false sense that you are not having enough success, so you need to change your approach; when in fact your approach has been effectively successful, and just fine.

A then-naturally-inclined amendment of your processes that this may lead to, may actually amount to shooting yourself in the foot; simply due to your not having more fully acknowledged your current level of competence, as evidenced by the favorable results, of which you unfortunately seem to have discounted!

Even if you could fully eliminate many of these types of pitfalls, and your continually-conservative bent only brought you more success and good fortune, financially-speaking; this would only mean that, by the moment of your death, you would have amassed a lot of assets, but you would not have allowed yourself to experience much in the way of satisfactions and happiness in life; and you can't take money with you into the grave! I'm just trying to illustrate how life is about much more than financial gain and protection. Delayed gratification should rightfully have its limitations, in the scheme of life's healthier potential balance; who could reasonably disagree?!

So, all of this comes under the heading of conscious disturbance; and as we can see, the conscious mind wants us to be disturbed to keep us in a vigilant state; but at least on a theoretical level, I don't believe the subconscious mind would want this for us; alternately, I imagine we could reasonably assume that it wants us to feel comfortable, happy, and undisturbed, to the extent this is possible for us at any moment.

I think we could also assume that dreams are creations of the subconscious mind for the purposes of bringing intelligent insights and perspective to the conscious thinking mechanism. The more I embrace conscious-subconscious theory, the more it seems clear to me that the subconscious mind becomes disturbed over the apparent trouble we are headed for, if we continue to develop our basis for strategizing, according to the unaided devices of the more simpleminded conscious thinking mechanism; which may often simply be inclined to stubbornly go its own way, to our whole being's detriment.

But this theoretical "internal communication process" I describe certainly does not appear to be a purely one-way relational process. Undoubtedly, the subconscious mind may become educated too, by the consciously-attempted solutions to the dream scenario problem set up by the subconscious mind, for example; and I consider that there are many other ways in which conscious input brings value to the subconscious entity it theoretically serves.

In fact, dreams appear to be a good example of how we are most capable when we "team-together" our conscious and subconscious resources. Conceptually, each of our two minds comes to the table with potentially- complementary strengths and skill sets; but I imagine that they both share many of the same thinking capabilities as well. Let's look at some of the theoretical similarities and differences:

As I consider it, both can have independent thoughts, integrate thoughts with each other, and arrive at resulting inclinations and other feelings; which can potentially be run down; or in other words, broken down into the component thoughts making these feelings up.

Both can reason, both can rationalize, both can develop fear, anger, jealousy and the like, both can project into the future, both can consider the past.

However, one huge difference is that the subconscious mind theoretically has a much larger database of ready-information to draw upon, as I imagine it.

In order to be most successful, as I imagine it, we must make good use of both thinking mechanisms on these levels; and we must have some facility in passing ideas, and reflecting thoughts back and forth, for best results.

However, let's think a little more about the mental processes I imagine are unique to each: First, it seems reasonable to consider that the conscious mind alone has the ability to sense what is happening in the outside world around us; and of course this is paramount. –And I imagine that the subconscious mind must rely solely on the conscious mind's perceptions; making it wholly dependent, in this respect.

Yet, there is often so much going on around us; and we know that there is a limit to how many things we can turn our conscious attention to at the same time.

When we decide to pay attention to one of a dozen things going on around us at a party, for example, we may not even know why we have chosen to key in on one given nearby conversation, as opposed to another one which is also going on nearby, at the same time. –But we seem to feel moved to bring our focus to something we sense may be of importance, or we might focus on some action, that we feel inclined to think, may be otherwise advantageous for us to turn our attention to, in the moment. Where does that inclination come from?

Maybe it could at least sometimes be consciously- motivated; but it occurs to me that our subconscious mind would be the main facilitator directing the focus of our attention, moment by moment, in this manner.

Looking at one aspect of competition between our two minds, suppose we come to this party with an initial objective of looking for our spouse. Then, we see someone very beautiful and sexy in the crowd in front of us. You know very well that you are already married, and on one level, you know you shouldn't be looking for involvement with anyone else in this capacity. So I ask you, assuming we have two minds, and the conscious mind is supposedly simpler, or less intelligent than the subconscious, which mind has suddenly hijacked our plan of action?

If we then approach the attractive one and strike up a conversation, we have then immediately developed the potential to sabotage ourselves. Maybe we get a nagging feeling about this as we are trying to decide whether we will take a detour and talk to this attractive stranger; or maybe if our conscious mind has become powerfully-enough compartmentalized unto itself, and able to cut us off from getting (or staying) in touch with the subconscious mind's objective of finding our spouse, we won't even be thinking of anything but how we will approach the sexy one, and what we will say.

Then, say we ultimately end up going home with this attractive one and sleeping with them; the next morning, we wake up really upset with ourselves for having done so; filled with guilt and remorse. Who won that competition, and who lost miserably?!

That's the problem, as I imagine it; our conscious mind can so easily win at every turn, to our detriment. – But that's not the end; the conscious mind maybe won that battle, but the war rages on!

The subconscious mind can apparently punish the conscious mind; and as you can guess, it must make sacrifices in order to do this. –But is it worth it? Yeah; on a deeper (or subconscious) level, we can become convinced that making these necessary sacrifices, serves us better in the long run.

Let's say you go home late the next morning; and your conscious mind has concocted a foolproof story to explain your whereabouts. You are so confident that you can easily explain your way out of trouble, that you feel pretty nonchalant as you arrive home and see your spouse. Your explanation goes perfectly, and your spouse seems satisfied; but then later that day, after she has thought further about it, there was something about your countenance as you were explaining, that tipped her off that you were hiding something; maybe a slightly guilty look or something.

Perhaps it was something subtle in your body language, that you couldn't even be conscious of; but then suddenly there is upset toward you.

If the relationship was pretty strong, you could quite possibly patch things up; but if your conscious mind became pretty overwhelmed during the ensuing related discussions, perhaps it would now feel it best to put its full trust in the subconscious mind's ability to reconnect with your spouse on a deeper level; consciously attempting to draw upon the subconscious mind's memory holdings related to the long-term history, of all you have shared together. In any event, theoretically, in all of this, I imagine that the subconscious mind may-well be strategizing all on its own, in an attempt to force the conscious mind into facing its shortcomings, and to ultimately take more direction from its subconscious master, in the future.

Even in the extreme case where the episode caused your spouse to end the relationship with you, the sacrifice that your subconscious mind (theoretically) has made, possibly in tipping-off your spouse using (undetectable-to-your-own-conscious-mechanism) body language cues, for example, would, even so, have good potential to, in effect, leave a lasting and severe impression on your conscious mind; that thwarting important subconscious considerations and objectives is foolish and troublesome, if not disastrous!

We should consider that, <u>minus</u> gaining greater understanding of these kinds of competitive syndromes, which may lead to more successful cooperation between our two theoretical minds, there may be no end to the serial ongoing battles between the conscious and subconscious mind within a person; in the case of someone with a particularly obstinate conscious thinking mechanism.

Yet, it is potentially a power struggle with only minor and temporary victories, for either the conscious or subconscious mechanism; which are also pretty certain to be accompanied by bitter defeats and great overall loss, for the person as a whole; unless and until the conscious mechanism can become clued in, as to its much better option to give-in; developing more-healthy levels of subordination to its theoretical subconscious master, more commonly.

We might theoretically ask ourselves, is it any wonder that our external world is an incessantly torturous and consequential battleground, when this kind of nasty competition is going on personally within so many of us, between the conscious and subconscious thinking mechanisms within each of us?!

If this is ever to get better, I see it, that we owe it to ourselves and to each other, to develop good ability to distinguish between conscious and subconscious disturbance; and to behave with more consistent respect to this theoretical subconscious source of greater intelligence within us.

CHAPTER 7

EXPLORING MENTAL UNCERTAINTIES, AND ARRIVING AT THEORETICAL CERTAINTIES; AND VICE- VERSA

I am hopeful that by now, readers are beginning to feel as though they have become in better touch with the "inner you;" if so, we have perhaps cracked a door open where the light of reason may shine in; and I would hope that, by this point, many of us have arrived at an updated "conception of the true reality" related to our theoretical understanding of how the human mind works, in this day and age.

Yet, at this point you may be wondering how to even make a beginning at unwinding this strong-armed position; such that your conscious mind has evidently stacked the deck against the true, substantive individual within. Hopefully, we have begun thinking we might safely assume that this subconscious individual within should really be mainly at the helm; in terms of how we might base our decisions, and coordinate our actions, going forward. Perhaps you are also now wondering, considering the history of its pretty consistent stronghold; whether at this point, is it even possible to render your conscious mind a capitulating servant, to the greater entity you would perhaps do well to consider as being the true essence of "you"?!

-But let me offer, in case you are feeling more- than-a-little apprehensive about your potential ability to remedy the questionable prior-effectiveness of your conscious self; or if you are feeling a bit lost, as to how this powerful, yet inferior conscious thinking mechanism of yours, might ever capitulate, and sacrifice some of its control; when perhaps it seems to have been ever- errantly out of control in the past, in many ways; I can tell you from experience, that the conscious self is always ready to grow and learn; and that it never really intended to do anything against the entire organism that is you!

If you are like me, your "conscious self" will wholeheartedly want to continually cooperate with becoming educated; once it has come to a revelation, of how its cut-off, compartmentalized thinking has possibly led to a serious degree of unwitting self-sabotage.

And by the same token, given that none of us can really do anything without the assistance of our conscious mind, I can only imagine that; deep within ourselves; we certainly must each realize that our subconscious mind's objective is only to partner up; and not to have any kind of ongoing power struggle with its conscious counterpart.

It may sound a little ridiculous to refer to our conscious and subconscious divisions, each as "it;" but then again, earlier I referred to them as separate individuals; separate persons, so to speak; and this is probably not entirely appropriate either. These ideas, of course, are merely theoretical constructs; and I only say these things to help us better-grasp conscious- subconscious theory.

The "it" concept may further be useful, in that it suggests that neither entity literally "is" who we are; yet perhaps we can appear more one, than the other, to a given observer. Up to this point, perhaps most of us have made ourselves appear to entirely consist of what is merely the conscious component of ourselves; but now, we are learning that there is much more of ourselves to reveal and interact with.

However, of course, complete subordination of the conscious entity should not really be our true objective; it seems that what each of us should really be aiming to endeavor, is to form a more advantageous partnership between the conscious individual, and the subconscious individual, both residing together within our single body, so to speak.

And it also occurs to me that we don't have to think of ourselves as two individuals at all times either; it appears we can be quite successful while continuing to run on autopilot, as usual, much of the time.

We should keep in mind that most others are going to consider one body to be equipped with one mind, in their dealings with other individuals, at this point; yet most people are also familiar with the concept of a subconscious division of ourselves; as when we refer to our dream experiences, and things like a "Freudian slip."

To the extent that we may become somewhat artful, it appears that we will also develop some capability to often avoid seeming weird to others, as we begin more-often revealing to others, at least at times, some of the conflicting thoughts, feelings, and ideas we will (from this point on) now want to stay in better touch with, given that theoretically, a person's conscious mind is bound to own a different set of thoughts, feelings, and values from the subconscious mind within us. As we begin dealing with our ongoing situations with a new, more complex perspective, in this manner, we may start to become in increasingly better touch with internal conflicts, and other differences in values, that we were quite unaware of previously.

To be sure, the fact that we have now opened our minds to considering possibilities that we had never before had the capacity to be open to, this is such a great new benefit! It allows us to introduce our two selves to each other; as crazy as this might sound! -But in very basic terms, for the subconscious, it amounts to becoming wise to conscious short-sightedness and trickery, perhaps mainly centered around goals involving immediate gratification; and we must also effectively train our subconscious, in terms of its learning to become more effective at prompting the conscious mind in ways that are successful at getting through to our conscious awareness, when we are consciously running amuck.

Alternately, for the conscious mind, our newly- developed capacity to sense the existence of our subconscious counterpart basically amounts to the gradual development of your continually-growing awareness of an adept and capable superior partner at its disposal; one who should be listened to more intently, including making and keeping an ongoing commitment to satisfy the objectives of, and pay more attention to, the inclinations of this inner self; as opposed to your previous idea that our conscious mind is the only resource we have, to make every decision, and call all the shots; as is perhaps the usual chain of command, for the vast majority of us, at present.

Even having gained this much insight into our dual workings in this manner, at first there remains a plethora of unknowns regarding which of our two minds controls what, within our body. I find myself constantly in a quandary over where one thinking mechanism starts and the other leaves off. Yet, I also appear to be gaining a growing awareness of how I can determine conscious versus subconscious thought processes; and as more certainty in these matters slowly begins to solidify for me, I also seem to be gaining added self-confidence, as well as added success at minimizing stress, managing more comfort, and enjoying more significant progress.

I have found that, as I look to the source of any particular inclination, it will often appear somewhat evident whether it was the product of conscious thoughts, or subconscious ones. Although we cannot distinguish with utterly dependable accuracy, which of our two minds has developed a given inclination, here is a time where I have found that playing the probabilities can often be a very effective and useful strategy.

The way I parse my inclinations out in my mind, conscious inclinations will usually be centered around more-immediate benefits, for example; or around providing more immediate relief, or a quick solution; whereas, subconscious inclinations will often point to exercising patience, in a tricky situation, for example; or to devising strategies that will ultimately culminate in various forms of delayed gratification, perhaps.

Further, a subconscious strategy might more- typically involve a strategy that will buy you some time; as on a deeper level, you are sensing there are yet possibly some more considerations that might be important to mull over, than you've been able to consciously take into account so far, regarding the situation.

I have also intuited that subconscious inclinations often involve strategies for gathering more information, or looking for further possible evidence, either confirming or disproving an intuition you sense regarding someone's hidden agenda, or regarding a contended truth that you actually have some doubts about, for example.

Let's say you are in a relationship as a heterosexual woman, for example, and you have come to discover that your partner was seen having dinner at a restaurant with another woman; say your best friend calls you to report having seen them out together.

The conscious inclinations would more likely be of the type that you should mistrust your partner; you are instantly filled with anger and jealousy, and you want to confront your partner angrily right away;

especially if your partner had apparently lied about where he was going that night.

However, subconsciously, you would be more apt to be thinking about the history of your long relationship, and the closeness that has developed between you two; and that you should be careful not to blow out the relationship with an immediate angry tirade, based on a preconceived notion that your partner is cheating on you.

Perhaps, subconsciously, you would feel inclined to do a little checking, to see if there was a legitimate reason why he went out with another woman; maybe it was simply a business-related dinner; or maybe it was even an unexpected visit from an out-of-town relative. Subconsciously, you would not be inclined to be hasty in your reactions just yet.

If you were to act strictly on your conscious inclinations, it would certainly result in an upsetting argument, rife with accusations and distrust. It would certainly be a negative ordeal for both of you; and who needs unnecessary stress and upset, over what perhaps was nothing?

A subconsciously-developed strategy (inclination), on the other hand, might be to casually mention that your friend saw the two of them at the restaurant; and to say that you are curious as to the nature of the encounter; waiting to hear their response, before you begin jumping to any conclusions.

So, let's continue on with this scenario; say that he seemed pretty nervous being found out and questioned; but that his explanation was that she was an old classmate from college; and when they bumped into each other at the grocery store, and he told her what company he worked for, she had responded that she was looking to make a career change, and asked whether he might give her some advice on looking for a job.

A conscious inclination, upon hearing this explanation might be to think this was a likely story, and warn him to not ever see the other woman again, or else. However, a subconscious inclination might instead be to ask what his advice indeed was to her? You see, each additional response to these kinds of questions would provide additional information and clues as to the true nature of his encounter with her; whether there have been multiple encounters with this same woman; all-the-while taking notice whether he seemed to become more and more nervous with this line of inquiry, etc…

Approaching this kind of situation according to a subconsciously-developed string of inclinations, as they naturally begin to unfold, one after the other, this would undoubtedly have better potential to protect and nurture the relationship; assuming there is a meaningful relationship between you to protect.

If further exploration and questioning begins to make it more apparent that he seems to be cheating on her and trying to hide it; then quite possibly it would eventually become both a conscious and a subconscious inclination to end the relationship; but if nothing shady is really happening, a blow-out could have reasonably been avoided; and it wouldn't have become a vulnerable point of oversensitivity, quite as easily.

Of course, it is equally possible that her partner was in fact cheating on her; but without too much cajoling, he came clean about it; and having newly realized how much he had to lose, by continuing to see this other woman, he could have (subconsciously) developed a strong inclination to resolve not to engage any further in behaviors like this, (that would probably end the relationship), because he has newly come to realize that their long-standing relationship is too valuable to him, to risk engaging in these types of encounters.

Either way, the consciously-inclined blow-out confrontation would never have been the best way to deal with things; yet, in this day and age, it appears to be a much more common reaction, when a woman discovers her partner has been out with another woman. Perhaps more commonly, for most of us, it seems all too easy for deeper intimacy to be thwarted, in favor of bowing to an immature fit of jealous rage.

This is just another example of how the "two individuals" theory can help us to a better way of life; by leading us to discover and act consistent with our more mature and intelligent set of inclinations (the subconscious mind's variety), in each circumstance.

We could only imagine how much more consequential, that immature consciously-inclined reactions could potentially be, when the individual involved is a country's leader; or an otherwise greatly- influential person in Government, for example, responding to such others in a different country. It seems pretty clear to me that this is how large-scale senseless killing and other suffering comes about, on a national level.

-But I digress; referring back to the chapter heading, "Exploring Mental Uncertainties, and Arriving at Theoretical Certainties; and Vice-Versa," to illustrate what I mean by "uncertainties" in this sense; for example, let's say I find myself having uncomfortably-tensed muscles in one part of my body; but the moment I become aware that I have subconsciously put myself in some amount of pain in this manner, I suddenly become (consciously) inclined to relax the muscle for relief. What thoughts and feelings triggered the subconscious tensing of the muscle? How is it that I was initially unaware that I was painfully tensing it, and how did I suddenly become aware that I was in pain due to the tensing?

Any of us could potentially trace back a series of developments such as these; but I tend to think that, normally, most of us probably don't bother ourselves with such distractions. -And even if we did try to trace this, we could not know for certain what thoughts or feelings were at play. We could only guess; yet, I also see that our guesses, in these respects, can often be helpful.

In attempting this particular "search-of-self," we could ask ourselves to try to become consciously-aware of what thoughts were on our mind that could have subconsciously inclined us to tense up certain muscles?

These kinds of questions could be seen as a good starting-point toward developing further insight into what is going on within.

Just so you know, I don't entirely rule out that there might be external psychic forces affecting our thinking perhaps; such as brain waves of others nearby, or God; but that all does actually sound pretty silly; I tend to believe that everything going on in our mind, is purely as a result of the life process going on physiologically within our brain; I am not going to comment on any possible outside psychic influence; I don't think we even have to go there, in order to figure ourselves out pretty adequately, and live a happy and successful life.

Yet, what I've keyed in on, is a very useful concept; this concept of two separate minds within us. I see this conceptualization as a mental organizational feature to embrace; and to this extent I strongly believe the two-minds orientation is very real; and I might imagine that perhaps the conscious mind may not initially even want to consider having a partner in this manner; perhaps, it desperately wants to believe it is the sole life force enabling us to live, controlling every facet of thought and action we will take, independently on its own.

And when I refer to the conscious mind, of course this is just another way of referring to the awake "you;" so what I am really saying is that, minus any possible belief, that you appear to have an additional separate individual living within you, mentally-speaking; or in other words as having a second personality existing within you; then perhaps the conscious "you," as the only person you have ever considered yourself to be, might well be desperately inclined to throw out any possible validity to these types of ideas and suggestions; so if you are not convinced yet, in the slightest; that I may be onto something; this might be one possible reason.

But assuming this severe form of denial has set in, (your consciously-having- developed a strong defiance of any idea that there is an additional point of view, or force of reason within you); it would only make sense that, if indeed there is another thought mechanism which is "in any kind of competition," as far as vying for a "controlling influence" over our expressions and behavior, this subconscious individual, possibly also occupying our psyche, or living a shared existence, within our one physical brain; perhaps would get pissed as hell that it was being defied and kicked to the curb; and it would do what we normally do when this happens; yes, I mean start a war!

It would also follow, that our body would serve as the battle-ground for this war, including all of its battles. We don't have to look too far, to find much evidence of war-torn bodies, rife with stressed-out deeply-wrinkled brows and such; but perhaps this can remain all-too- easily hidden from us, as well.

Consider the career boxer, for example. In terms of my suggestion that we newly begin "considering the possibilities," in more of an openminded fashion, perhaps this man's defiant refusal to try and detect subconscious prompts have unwittingly inclined him to put himself in a position where he will be relegated to suffer continual beatings until he might come around more, to realizing that quite possibly, there is truly another psychological entity, so to speak, living within him; he didn't give himself cauliflower ear!

So, I suggest that if you consider that you seem to be plagued with ongoing suffering, living some form of tortuous existence perhaps, maybe you might be well- advised to look further, suspecting that a subconsciously- prompted continuing internal battle might be the true cause of an ongoing series of decisions, over the years, to keep being (something like a fighter) for a living, for example.

It seems we would have at least some potential to deepen our individual perspective, once we begin to use our imagination to newly-consider such types of ideas, as that possibly, we are subconsciously being caused to become beaten into submission until we give up our psychotically-conscious attempts at maintaining exclusive control over the expressions and behavior of ourselves as an individual; yet, perhaps we have consciously taken the position that we just "ain't gonna submit;" and so the battle rages on, even for decades maybe.

At first, this may sound too-stupidly-Freudian, and indeed, the consideration of such symbolic theoretical themes is probably more-appropriately posed by your therapist, perhaps as a rhetorical question; but I see evidence of human battleground wreckage all around me; and often, when I am able to get to know more than a little about the nature of one of these individual's background and general state of mind, (in terms of their most important beliefs, values, and goals, and the roots of their struggles); enabling me to become more privy to the vicious cycle of their continuing defeats, and their many bitter and painful disappointments; at this point, the nature of the division within their psyche seems to reveal itself to me pretty clearly. This is often when I begin to think I could be of help, if I ever get the chance.

I see that in order for anyone to begin interrupting this torturous vicious cycle, they must begin making ongoing attempts to face the stark reality of the somewhat-elusive truth, regarding their current conceptions, perceptions, and beliefs; and the values that seemingly would naturally develop, as a result.

For example, say that a near-death, or a quasi- death experience leaves them telling others that they have hard-and-fast knowledge that heaven exists; and it is a wonderful feeling to arrive there after death. This person tries to convince everyone else, and especially themselves perhaps, that Heaven truly exists, and that God is real and present in the lives of each of us. –And they feel absolutely certain of this; or so they think (i.e.- a "belief-become-fact"). –But let's get real; if this were a true, unquestionable certainty within them, wouldn't they then logically be inclined to do whatever they could to get there as soon as possible?!

If they continue to devote their energy to forge on living, and have the outlook that they will continually strive to have the best life possible in the here and now, then it becomes somewhat obvious that they would not feel completely certain of the existence of God and heaven; although perhaps they may rationalize otherwise.

Their continued refusal to acknowledge this, even to themselves, much less anyone else, appears to me as evidence, of an internal defiance of their own truth; they want to believe in God and Heaven; but it seems evident that they honestly don't believe this, in the most whole- hearted sense (i.e.- they remain unconvinced subconsciously). So, although they try desperately to negate it, they are truly agnostic; as any halfway intelligent person probably should see themselves.

In order to begin to improve, it seems they must become able to grasp this; and stop trying to deny it. In so doing, they are probably doing themselves a terrible disservice.

I suppose it is a bit of a paradox; I start out saying that in order to save ourselves from eventual ruin, as individuals and as a people, we must strive to make determinations, at least theoretical ones, although we would commonly be initially starting with much uncertainty regarding the more-probable distinctions which would define the boundaries of conscious-versus- subconscious mental processes; and then I say we must become aware of our uncertainty about things we have misguidedly become sure of, consciously; and embrace a continual uncertainty in these respects! But both seem to be true. This perhaps gives birth to a new one of those pithy platitudes: We must learn to become certain about what we are (falsely) uncertain of; and we must learn to become uncertain of what we are (falsely) certain of!

CHAPTER 8

DETECTING OUR INNER NATURE

For practical purposes, in terms of terminology, we could substitute our "inner-versus-outer nature", as an equivalent term to describe our "conscious-versus- subconscious" selves; and maybe this would be more palatable for some. As one terminology-related complication, the term "subconscious" seems to connote a part of our being that we cannot be in touch with, at all, during our conscious waking state; and whereas, unfortunately this is probably the case for a lot of us in the present day and age, the whole point of this book is to help people gain a much greater conscious awareness of the subconscious component within them, even as perhaps, actually constituting the great portion of their true identity.

Although I believe it is probably most helpful for us to consider these two aspects of self as pretty separate thinking mechanisms; (the conscious mechanism certainly far more familiar to us, in defining what we see as the overall characteristics of our person); I have long- since-discovered that if we keep trying to look within while we are awake, we appear to have much potential to become quite knowledgeable about the nature of this greater inner "us".

However, a huge proportion of us are not even acknowledging, much less embracing the existence of an inner partner, of whom each of us are attached at the hip to, so to speak; and indeed, one which perhaps usually owns quite a different set of (deeper-perspective-related) perceptions, values, and goals; the culmination of which also resultantly becomes the basis for a completely different set of inclinations, than those we might tend to harbor consciously.

We know that, operating based upon good assertiveness-training principals, any of us can learn to develop a healthy and constructive partnering bond to another individual; be it a spouse, or a business partner for instance. I find these same principals will make for a layup in developing the same productively-cooperative partnership between anyone's inner and outer selves; (or between your inner and outer nature, if you prefer).

I find it helpful to keep in mind several consciously- detectable types of signals from within, basically prompting me to search myself whenever the thoughts, feelings, and perspective of the inner me are thought, by this "inner self" to be most helpful to bring to mind, consciously; or provided my inner self considers that its input would be otherwise-important to enter my awareness.

These prompts are all sensation-related; as of course, sensation is one of the premier characteristics of consciousness. The first one of these prompts that my attention was turned to was suggested by Dr. Hans Selye, in his book, "Stress Without Distress." He called it "Butterflies in the stomach." But there are many other "prompting" sensations we can pick up on, when our inner self attempts to incline us to conduct a conscious search to become more aware of its presence, and its more-extensive degree of information and considerations, pertinent to what we are consciously trying to deal with, at the current moment.

In terms of the inner self's prompting mechanisms, just think of them all: Anger, fear, torment, jealousy, worry, anxiety, uncertainty, indecision; there must be a dozen or more of these types of sensations; and perhaps the prompting of us to search our deeper (inner) self for further insight regarding its thoughts, feelings, and its ideas in general, is arguably the main function behind our ability to discern the difference between these types of "alerting" emotions; also probably affording us all the potential there is, to better-become-connected with ourselves in this manner.

Yet, how unintelligent, if we only go as far as identifying which one of these emotions we are feeling at the moment; without exploring further what is at the center of our upset! -And of course, many of us will realize that limiting ourselves to merely a shallow searching of ourselves would be pretty neglectful!

I would certainly advise that we try to avoid leaving any important stone unturned, in our wending search through our thoughts and emotions, related to any significant situation we might find ourselves in.

However, all of this searching will often require perseverance and continued resolve, to keep working at making pertinent discoveries about what is bothering us, on different levels. Maybe we'll run down what's behind our twisted emotions for a bit, until we start to tire; but for many of us perhaps, it may well be that our consciously-conceived-of convictions to serve our inner self are, at best, half-hearted. It seems that many of us fail to see the point of ruminating to any greater extent; we try instead to distract ourselves, or make this process within us stop.

-And this disengagement is probably not truly from fatigue, as much as it is probably from laziness. Maybe we lull ourselves, conceding that we've worked hard enough for now; we are comfortable enough with our surroundings; we have food to eat, and a place to sleep; what need is there to occupy ourselves with trying to resolve any further issues of our discontent?

Here we are, back again, with our old pal rationalization! Well, I am trying to suggest that we owe it to ourselves to not buy it! Once we have become open enough to the possibility that we do have an alter-ego of sorts; and if we won't take the time and energy to listen to it and interact with it like it wants, (well we've already assumed that it is much smarter than the conscious part of us is), it seems only reasonable to also consider that it may well punish us, in some form, for disregarding this more-major part of our overall psyche.

I realize that perhaps it sounds a little nutty to imagine, that this might really be the true reality of our mental makeup as human beings; but trust me, I find this to be a very valid assessment; or at very least, we might at least find that relying on this theoretical assumption becomes a valid basis for determining our actions.

But despite the notion that our inner self might purposely punish us, (therefore, it too having to make consequential sacrifices even), it *is* fortunate, that for many of us, we may (only now) be waking up to fact that there is so much more to us than the conscious part of us. Among other things, it means that going forward, we will now have better access to a considerable pool of resources, to the extent we can eventually get in pretty- close touch with our inner self, and learn to use its devices to our advantage more consistently.

In the private world of my own mind, I have found it most helpful to consider my subconscious as an additional individual living inside of me; but certainly, I also know that if I were typically to disclose this private way of thinking, socially, or in business, it would undoubtedly work against me in my dealings with others.

Regarding romantic relationships, I'd have to say that at this point, I actually have no way of knowing just how disclosing my "two individuals" conception of myself might affect an intimate personal relationship; as I have not been in one since I figured these newer things out for myself. However, I do feel pretty certain that developing this new perspective has not decreased my potential to successfully relate to an intimate partner; in fact, I think that understanding myself in this manner would be a wonderful catalyst to maintaining a good relationship, just as it seems to be in all other matters.

Back to further considering how we might become in touch with our "inner nature;" of course, this involves how effectively we might better-learn to access our personal "subconscious database," of sorts; and here we are really talking about improving memory recall; and then in the process of considering a memory that we have recalled, we will also become aware of thoughts and feelings related to this memory.

When I refer to our study of any specific "memory;" at least in connection with a memory of one of our experiences; this also encompasses studying memories of the emotions we were feeling before, during, and after each given experience that we will recall; or in other words, memories of the feelings that we had, attached to one of our experiences that we have brought to mind.

Our ability to analyze these "emotions-attached-to- our-experiences" provides us with a greater potential connection with aspects of our subconscious intelligence. But of course, I'm not recommending that we try to analyze each emotion we felt before during and after an experience that we have brought to mind, in the process of trying to solve a current problem, for example; but rather that we allow ourselves to be directed consciously, to think about the emotion that appears to stand out as most significant; that you seem most interested in thinking further about; in other words, your sensing of an inclination that you should probably be running down exactly what thoughts led to the development of this particular emotion, for example.

I think it's important to theoretically consider our emotions as prompts, methodically given to us by our subconscious mind. Certainly, we also need to weigh the relative impact of our various emotions surrounding an issue we are consumed with thinking further about; and that is one particularly important function that thinking about our emotions can serve; but I also see our emotions as having greater potential to direct us to "consciously examine" what has led to their development; and in so doing, this theoretically gives us a window into the workings of our own subconscious mind; which becomes so educating and useful.

And concerning the way we can allow ourselves to <u>be</u> directed by our subconscious mind, I think it's important to realize that we should attempt to become more sensitive to the relative strength of our emotions; meaning that in one given circumstance, for example, it may occur to us as more important (or in other words, we may feel more moved at the time) to study the probable reasons why the emotion we felt <u>just after</u> going through a certain experience, had developed; or in other words for us to think about the group of thoughts that had seemingly formed this emotion.

And yet, in another circumstance, maybe we are sensing that it is more important (i.e.- we have become naturally moved) to consider just what led to the formation of some certain emotion we were feeling <u>during</u> some experience that we had gone through; this particular experience having come to mind, in the process of our dealing with some current situation; and assumedly for this purpose we have intuited that our memory of this specific experience could be useful to us.

Theoretically, we could consider that the "relative strength" you can discern, of the emotions that you had felt, just before, during, and after a given experience, can be used to guide you toward analyzing what your "subconscious self" thinks is probably most important to turn our conscious attention towards, and then thinking more about, to help you deal with your current problem, or challenge at hand.

Earlier on, I was talking about how any of our inclinations will become formed as a result of our consideration of a certain group of thoughts; but in like manner, each of our emotions of any particular moment, is also a product of a group of thoughts that led to its development.

For example, let's say that a construction worker just picked up his paycheck, on Friday afternoon. Walking to his car, he is feeling happy; and this is not only because he just received a paycheck, but also because he knows it means that he will go out to the bar tonight perhaps; or take his wife out for dinner; or pay for his son's new baseball glove; or make his mortgage payment on time; or whatever group of thoughts might come to mind, in concert. -And further, in terms of the strength of an emotion such as feeling happy, it would also follow that the more of these happy thoughts that additionally come to mind; while you are sensing being happy at this time; the stronger the emotion will feel to you. (i.e.- the construction worker's happiness comes about just after he has realized that several pleasing things can now be accomplished because he has his paycheck in hand.)

Perhaps, a similarly-strong emotion of sadness would be felt if the construction worker went to collect his paycheck, and he was turned away, empty-handed. Now he would be unhappy because he could <u>not</u> do all of the things he was planning to use this money for, as I had just listed above.

So I suppose that the hierarchy is that first, a thought comes to mind, and then perhaps that thought triggers other related thoughts; and then in considering this group of thoughts, an emotion becomes formed within you, attached to this specific group of thoughts; and then maybe this all has triggered an additional related thought, which triggers a different group of thoughts, and then considering this new group of thoughts, perhaps some different emotion becomes formed within you; and then on the final level of the hierarchy of our intelligence, we consider the group of emotions that has developed related to our current situation or circumstance, and from this consideration we develop an inclination; or perhaps multiple inclinations; but one of these inclinations is usually discerned by the individual, as the one which will most-advantageously move us to act based-upon.

If we have mixed emotions surrounding a certain issue, maybe we have a few different inclinations in the mix; let's say our construction worker is inclined to go out drinking with his buddies at the bar, he's just received his paycheck; but then he knows that his wife will be upset, and he is not inclined to upset her either.

But ultimately, theoretically he would be tapping into his greater sense of intelligence if he could consider which of those inclinations is strongest, and go with that one. Of course, weighing different related factors, and how strongly you feel inclined to do one thing, versus another instead; this can be a messy business; but of course, this is what we are each naturally charged to do. All I am suggesting is that the more we understand about what is behind some of these more complex influences, the more well-informed our decisions and future choices are apt to be.

And I suppose that after all, we will still ultimately be making whatever choices, and taking whatever actions, via the utility of our conscious mind; but through our employment of conscious-subconscious theory, we will have been directed primarily by our subconscious mind's prompts, in the form of emotions we will sense in connection with our experiences, and inclinations that we will sense, being come-to by a natural thinking process that bears some similarity to solving a math equation perhaps; but all of this appears to be, to our great advantage!

Now, can I say, with any definitiveness, that our every action is carried out according to this pragmatic "thought-emotion-inclination" developmental-process I have been describing? Who knows; all I know is that whenever I have analyzed my own thinking and behavior with this theoretical model in mind, I can invariably make sense of myself; in terms of the development of my various considerations and interests, my motives, and the inclinations that have driven my behavior; and of course, this perspective also helps me in considering my possible future behavior, as well. I believe it is safe to assume that this would hold true perhaps for any of us.

Although this may be a bit after-the-fact, I'd like to take a moment to talk about my connotations of the idea of "thoughts" versus "emotions" versus "inclinations." We could really say that all three of these are "thoughts," in a manner of speaking; because for example someone could say to you, "I want you to come with us to the beach;" and your first thought might be, "I don't really want to do that!" That particular idea is an inclination of course.

And then maybe in the next moment you're a bit surprised at how quickly and automatically you came out with this response; so you start to ask yourself why; and the first thought that pops into your mind is that you really don't like one of the people who is going to be in the car, if you were to go. This of course is an emotion.

So technically speaking, emotions that occur to us are "thoughts," and inclinations that occur to us are also "thoughts." However, I would obviously like us to focus on aspects of our possible differentiation between thoughts and emotions and inclinations, in the most useful sense. I would advocate that we keep in mind the "building block" structure of how the three (theoretically) work together. Individual thoughts trigger other related thoughts, and then our consideration of a related group of thoughts culminates in an emotion; and then a little farther down the road, our consideration of a group of related emotions surrounding the topic we are thinking about, culminates in the development of an inclination.

I also want to take a moment to clarify, that the word "emotion" is obviously pretty interchangeable with the word "feeling;" but because I started out, in the early part of this book, mostly using the word "feeling," I will mainly continue using this word. When I use the word "emotions," this will generally be referring to the wider variety of feelings that we will have; while the word "feeling," when I use it as a noun, refers to one particular emotion that I am isolating for discussion.

Continuing on, I theorize that the capacity of our memory-recall abilities has more to do with organization within the subconscious, than with any conscious function, perhaps. I say this because many of us have seen television interviews with extraordinary people who have the ability to remember the chronological order of their experiences, down to the minute on the day they had experienced these events. This "complete and accurate specific recall" ability would seem impossible for the rest of us; but when some of these reported past- experiences are checked out for accuracy, amazingly it is discovered that this ability is real, for a few of us.

It may more-commonly appear, for most us however, that we will generally remember, quite vividly, only those experiences which have left the greatest impact on us; being that, at any given moment we search our mind, there will usually be periods of months, or even years between many of the chronological events we are limited in our ability to remember, if we are trying to remember everything (during some time-period requested of us) that we had experienced, in sequence; had someone challenged us to recount this during an interrogation, for example.

Yet, scientists actually have theoretically determined that basically every event we have ever perceived is in fact stored within our memory; it's just that; also theoretically; it would take way too much time for any of us to remember all of these "consciously- regarded-and-therefore-recorded" events; and we usually only have a limited amount of time to search and recall some event, circumstance, or experience, in the heat of the moment, when we are trying.

Perhaps more recently, this theory has become widely-regarded as bearing validity; that we will store memories of basically everything we have ever seen, heard, or felt; while we were awake; this idea having been considered while examining the best ways of storing and accessing information in a library, or a database. (Computer programmers chose to study human memory storage and recall operations, to aid them in creating a new design for computer software which would be used to access a computer database).

Of course, we could potentially design a search mechanism in any of a number of ways; and when it comes to exceptionally large databases, for example, at least a few of these search designs would eventually allow us to access any piece of information stored within the database; yet for most of us, some of our cognitively- stored experiences, and some of the information and processes we have previously learned, would undoubtedly take an extraordinary amount of time to locate and retrieve; even provided we have put into place, perhaps the most-effective type of conscious-search-mechanism we could imagine.

Yet, perhaps we can depend on this "all of our memories are stored within us" idea to hold true, as evidenced by the fact that if we try to remember all that happened in a given time period, in one sitting; and then later try to remember what happened during this same time period at a second sitting, we usually will be able to recall additional events or detail.

Just in case you might still have doubts, as to whether all that we consciously experience, becomes stored in our memory; and also, to provide further possible evidence that our memory storage is not limited to just the things that were of most significant impact on us; we might consider that, in addition to the impactful details, we also seem to remember things that aren't of any importance. Let's say, in one of your experiences, you were on a sailboat on a windy day, and your boat capsized. You may vividly recall that the color of the sea water had a green tinge to it. Of what importance is this?

So, if we might theoretically assume that all of our memories are there, stored within our mind; then our recall ability would come down to how efficiently our mind has organized the storage of these events, right?

Thinking further about aspects of our naturally- developed (physiology-corresponding-to-mentality) design, the degree of impact that a given experience had on us at the time, certainly seems to be made a significant factor in our ability to recall this experience; and this is certainly one important aspect of memory storage organization.

What might be some other features of our memory organization? What I am trying to get at, is that there are "organizational" features that, while many physiological components of our brain, and of our brain chemistry are somewhat-universally shared in common among us all; but then, just as we each have unique fingerprints, there would also would appear to be some organizational features which are uniquely tailored to our personal best interests, in terms of how our methodically-structured minds have grown and developed. It would also appear; at least theoretically; that the more we are able to realize about our own personal memory structure; through making conscious searches of self; the more effectively we will be able to recall our pertinent memories when this becomes advantageous.

Another thing we have learned about the human mind, from looking at fMRI brain scans of different people's mental processes in action, is that, for two different people asked to do the same task during an fMRI scan, mental activity as indicated by certain areas of the brain that light up with chemical and electrical activity during the performance of the task, in many cases will be taking place in two completely different areas of the brain; measuring one person versus the next!

What this indicates is that each of us learns by uniquely different means; in terms of the routes of neural pathways utilized by a given individual. Perhaps, it could be that as our brain neurons touch each other off, in chainlike fashion; and as the resulting electrical signaling moves down the line toward the end of the firing chain, so to speak; maybe we are further-enabled to gather details of a memory we are recalling; as well as adding intelligent consideration related to the memory's potential to aid to us in figuring out what we might need to determine, related to our current situation, for example.

Thinking further along these theoretical lines, it would follow that each of us may organize and store some of our various memories, also using some uniquely- personal neural processes, and other uniquely- personal aspects of "physiological-corresponding-with-mental" structural organization.

Many of us probably do hold the conception, that the formulation of who we become has much to do with what we have individually experienced, in the order and magnitude of impact this has had on us; and this has been scientifically determined, through many different studies of identical twins; who invariably will yet have, by definition, identical genetic makeup; so, minus a different set of experiences for each twin, we might otherwise expect that the psychological development of both, in terms of personality characteristics, would also appear to be, at least, pretty similar.

Even given that many of the sets of the identical twins who were studied over the years were raised spending much of their chronological past in a mutually- shared family environment, having shared many of the same experiences, at the same time, over their formative years, it has been shown that very different personalities will often be formed, between the two.

One further discovery of note is that; while anyone's genetic makeup will not change during their lifetime; of the hundreds of genes that will make up one's personal DNA, some genes will become "expressed," or turned on; activated basically; and some genes will become prevented from becoming expressed. As I understand it, in the case where a gene is effectively helped to become expressed, through the process known as "histone modification" which facilitates a certain genetic property to become turned on (to be expressed); or alternately, in the case where a gene is kept from being expressed due to "DNA methylation" which basically wraps around and encases the gene, to keep it from being expressed; both of these influences are termed "epigenetic" processes. This, for example, is what will make the difference between one twin having, or not having, a physical or psychological trait, that the other twin will yet have.

Learning about this phenomenon has solved the mystery of how two identical twins could have the exact same genetic makeup, yet become very different from each other; especially in later life, after many independent personal experiences.

Recent discoveries show that both of these naturally-automatic physiological processes, Methylation and Histone modification; which may alter the individual's gene expressions; are apparently greatly-influenced by a person's experiences, and by the various changes in the ongoing conditions of their living environment.

Of course, we had already known that our impactful psychological experiences will greatly influence the character of our personality; including, for example, what we consequently will avoid, out of fear perhaps; or what we might consequentially be drawn to, in terms of our interests and the focus of our endeavors.

Additionally however, related to the ways that many of us will also <u>physiologically</u> evolve during our lifetime, in terms of our personal brain-structure growth and development, and our "epigenetically-influenced" gene expression; both will be affected by the influence of our impactful psychological experiences, as well.

My point is that, given, each of us will have a unique set of life-experiences, as well as a unique set of changes in the ongoing conditions of our personal living- environment, as time passes; then in terms of our ability to achieve our potential; at least theoretically, it would logically follow that each of us would uniquely have the greatest ability to understand who we have personally become; as well as how this development has come about; mainly via searching ourselves more effectively; our conscious search endeavors having been often dictated by our subconscious self. This is just one further reason, This truly being the case perhaps, is why it would be of great importance to spend a lot of time and effort becoming more familiar with the "inner you," in this manner.

-And as far as our consideration of which of us might have the greatest ability to achieve their full potential in this respect, it would logically seem that the most intelligent and well-educated among us would also have the greatest ability to come to a more-abundant understanding of how the human mind works, in all of these respects; whereas, perhaps a lower-level factory worker might not ever learn much about the intricate chemical and electrical workings of the brain, for example.

However, I imagine that almost any of us can learn enough about the theoretical basics of our individual thinking mechanisms, to gain a much keener sense of the psychological positions we have arrived at, at points along the way; and I am suggesting that anyone with an adequate willingness to try and gain some of this valuable insight, would do well to begin working toward connecting up better with their inner self, in ways that will perhaps greatly-improve their standard of living; enabling them to "hammer out" more success, in their attempts to achieve their various personal goals and initiatives; and it would also follow, that enjoying these marked improvements would also bring us substantially greater levels of comfort and satisfaction, as well.

I will concede that this must seem as a pretty lofty ideal; maybe even too good to be true; in the minds of many, at this point. I am not suggesting that all of this can come about overnight; but I am suggesting that, as we learn increasingly more about the inner workings of our mind, we might-well increase our personal potential to enjoy at least some of these benefits.

CHAPTER 9

GOVERNING YOURSELF, THROUGH DEPENDING UPON THEORETICAL CONTENTIONS REGARDING THE SUBCONSCIOUS MIND

As we further-advance at putting conscious- subconscious theory into practice, once having become more-acutely aware of our subconscious trains of thought; and also having conceptualized the possible degree to which we might develop new goals accordingly to serve these more intelligent, and fulfilling purposes; I would suggest that a large part of how we might plan to govern ourselves, going forward, might likely be predicated upon what we have become reasonably assured that our greater subconscious self would want for us; and also what we might sense that our inner self would not want us to persist in, any longer; such as various aspects of how we have allowed ourselves to consciously think-in-somewhat-malignant-terms perhaps; or maybe we will begin thinking in terms of eradicating disadvantageous behavior patterns that we have been habitually and repeatedly engaging in historically, over the course of our daily lives, in the past.

I imagine that the types of inclinations that I have just been describing, would tend to naturally develop within you as a result of having already become in better touch with (your expanding conception of) the "inner you," that you had never really been able to focus on, ever before; because you were simply unaware.

For example, you may have persisted eating poorly, thinking, "What the Hell, I've eaten this way all my life; and I enjoy eating sweets and things; even if I know that they are bad for me." (You love these foods and treats, of course!)

But if you come to realize, from talking to your doctor for example, that due to your condition, your current eating habits may well be heading you for a stroke or a heart attack, or a detached retina or something else awful; you could at least aptly figure that your more-intelligent inner self would want you to discontinue eating the bad stuff heading you in this direction!

Yet, your inclination to trust that this subconscious greater-part-of-your-person would think it important; and wholeheartedly desire to substantially lower the risk of endangering your health and well-being; and the fact that, from having made that assumption, you are finding resolve to diminish your ongoing willingness to keep eating a lot of sugary things; this internal message would certainly be different, from telling yourself it's time to go on a temporary diet; which maybe you might revolt from in short order, perhaps.

Instead, at this point you may personally come to realize that it is not necessarily because your doctor wants you to stop eating sugary foods, that you might now start considering paying heed to his recommendations, (granted, yet against your will on some important level); and it is not even that we have to consider sacrificing, to our consternation, some form of immediate gratification that we overwhelmingly value; instead, it is in the spirit of valuing more, our potential longevity, along with the realization that many people can still live relatively happy long lives, without necessarily eating a lot of sugary foods; and perhaps we would prefer to be one of them!

But coming to this sort of an epiphany, is not anything set in stone either; in my own experience, going through the string realizations that I just laid out above, has constituted a significant positive influence upon my overall eating habits. However, I tend to compromise these lofty ideals, at points; meaning that I sometimes follow what I sense are stronger inclinations to have a piece of cake or some ice cream, for example; and I am not a model of optimum dietary example, by any means!

But I can only imagine that if I had not had the benefit of being able to apply conscious-subconscious theory to aspects of my everyday living situation, I would probably not be in anywhere-near as good health as I am, at this point. The above dietary scenario is just another good example of the welcome improvements in my thinking abilities, and in the further-advantageous nature of my behavior, afforded by embracing this theoretical perspective.

Even though doctors warnings or other people's entreaties for us to eat better have never swayed us before, for any length of time anyway; in terms of keeping to some long-term commitment to eat better; given our new angle of consideration, it is rather that we have come to realize that it is (a more intelligent division of) ourselves, not anyone else, that finds it the lesser of evils for us to stop doing ourselves harm in this manner.

What I am saying is that we can grow to depend on the theoretical fact that our smart inner self would most- importantly want this for us; and indeed, if we want to live the best life; going forward we must certainly do our best to become willing to make some of these kinds of sacrifices; in terms of reining in our conscious mind's unbridled prior-degree of immediate gratification; for our own long-term benefit; and of course we can currently enjoy the idea that we are taking better care of ourselves, and paving the way toward a long happy lifetime.

I would suggest that this type of dependence, upon our personally-developed theories of probability, regarding what we could think of as the more-logical-and- intelligent subconscious thinking mechanism within us, will obviously have the tendency to start us on a much better path to model our future behavior based-upon.

Still, this example emphasizes the reasonable need for compromises to be made, between these behaviors that would perhaps seem ideal; from the subconscious mind's point of view; and our present-moment enjoyment, on a conscious level.

Because it probably wouldn't be a very good idea to "self-engender" our conscious self to feel mutinous toward our subconscious self over such matters; this would only seem to create discord within us. Related to my scenario of thinking in terms of eating better, for example, we could probably instead become pretty comfortable with allowing ourselves to have desert on some occasions; having given yourself some reasonable guidelines, as to upon what circumstances you might allow this grace, for example.

But we should probably begin to view it, that we actually owe it to ourselves to experiment with "how seriously" making any particular one of these sacrifices goes counter to our conscious inclinations. If it seems too overwhelming, it may be more advisable to hold off on making this rash of a change, at this time.

Of course, since "matter of degree" is significant, concerning any of our offenses, we may reasonably grant ourselves some latitude to compromise enough to keep ourselves fairly comfortable, as we forge our way to a lifestyle that perhaps begins to ensure our more-healthy longevity.

Just for illustrative purposes, let's look at how you might respond, under a different set of personal circumstances: Let's say that, in the hours following our learning of the dangers, as a newly-diagnosed type-two diabetic, of continuing one of our disadvantageous habitual behaviors (eating sugary foods), we may newly become (even consciously) inclined to cut ourselves one last piece of cake; and then throw away the rest of the cake, as a symbol of our commitment to our greater self, in this manner.

Of course, our conscious person is not that greater self, and we may even feel pretty divorced from being in agreement with our subconscious mind at these times; but even at these times, we can at least view our consciousness as <u>part</u> of our greater self, or as theoretically having been created by our subconscious mechanism; perhaps during our earliest brain development phase; which may also help us develop the ever-increasing conscious inclination to begin considering ourselves as, at least gradually, becoming more-serving of our subconscious self, going forward. I am suggesting, why not at least "try on" this type of living, for size; and see if you can remain satisfied enough, consciously- speaking, while beginning to live a bit more-healthy?!

For one thing, you must know that, on some level, you <u>will</u> feel better; even psychologically; perhaps pretty quickly, for having resolved to make one of these kinds of healthy changes to your routine, alone. No, you don't have to become a complete "goody two-shoes" or anything; but just try it; put your toe in the water, by changing one unhealthy thing you do regularly. You may well find that you are okay with it in pretty short order, after having gone through the initial discomfort associated with this behavioral change.

Baby steps; progress, not perfection; easy does it; all that good stuff. These are AA slogans, of course; and although I am pretty critical of this program; for a plethora of good reasons which I express in the second part of this book; I would have to concede that many of the people who work this program in the spirit of self- improvement, certainly have also embraced a number of relatively-healthy ideas and ways of thinking, suggested by AA literature, over the past 100 years or so, since this program was first introduced.

In any event, I would suggest that, due to our great capacity to compromise, in the spirit of making reasonable progress while maintaining adequate comfort, these kinds of ideals appear to be of very good value to put keep in mind, in forging our way toward a wide variety of healthy changes that we might become inclined to aim toward, in an ongoing manner. As it is said, the hoop you have to jump through is wider than you may initially think! Why not work with yourself?! (To make some sacrifices to your (consciously-sensed) levels of comfort or enjoyment, of the current moment; for your longer-term benefit.)

CHAPTER 10

REVISITING MORALITY, FROM A DIFFERENT PERSPECTIVE

In his recently published book, "Secrets of the mind," renowned neuroscientist Mariano Sigman provides some interesting information and contemporary ideas; most notably for my purposes, Sigman discusses morality in an interesting light. He points out that our sense of morality is based on various inconsistent principals that have evidently been sociologically programmed into us; and they don't necessarily make rational sense, in some cases.

Sigman offers that the more serious the potential consequences of deciding which is the 'least disadvantageous' one of two alternative ways we might consider as our best behavioral options, (given a crisis situation for example), the more culturally unified people are in general, in terms of everyone usually deciding to act based on the same (most highly-valued) morality principals; leading each of us to make similar types of decisions and take (like) actions in (like) situations.

Sigman posits a few different theoretical situations a person could be faced with, involving two possible choices; limiting discussion to only these two alternatives for simplicity's sake. He paints a scenario which assumes that you had a choice of two possible actions you could take, where death would occur in either case. He gives an example of an accident about to happen, where a fast- moving object is heading right for a group of ten people; but there is a person in-between, and it is realized that pushing this person into the path of it would cause it to veer off, and not strike the ten people otherwise in its path.

Of course, this is a ridiculous example; but although it is a quite farfetched possible scenario; it is perhaps useful in helping him to make a few points about morality. He points out that, certainly for people in the U.S., (culturally speaking), it universally would not be considered the least bit proper or acceptable to push such a person into the path of a train in order to derail it, so that it would not otherwise certainly kill ten people in its path.

One major psychological force in this type of situation is that if someone was to consider such an action, this would be accompanied with great fear, and a strong consciously-perceived disinclination to purposely take any action which would kill someone; especially not an undeserving soul!

For added perspective, Sigman proposes a few other different scenarios involving similar situations; one where you are operating the train; and you have the option to switch tracks in order to avoid running into ten people; but the other track you could switch to, has one person on it who will be killed if you switch tracks. In a situation such as this one, it could be considered a reasonable choice, to make the decision to kill the one person instead of ten, for example.

As a third scenario, Sigman posits a situation where five people need transplants, or they will die; and a sixth person comes into the hospital with a minor malady; but it is realized that this one person has all five organs needed in order to save the other five patients; but the surgeon would be killing the one with all of the organs you would be taking out of him, in the process, of course. This would by far appear as the most morally reprehensible to go through with, as a surgeon, because how could anyone think in terms of cutting into and killing a perfectly healthy person, for any reason?!

But of course, we have been looking at these situations through the lens of our typical conscious considerations, and from a U.S. cultural perspective, in each of these scenarios. Whereas, certainly the third of these three scenarios, would never seem the least-bit justified in any event! However, given I have theorized that we may depend on the subconscious mind's less- emotional (and more objective) inclinations to incline us toward taking action consistent with the lesser of evils, as well as the greater human good; and thus, in the scenario where we would have to push a person to their death in order to prevent ten other deaths, then we might assume, theoretically speaking, that we would be subconsciously inclined to carry through with this idea, when push comes to shove. (Excuse the pun!)

So, this is one example illustrating just how different life would be for all of us, if we all began to serve our subconscious mind's objectives, instead of running ourselves (quite-so-largely) based solely upon the values and perspective of our conscious thinking mechanism. In this case, humanity would be more- consistently finding it a better option to choose to sacrifice one person's life, rather than standing idly by, watching ten people go to their death because you did nothing.

Of course, any rationality possibly associated with this choice must certainly be very hard to fathom for many, in the current day and age, perhaps mainly due to how we have socialized ourselves based on consciously-determined objectives; (and this is just another example of why) I wonder if it is really best for us to think in these consciously-driven terms?

Going a step further; here in the U.S., if you had taken the action to take one person's life, in order to save ten, as in the first train scenario above, you would undoubtedly face a murder charge; quite possibly being convicted and suffering the maximum penalty for murder.

This is also quite obviously an example of how a consciously-driven set of laws we have developed, will guide us consistently to a universal default, which may or may not always involve the greater good of humanity, perhaps.

I'm just pointing to these aspects of both individual and societal guidelines (and the current universally- accepted inclinations to act upon), as constituting further inescapable evidence of how the conscious mind has stepped in, and I say it has often stepped in way over its proper bounds, evolutionarily-speaking; and taken a disadvantageous degree of control over (both our personal and societal) governance.

If society were to somehow stop dictating, through consciously-conjured means, that someone necessarily will be charged with murder and ultimately be convicted, if they took a life to save ten, in such an unusual circumstance for example; and alternately there might be ten times less premature deaths annually going forward, would this really be so awful?

Of course, I can probably be pretty sure that once this book comes out, some number of people will write scathing articles condemning me, stating some distorted impression that I am advocating murder; simply because I asked the question whether it would really be so terrible that we change to act (consistent with a less overly- emotional, and more reasonably rational inclination, when prompted by the subconscious entity within), such as to more often in a grave crisis, for example, end up sacrificing one life, if by doing so we can save ten lives in the process?

-And what would be the most important motive for why this scathing and distorted attack on me would undoubtedly occur? —Perhaps it would be because the conscious mind seriously wants to prevail, at all costs! - And perhaps, we could reasonably predict that less- sophisticated thinkers will feel threatened, or otherwise uncomfortable with it, when beginning to consider being differently dictated to, and more influenced instead by inner-inclinations coming from a deeper, less familiar source, in some ways. I can only imagine that the conscious mind will want to cling desperately to what it has always been comfortable with, in its challenge to go about independently determining what is to be done, at any given moment.

Concerning any suggestion of perhaps alternatively depending on some other force, to go by; even if these ideas are coming merely from a division of the same mind it that this conscious entity belongs to; initially, a person's conscious mind will likely have a tendency to recoil from deciding to, and carrying through with, taking actions in some manner other than the way it has always historically been comfortable with (i.e.-completely running the show).

-And I also might question; from the point of view of the individual's conscience, do you think you would feel better or worse, knowing that in a crisis situation where ten people died, you had avoided directly taking any action that would have led to someone's death, (so you could perhaps feel good about that), even though ten people died who you could have quite probably saved, provided you acted differently in the situation?

Or would you rather have had it turn out as being a situation where you took a calculated action that, while it unfortunately sacrificed the life of someone who would not have died otherwise in this crisis situation; yet, this action (that you took anyway), saved the lives of ten people?

Obviously, for anyone who can possibly get beyond feeling completely horrified that any person at all was willfully killed, for any reason, as a paramount moral principal in itself; certainly the virtues of the second scenario (the advantages versus the disadvantages overall) make it seem like the better option; for anyone who might have had the courage and fortitude to sacrifice someone for this type of worthy cause.

This is an example making it very easy to see that rationally speaking, perhaps we would be better off living according to something other than our current (consciously-driven) sense of morality; where we all concur that not only is it a better choice, but it is the only proper choice, to let ten people die when we could have saved them, and didn't take action to do so. I'm just continually trying to paint a bigger picture that, in many ways it seems, the world is a far cry from the way it should be; and conscious logic, which in many cases, really is an unfortunate form of irrationality at the same time, is perhaps mainly to blame.

All of this notwithstanding, it begs a very pivotal question, as to whether it might, in some cases, even possibly, at all, be a moral right; much less a moral duty; to interject our personal judgment over who we might think is more deserving to die at our hands; either by acting, or by omitting to act when we could have, to save someone.

Just to illustrate this moral dilemma a little further, let's suppose that the one we could possibly send to their death in order to avoid the certain deaths of ten others, let's say he was one of the greatest minds like Albert Einstein; then perhaps you would think twice about sacrificing him, in the situation. However, if Einstein was one of the ten you could save by sacrificing some more ordinary soul, this would undoubtedly become a factor in the dilemma. -And you could ask, who am I, as a mere ordinary individual, to take such consequential matters into my own hands?!

But you see, if we conceptualize ourselves as best- off trusting that the smartest possible decision would come to us in a moment of decision, in the form of an overwhelmingly-strong inclination to take action in one direction or another; and that it would therefore be our charge to consciously allow ourselves to be decisively moved to act, when we would otherwise be consciously paralyzed, like a deer in the headlights; it would be easy for us to believe that we had made the most-intelligent decision possible, in the heat of the moment.

Looking at another oddity of human morality, (or rather the apparent lack of it in this context), in A.C. Grayling's book, "War," he writes that we have become more clever (skillful, adroit), but not more-wise. He states that our weapons have become more potent, but our judgment is (still quite) lacking. I take this to mean his acknowledgement that the conscious mind, (that yet we all typically lead ourselves with), only has a limited capacity to help us to avert self-destruction. When he says that we have failed to grow wiser, I take that to mean that we simply won't seek the wisdom that each of us probably does have the potential to tap into, if we could better listen to and obey the subconscious component of ourselves.

Presently, it seems obvious that, for most of us, our impression is that the conscious mind is the end-all, and it represents our full potential to act to good purpose.

Yet, when the greatest minds of the age recount how "war represents failure- failure to resolve a conflict by any less extreme means; failure of the ties between countries supporting free trade and national supply and demand features, and failure of (the potentially healthy exchange of) complimentary resources among the two countries in conflict," the best minds can surely see that this limitation amounts to a serious shortcoming of our conscious capacity to take good care of ourselves, one and all!

We know that "shooting starts when talking stops;" that (winning a) "war may <u>not</u> determine who is right" (only who can reign more terror). Some of the greatest minds among us ask, "is there a greater evil than war itself?!"

It is stated in Grayling's book, that we must all learn to identify war as a futile effort in every case. By one definition, "war can be described as armed hostility." We hear intelligent platitudes such as "the first victim of war is truth. (The next is human rights)"

We also know that once a country enters into a state of war, it considers itself as having a license to commit any of a huge list of atrocities against its foes.

These days, going to war can cost upwards of $60 billion per year. The war in Afghanistan has cost us over $500 billion already! War condones our stepping outside of the "moral universe." The aim of winning "justifies any and every act."

It was also stated in this book, that great generals are not so, due to military training; but due to some other personal form of talent and creativity. I suppose that Grayling means "creative strategy;" and he states that this resourcefulness is apparently considered as a manifestation of a warrior's personality.

However, perhaps most us would consider one's personality as being mostly comprised of a person's conscious mind's attributes; whereas, I imagine the genius of successful battle strategy is probably due to a great war leader's unusually-greater connection with their subconscious intelligence, than most of the rest of us. – But even here, the conscious mind of such a person obviously manages to badly distort this more-intelligent subconscious line of thinking, anyway; because as I said earlier on, personally, I can't believe that anyone's subconscious mind would naturally have a motive to kill others. My theory is that this idea may only be embraced within the lesser-intelligent conscious mind.

In Grayling's book, they call this conjuring up of atrocity using creative means, a "romantic" type of thinking. How curious?! –But obviously what they mean is that committing war's atrocities could not be a plan based on reasonability or rationality of thought; just like romantic feelings toward someone, I suppose.

Great war leaders are said to have "audacity," to clash wills (with another great war leader on the other side). War is, of course, "an act of violence… to force our opponent to perform our will." According to some of the most ruthless war leaders, war's object is "total annihilation of the enemy." Hitler was one of these types of thinkers; yet even after Hitler has long been gone, there are still many others more than a bit like him, who have the ill capacity to think in these vile terms. Within this book, it was stated that war is a "trinity:" Primordial violence, Hatred, and Emnity (a blind, natural force).

Grayling's book goes on to express the ideas of Giulio Douhet; who considered that "command of the air" (his book title) was most advantageous in war. He thought that "bombing should target the civilian population… to break the enemy's morale; or to cause a complete breakdown of social structure." "The nation that can stand being bombed the longest would win." What barbaric ideas!

At least, in more modern times, we have tempered our warring approaches, to try and avoid other than military targets (only sometimes, though); but this seems really to represent a ridiculous form of rationalizing, that war is anything but unacceptably disadvantageous, cruel, and inhumane, in every case!

CHAPTER 11

INCORPORATING CONSCIOUS-SUBCONSCIOUS THEORY INTO AN INTIMATE RELATIONSHIP

Perhaps it is easier to bring these considerations into play when we are thinking, by ourselves, about what behaviors we are inclined to move forward with; where our thoughts and motives will not even necessarily become known by, or discussed with others, to any degree.

However, bringing communication regarding this new way of thinking and explaining things into interpersonal discussions or transactions, in a more- intimate personal setting, is of course, certain to become more complicated and challenging. Saying something like, "I sense that my inner self likes you well enough; but my outer self is actually afraid of you, at this point;" would perhaps leave a potential intimate partner, in a developing relationship, looking at you cross-eyed!

It is easy to see that there will obviously be personal situations in which, pretty early-on, we will need to explain a little about your newer awareness; of how you have come to understand it, that each of us exists as two fairly separate individuals in principal; and that, the way you have come to see things, the conscious "you" is only a mere component of the overall you; and that it is also of considerably less capacity than the "subconscious you;" in terms of its intelligence and available resources. Of course, you would also need to explain that you certainly realize that these ideas are purely theoretical; however, that you have been led to believe that "acting- as-if" this theoretical perspective were a true reality of the human mind's mental structure would amount to a substantial improvement in your ability to evaluate your circumstances, and act most-advantageously; and that you are "trying this psychological position on for size," so to speak.

While getting to know any new friend, for that matter, it may well be advisable to find some way to put forth this disclosure fairly early on, within this potential developmental stage of the new relationship. That way, there is at least some chance that your new friend might come to understand enough about these ideas, to follow some of your lines of thinking, instead of becoming hopelessly confused and put off whenever your behavior departs from convention, at points; thereby snuffing out any potential for a closer relationship to ever develop.

I imagine that if, earlier on, you have done an adequate job of explaining how you have been developing a keener sense, more newly attempting to distinguish between two separate sets of thoughts, feelings, and inclinations (a conscious mind's set, and a subconscious mind's set); hopefully, (instead of alienating them), this will incline your new friend to inquire further into what seems to be going on within your mind in these respects, as increasingly-intimate relations may ensue.

Of course, it would also be important to offer your realization that attempting to distinguish one set from the other is not an exacting science; but perhaps the laws of probability can often help to indicate which of our two conceptual minds is thinking and feeling what, given various types of dilemmas and situations we will find ourselves in.

As you might imagine, having developed your mentality in this more complex light, you could seem a little weird, to some people whom you will encounter, as you begin to talk in these terms, at times; and unfortunately, you would, no doubt at least temporarily put some people off, in so doing. However, perhaps those of us who have come to this more complex realization about how our minds evidently seem to work, will undoubtedly have a prevailing ongoing tendency to figure out various creative ways to successfully rely on an increasing number of new (theoretical) determinations, of which perhaps we now might pretty-undoubtedly be making; as we continue to propose different theories to ourselves; drawing upon our experiences; along with what we may newly learn about our inner self, going forward. These types of theories seem to be constantly coming to light within me; born out of a natural creative intuition; and I imagine this would also hold true, for many others.

And I can only imagine that, as more and more of us grow to embrace these somewhat universal ideas and concepts, the dimensions of intimacy between individuals will grow increasingly more rewarding for each of us; as we grow in our ability to communicate the sources of our thoughts and feelings more succinctly; and as we become further possessive of a growing ability to develop a deeper perspective on ourselves, and on humanity in general.

Perhaps in the not-too-distant future, for example, most of us will begin to be able to follow, when a friend says things like, "My outer self would normally feel the social pressure and move me to make a (reasonably expected) commitment to go to their party; at least when I'm invited by someone I have gotten to know, a bit more personally more recently; but I am actually sensing an awareness of disinclination to go, existing within my inner person."

Now granted; once hearing this said, you might start thinking this friend is maybe a little dorky; but still, this disclosure might give way to an inquiry of, "What do you think might be behind that disinclination?"

-Which might be answered by, "I feel like I am being pulled into an intimate relationship, by this person having the party and putting pressure on me to make a commitment to go; and I am not really inclined to expend the time and energy I anticipate would be entailed, in dealing with the intimate partnership I am sensing she wants to develop with me."

Your friend could then say, "It sounds like maybe your inner self senses that you have quite a bit of conscious fear, of getting manipulated into fulfilling her needs at the expense your becoming encumbered, and feeling no longer on your own, to do entirely as you please, as an autonomous individual."

"Yes; there's that too. —But of course, I consider that my subconscious mind runs more on desire; and if I subconsciously was inclined to start up another intimate relationship, it's not likely that it would seek to serve its conscious counterpart, as much as to have things work the other way around.

However, I do sense that, subconsciously as well, I really have a strong desire to hold onto my independent lifestyle, at this point in my life. After having had one- after-the-other intimate partner relationship, pretty constantly throughout my adult life; and now I am divorced, I feel I have had my fill of this lifestyle choice; and at least for the time being, I suppose I see myself as better-off devoting my time and energies to working on accomplishing my independent personal priorities; as well as enjoying not having to endure an intimate partner's potential demands, including the inconvenience of having to work things out and compromise, as seems to become necessary so much of the time, in the interpersonal setting."

Then, your friend could surmise, "Well, at least it doesn't appear that you are avoiding working toward forming some relationship that you sense might well be rewarding and enjoyable, just because of some greater level of conscious fear; in which case if it was that, instead you might make more of a concerted attempt to incline yourself to move through this fear, and not let it stand in the way of inviting further intimate exchange with her."

This type of interaction says so much more than, "I think she wants to suck me into a relationship with her, but I don't want that." -Not that this statement might not be the better option, to "keep it simple," when talking to someone whom you only know pretty-superficially, for example.

The former deeper exchange I just laid out, might seem to you more like what would go on as a conversation in a therapist's office; but why must we limit our therapeutic exchanges to the environment of a therapy appointment; given that commensurate with the development of the kind of "mentality expansion" (of sorts) that I have been discussing, we may well develop good potential to help each other out on these deeper levels, in our day-to-day life experiences among the people we care about most; be it close family members, intimate friends, or an intimate partner. It may not necessarily take a therapist, to share a hunch of what might alternatively be behind each other's questionable thinking and actions, at times.

In this last scenario, for example, the comment about sensing some greater level of fear, possibly distorting someone's perception of their main motive, has good potential to incline this person search deeper, possibly to "smoke out the real objection," as it is said in the sales world; in the case where a short-sighted rationalization might indeed appear to be blocking an advantageous initiative.

For example, perhaps as a result of having this kind of interchange, you might instead have become inclined to think further, which might have led to the realization that you really were finding good enjoyment from sharing more-intimate ongoing exchanges with this other person; granted whom you are, at the same time, also afraid of becoming day-to-day partners with; thereby becoming in touch with the idea that if you continue to take this tack, of cutting off any possible development of rewarding intimacy, your greater subconscious self would suffer unnecessarily for this. You could start think that, at very least, perhaps it would mean snuffing out some potential for a greater level of fulfillment and enjoyment otherwise possible for you; unless you were instead to allow the intimate exchange to continue.

Maybe, in a situation such as this, you could attempt to discuss more-specifically with this friend, what aspects of their behavior typically bother you; while also telling them that you have yet, enjoyed your interactions with them; perhaps ultimately offering, "here's what I would suggest, to keep it more comfortable for me, so that we can continue"…

Here's another piece of theory- If we consider the idea that the conscious mind initially was a creation of the subconscious mind, for the purposes of serving it, then theoretically, our subconscious mind would not ever be wondering much about what is going on within our conscious mind. We could consider that, theoretically, our inner self would already know what thoughts it has prompted the conscious mind to consider at any point in time. If we were to possibly assume that these theoretical contentions are indeed true, then it would seem to follow, that any time we ask ourselves a question, of which most of us find ourselves doing this pretty frequently perhaps, we could assume that the conscious mind must be the one always asking these questions, of its subconscious master.

This is just another example of the types of things we can "theoretically-figure-out" for ourselves utilizing conscious-subconscious theory; and how we may increasingly grow in our potential to develop some amount of certainty about (in this case) "who's asking who," which may be of good assistance to us, when we are trying to get an increasingly better handle on determining which thoughts are coming from which of our two thinking mechanisms; at times when it could be useful to be able to feel, at least, some certainty about this.

I, of course, consider that my subconscious mind provides the bulk of input, of what my conscious thinking mechanism will be thinking about at any moment.

However, if, as I have proposed, my conscious mind has sometimes taken this input and has developed its own independent lines of thinking, (possibly contrary even, to the most important values and understanding of its subconscious master), then I figure that for starters, my subconscious mind must learn how to keenly sense this opposition, in order to effectively gain some potential to reign-in this somewhat aberrant conscious mental activity.

Yet, even subconsciously coming to understanding more-fully, what is behind these opposing consciously- developed inclinations, this obviously may not be enough, in itself, to necessarily enable the subconscious thinking mechanism to be able to reign-in different forms of problematic independent conscious logic and rationale. (Our review of mankind's worst consciously-rationalized destructive acts that even some of our most powerful leaders can become moved to carry through with, certainly would constitute evidence of this, for example.)

This of course, is our paramount human predicament, of which I see is presently wreaking havoc in our world, in a huge way. The fact that the conscious mind apparently has great power to make pivotal decisions, and to take our every action, yet with comparatively miniscule capacity to think anywhere near as intelligently as its subconscious master, this seems to represent a poor natural design, in many respects.

In an evolutionary sense, ideally, this unfortunate dilemma would obviously not have been an intended result of the subconscious mind's (theoretical) development of the conscious mind, to better serve its objectives; I consider that it constitutes the "running amuck" of the conscious entity, which has become responsible for so much human trouble and destruction, in my view.

Therefore, it becomes the subconscious mind's ultimate challenge to find ways to incline its component conscious mechanism to work more cooperatively, and for the most part, pretty-consistently within the guidelines of the greater subconscious self's (infinitely more-complex) understanding, to the extent the individual can grasp.

CHAPTER 12

CHALLENGING OUR SOMEWHAT STANDARD DEFINITION OF WHAT IT MEANS TO BE IN A "RELATIONSHIP"

Many of us can probably agree that there seems to be a widely-understood singularity among us, of what "being in a relationship" normally means; and we seem to embrace many common ideas of just what is expected of each partner, when we consider that we are "having a relationship" with someone.

Some of the parameters might be that each party feels somewhat possessive of the other, in particular ways; namely that there is a mutual commitment involved, that it may continue on indefinitely unless or until one of the parties violates it in a significant way; that it involves romantic interchange, sexual interchange, and contiguous contact, usually daily contact at several points during the day; perhaps often that you each come home to each other at the end of the day, and spend the night together, most of the time, at least.

Looking at these characteristics, it is easy to see how relationships can be scary at times; or at least pretty-uncomfortable, for either or both parties at different points.

Of course, courting used to be different in the 1940's, for example; and back then, apparently it was pretty common for relationships which eventually became marriages, to have started out merely as social relationships and dating, perhaps much more often than by a single romantic and sexual encounter; but starting in the 60's perhaps, it became more commonplace perhaps, for relationships to develop quickly; usually after the first "romantic and sexual" encounter which had been mutually satisfying for both parties; or at least, this is how it is generally depicted in many movies.

It certainly has been this way for me, over my adult life. It starts with a kiss; and by the end of the night, the deal is assumed sealed by the good sex. Don't get me wrong; there are many meaningful dimensions to having formed a close bond with your partner; but I would say that more usually these days, good sex starts it off. I consider this to be a universally-understood sequence of events that has full potential to lead to a longer-term relationship; although many of these types of encounters do, of course, end up being short-lived; such as a "one-night stand."

Also as a fad, starting in the 60's, the concept of having an "open relationship" came into being, and some people started experimenting with liberally sleeping around; but we all know that engaging in this practice, adding this liberal parameter to the more-usual confinement inherent in a conventional monogamous relationship, becomes fraught with complications and ill feelings; fear, anger, jealousy, and the like. Trying this, is not for the faint of heart! Perhaps, we don't commonly hear about this type of relationship so much anymore; but we have an offshoot of it, in the form of "friends-with- benefits" relationships; although movies also depict how this often doesn't turn out well.

But I wonder how many of us avoid getting tangled up in a relationship like the plague; because of what it will probably cost us, to end up in one. There is our conception of "the pursued," and "the pursuer" in the relationship; and being in either of these positions has its accompanying package of advantages and disadvantages.

There are countless possible assumptions that either party may make along the way; and these can cause problems.

But if our sense of fear and our inclinations of avoidance leave us with a breakdown in the possibilities for rewarding intimacy, with another who's company we have enjoyed, this becomes a loss of some degree of our potentially-improved standard of living; and I consider that a general lack of deeper intimacy between us as individuals is another big reason why we can't get along; or at least respect each other enough to avoid such hurtful and destructive actions and initiatives such as passive aggression, physical beatings, and acts of war, for example..

Therefore, I would say that we need to redefine our standard definition of a "relationship" in an effort to make it safe and comfortable enough to engage in rewarding forms of intimacy.

Our language developments over history give us a hint of what intimacy truly is: In Time Mate. This suggests that if we are doing it right, in time, we will become "mates" to each other.

Even that word "mate" could stand to be redefined. It seems to be another slippery slope, when we consider what it conventionally means to refer to someone as our "mate." This is perhaps mainly used by people who are married, of course; but it appears as the ultimate statement of commitment and ownership of each other.

In any case, it can feel smothering, to be pursued for the purposes of becoming snagged into an ongoing position of inability to happily pursue attractive people whom you encounter in the course of your daily life; and maybe even worse, to become in a position where assumptions can be made, along with expectations to comply; like the expectation you will accompany your wife pretty much wherever she goes; in such situations as accompanying her to her parents' every party; when perhaps you don't like her parent much, for example.

Even when you are not inclined to head in this direction, if your potential partner is artful, and desperately infatuated with you enough to badly want you in their daily life, in the case of some people, and given some types of circumstances, you could pretty easily be manipulated into a continuing relationship; for reasons such as that you know this ardent pursuer would fall apart and maybe even be suicidal if you simply announced the end of your willingness to be with her at all, for example.

So, the fact that as a society and as individuals, we consider being in a relationship to consist of these expectations and attributes leads to two big problems: One, that it keeps people from getting anywhere close to getting into one; but more importantly, it may often become a form of oppression, alternately for either or both parties.

I would propose that, instead of two people molding themselves into conforming their behavior to the conventional view of the way you should conduct yourself in a relationship, the relationship probably should instead fit the needs and desires of the two particular people that are having it.

Its customization should probably revolve around aspects such as how attractive each partner finds the other; physically speaking, for one. If one partner doesn't find the other too attractive physically, but enjoys their company just the same, then the relationship may not even have to get romantic or sexual. In this case, maybe it wouldn't even be considered a relationship at all; assuming this is a necessary requirement in order to qualify as a defining characteristic.

But that's just the point; the intimacy of this type of relationship (romance-less and sex-less) may still be rewarding for both parties; it could be predicated on other things like having shared common types of experiences, having similar pasts in various senses, or both parties facing similar obstacles to accomplishing their goals; even having similar or comparable levels of chronic physical pain to deal with on an ongoing basis could perhaps be a tenet of a constructive and rewarding relationship.

As long as both parties continue to feel a deepening of intimacy; in other words they develop further knowledge of each other's past, their preferences, fears, hopes, perceptions, and a mutual sharing of the ongoing development of working toward their goals, expressing changes of heart; all of these aspects could be seen as parts in the puzzle, of what forms valid potential to form and continue an ongoing relationship. We could more conventionally consider that it doesn't even have to be romantic or sexual necessarily, in order to adequately serve the needs of two willing parties; whatever their different individual reasons for being in a relationship with a particular partner may be.

All of this being said, I can certainly see the validity of having developed a widely-held conventional view on intimate relationships; as observing these ideals and standards provides useful guidelines for those who do go into a relationship, both parties being very-much mutually attracted to each other. In this case, perhaps there is true potential for a very rewarding and satisfying full-blown relationship, including romantic and sexual passion.

This being the case, convention does offer some helpful, protective, and protective guidelines, to prevent disadvantageous developments such as affairs and other types of unfaithfulness, for example; and to engender healthy and caring support for both partners. Of course, we know that things can go quite smoothly, if both parties adhere to many of the unwritten rules inherent in these widely-accepted conventional standards, governing each partner's expected behavior within an intimate relationship.

However, I would estimate that this kind of ideal beginning point, involving strong mutual attraction, to exist in a smaller percentage of cases; it seems that most relationships involve settling for less than, what at least one of the parties would ideally want for themselves, as far as becoming deeply intimate with a satisfyingly- attractive potential partner, who might have many of the physical, mental, and emotional attributes and characteristics they might hope for, in an intimate partner; and this is why I believe we should develop more flexible standards, in order to better serve the needs of partners in an imperfect situation.

Endeavoring to make a relationship work effectively to satisfy both parties, in a non-ideal situation such as I have been describing, would require good understanding of yourself, as the double entity that each individual truly appears to be; as well as the development of adequate communication skills; in order to do things like set comfortable boundaries, as far as limiting the drain of the other's demands and uncomfortable pressures, which you could otherwise feel as though they are being put upon you; and you will need to develop good ability to establish how much regular contact would be comfortable for you, and the such.

Although, as I have suggested, it is probably pretty necessary to be forthcoming, with more-intimate friends, about what will perhaps more-commonly; at this point in the development of evolving human mentality; would be seen to constitute your somewhat-different and unusual way of thinking and communicating, in this respect; probably in most other dealings it would seem to work much better for you to avoid getting into how you are differently considering yourself, and your ways of thinking and feeling, in light of having come to newly-embrace some of the ideas discussed within this book; and more- commonly, perhaps instead of disclosing how you have come to the behavioral decisions of the moment, just give others the end product of your more-complex thought processes; as conversations develop.

CHAPTER 13

INTERNAL VERSUS EXTERNAL RECOGNITION; WHICH IS TRULY MORE VALUABLE?

When I was in the insurance business over 30 years ago, the Pacific Mutual training program conditioned agents to find great value in two things: Earning a lot of money, and "Recognition." I had long since forgotten about that; obviously, the conditioning never took; as is invariably the case, where I am concerned; however fortunately.

However, hearing someone talking during a gathering I was at today, reminded me of this value that was to be impressed upon us, as agents back then; and actually, I seriously doubt that Pacific Mutual's training program emphasis has changed in this respect, to this day; as our societal values seem to have stagnated for many decades, perhaps, in the course of our rogue conscious mind's takeover that seems to often thwart deeper inner objectives.

The type of recognition we were to value most, back then, was in being recognized <u>by others</u>, as society's having become impressed by, or greatly appreciating an individual, for having accomplished something publicly-regarded as formidable. Back then it was the "Million Dollar Round table," an elite commendation for those agents who sold at least $1 million dollars face value of life insurance coverage in a single year.

But in terms of becoming recognized for something that everybody can see, clearly amounting to a formidable accomplishment, I would not consider these types of accomplishments to be anywhere near as valuable as having uniquely created and developed something, perhaps of even much greater value, as a gift to mankind; such as a significant discovery you have made, or your possible development of some new useful set of concepts, or a unique methodology; which may actually have received no recognition at all, by the public, to date.

I can only imagine that Einstein personally "recognized" (or realized) things that almost nobody in the world would have the slightest understanding of, at the time; and therefore, perhaps society would have placed no particular value on many of his individual discoveries, by themselves. He only became outstandingly recognized by the public at large, once the bomb blew up in Hiroshima; but there were obviously dozens of realizations he made while on the way to this recognizable accomplishment.

The point is, especially while perhaps many other scientists were "poo-poo-ing" his uncommon ideas for years beforehand, it could only have been his own inner recognition of the significance, of perhaps what he alone came to understand, from following his fairly sound, unique trains of thought; that made it possible for him to egg himself on, to many brilliant discoveries and theoretical developments.

On the other hand, of course, how can we possibly recognize the ongoing genius of an Einstein, before any publicly-demonstrated accomplishment of greater value has become more-widely known?

I'm not trying to diminish the value of public recognition in the conventional sense; but my point is that maybe these after-the-fact accolades should probably not be thought of quite as much, as the gold standard; but instead, perhaps we should put more emphasis on scouting for ground-breaking new developments being made by uniquely-thinking individuals. It would seem to be a good future development, to form recognition committees, of sorts; searching out various types of personal and professional developments of this nature which would seem to have much potential to help humanity; assuming that such brilliant ideas, discoveries, and inventions could be more- quickly broadcast around the world.

Still, if you get that feeling like "you're on to something," it sure seems most exciting and potentially- productive to "follow your nose" further, on your own.

However, depending on the events or circumstances I could find myself in the middle of, at times, it can become pretty challenging to keep from feeling like the pace of the world around me is just steamrolling me into submission, to try and accept the way whatever "group" I'm up against sees things; even though I may have the overwhelming impression that the members of this group have simply been erroneously- conditioned to think as they do; without really having any solid basis for coming to such unquestionably-rock-solid beliefs, which may often go contrary to my own ideas, it seems.

Then too; moving forward, in light of these new ideas I have been discussing, becoming more-accepted among us, perhaps; we shouldn't be so afraid of appearing a bit flaky to one another, if in fact what is really happening within our mind is some developmental process, which is leading us toward truly what would ultimately seem to be the better decision, or choice available to us. Ideally, it would seem that all of us in- common will share a more-flaky appearance, in this respect; assuming the overwhelming majority of us might pretty-quickly become aware of how important it is, for us to more-regularly experience much deeper introspection; and it seems only reasonable to assume, that this level of expanded consideration would naturally trigger more of a back and forth type of internal conversation going on between what, by now, we should aptly be considering as our two minds.

This would not really be flakiness at all; even though it may appear so, to some of us, initially; I see this form of natural vacillation as developmentally constructive, and I believe it is the kind of thinking that actually seems to be of paramount importance for us to allow ourselves to develop and move through, as we go about negotiating the matters of our daily lives.

CHAPTER 14

MUSICAL CONNECTIONS; AND OUR COMMONALITY, IN GENERAL

I was thinking that, besides being enjoyable to listen to, music also teaches us more about our minds; to the extent we are looking to learn, perhaps. As I see it, the music that plays within our minds can be fairly-easily discerned as coming from our subconscious mind; as when some song keeps playing over and over again in our head. Even though it can certainly be monotonous when a song that has been reverberating through our mind keeps playing; and we can't seem to stop it very easily; this appears as evidence that this is a subconsciously- generated phenomenon.

When this happens to me, it makes me become more aware of the concept that I have two independent thinking mechanisms operating to, together, make up the entirety of my mind. This morning, a song that I had heard couple of times yesterday kept playing over and over in my head; and I found myself, my conscious self that is, making an entreaty for it please to stop; but it wouldn't; and it reminded me of another concept I have been discussing; that theoretically, your subconscious mind is not a servant to your conscious mind; but of course, it is the other way around.

When I had asked it to stop reverberating this song within me; and I had subsequently noticed it hadn't; at least, it almost suddenly became less pervasive within my conscious mind; showing me that for one thing, my subconscious mind certainly is respectful of its conscious creation to assist it; and it has no desire to torment me; but it obviously wanted to keep playing that song perhaps to itself; and I am also guessing that it must have its own sense of awareness within itself; otherwise, of what value would be for it to play itself some song that it likes, as it goes on churning with thoughts. I assumed that my subconscious mind must find its playing of music within my head to be helpful; and I also can only assume that it is somehow inspiring the further development of some important mental process it is going through in order to go about its incessant activity of developing my further understanding, augmenting my ability to forge on, in its never-ending process of increasing my overall intelligence.

I can also learn; based on my general appreciation of various musical styles and their harmonic content; by considering various aspects of the nature of my enjoyment, as I am listening to certain more well-liked melodies and progressions. For example, probably just like most Americans, I enjoy music in a major key, using progressions that are very-commonly used to write a great many popular songs, for example. I consider my enjoyment of listening to major-chordal progressions to represent that my mind likes order and symmetry. One of my favorite classical composers is Bach, and of course his music is quite mathematical in structure; and I can only imagine that this is one huge reason why I enjoy it so.

It reminds me that I also enjoy the symmetry of building things in perfect squares and rectangles, or triangles, or in any of the many symmetrical geometric shapes, for that matter. Major progressions also seem to inspire optimism within me; and this is a form of positive spirit which I sense is significantly helpful; often giving me a sense of increased energy, that I consider is perhaps most-importantly working within my subconscious mind, as it goes about accomplishing its tasks.

On the other hand, most of us obviously also appreciate music written in a minor key, such as the blues. Some musicians who play the blues a lot of the time, or sing the blues as their major emphasis in performing, obviously find this minor melodic content, even relatively more-gratifying than major progressions, probably.

And of course, most of us can relate to the emotions communicated through the playing and singing of blues songs. It is certainly one way that helps us to feel a greater connection among us, in that we all will have sad experiences which make us feel, at times, just like the emotion the singer or musician playing the blues song we are hearing, is being represented or communicated.

Of course, we all like feeling connected to one another; and almost any form of music which is more- widely appreciated helps us to sense this greater connection, and all that we have in common with each other, as human beings. In fact, I consider that perhaps, one of the many reasons why the idea of God was created by us in the first place, was to establish that we all basically think and feel the same way, as human beings.

I'm sure that this is one of the main reasons why I have gotten along well, and been able to identify with people for whom a strong religious sense is a major part of their conceptual reality. It seems to allow me to sense the considerable value that churchgoers receive, by listening to religious readings and sermons, in church; and I'm also sure that being able to relate to other church-goers in this manner, was one of the reasons why I could continue to come to church every Sunday, and sing with the church choir; even though I rarely had much of a sense that God, as a being, truly exists.

But as I said earlier, within humanity, we tend to get on the right track, long before we have more- thoroughly developed, in the most comprehensive sense, a more-completely-accurate understanding, of something important that we are considering, conceptually; and I tend to think this phenomenon is at play regarding our conception of God. Perhaps, we should keep in mind, that regardless of whether God, as a being, is a true reality or not, the <u>idea</u> of God was first thought up a few thousand years ago; and I can certainly appreciate the utility in embracing godly concepts.

I can see an even greater value in how the societal leaders of the very early generations of civilized man, could very effectively communicate what seemed to be the most wise and constructive ways for the individual to think in terms of and base their actions toward each other upon, in utilizing the concepts laid out in religious stories. Then too, the threat inherent in instilling the strong belief that God is real, and that if you don't sincerely try to embrace and operate exclusively based upon these religious ideas; strictly behaving in a manner that we might each conceive of, as what God would approve of; we might-well be punished severely.

Additionally, by suggesting that there is an afterlife, and that each of us will either end up in heaven, or perhaps having to live in hellish conditions forever; depending upon whether we acted constructively and benevolently during our lifetime, or whether we behaved badly, and caused much trouble and anguish to those around us.

These ideas would obviously have the effect of keeping the masses in line, and of keeping the fellowship of the society of man together; as well as discouraging harmful and destructive ways from persisting as a major basis for how we think of, and treat each other.

However, I maintain that there is nowhere near as much need for us to keep our focus so strongly on God and on religious teachings, in the modern day; as we have learned a great deal about our own humanity, since those early days of the creation of religion; where we each perhaps did indeed have a great need to be directed; but with the exception of a very few extremely wise and advanced thinkers back then, the vast majority of us quite obviously were pretty lost, in terms of understanding how to reasonably get along with one another; as we can see how the ancient stories in the Old Testament of the Bible describe the barbaric, awful nature of humanity, at that very early time in the development of man.

And I suppose there still remains some significant barbarism, in far too many areas of the world, even in the present day and age. However, by now, in the current day and age, perhaps the vast majority of people in the world have become more enlightened about how and why we should be more humanitarian to each other.

In today's society, among the many cultures of our 300+ countries in the world, it mainly seems to be those who are quite rich, or who have otherwise become in powerful positions; especially those acting in some governing or lawmaking capacity; who take such extreme advantage, wielding various oppressive strategies upon the greater body of people whom they lord over. But again, I think this has to do largely with the fact that these rich, powerful individuals may simply have developed a very powerful conscious mind; and without knowing this for absolute certain, I think we could be pretty sure that, as a rule, these people are basically out of touch with their own subconscious mind; and therefore they have perhaps cut themselves off, from a much greater source of intelligence, thoughtfulness, and compassion; that I think we all otherwise value, in common, across the entirety of the human race.

This commonality in our basic values is what I think really inclines so many of us believe in God; I think it is because each and every one of us has a subconscious mind which has developed; in an evolutionary sense; to hold, in common, so many widely-perceived and accepted values; naturally then forming many common general ways of thinking. Of course, this would make it very easy for us each to gain an overwhelming sense that there must be some coordinating force, conceptually in the form of a supremely-intelligent being of some sort perhaps, which universally moves us all; somehow communicating and interacting with each of us.

However, personally I have the very strong sense that this great common influence that we each may sense, is merely present within each of us because we are all cut from the same cloth, so to speak. Each of us will certainly have an identical group of biological brain structures under our thick skulls; and we are all quite- obviously the products of an identical environment, of course; in terms of the evolution in common, of our thinking mechanisms; as each successive generation adds to man's and woman's common knowledge and ingenuity. So, even if God may exist, it could seem that we kind of don't need him anymore; provided we can connect up much-more effectively; each one of us, with our own individual subconscious mind.

Back to the subject of music, all day long I have been running a classical theme, or rather a variety of them, sort of like a radio in my head, conceptually speaking; and this is quite common for me. I have a pretty-extensive musical background; my mother was a concert soloist and composer; and my father was not only a church-choir tenor soloist for many years, but also an avid appreciator of opera, and show music; as well as popular music of his time.

His Father was a professional singer, and my father's brother was a boy-soprano who later became a church organist. My own brother has made his living as a musician; starting out as a rock guitarist; and later getting heavily into jazz. He has performed all over the world, for that matter. Even my sister was offered a recording contract with RCA. Music has been in our daily lives, all along.

I suppose I was a bit musically-impressive even as a toddler. For example, I mimicked my mother's singing; even some of her most-complex coloratura runs; as she prepared for concerts, while I was yet in the crib; and she started giving me piano lessons when I was five. Then, I started learning how to play the cello when I was ten years old. I took private cello lessons through my college years; and I also learned how to play the guitar a little later. In my adult years, I have been a singer-songwriter, and I now compose contemporary orchestra music as well, utilizing my synthesizer setup.

Having had an early orientation to classical music, I eventually became an avid church choir singer; and later, I became tenor soloist. I have long been a writer of my own original songs, which I also sang while playing my guitar. My brother got into rock in early teenage-hood, and later he got into playing jazz guitar; and I followed his lead, in developing a strong orientation to jazz intervals, chordal structure, and rhythms.

Of course, having grown up in the sixties, I also learned folk songs and folk-rock songs; and I learned to play Eric Clapton and Jimi Hendrix licks on the electric guitar; I probably love rock just about as much as any other style of music.

I mention all of this so it can be understood why I might have developed, like a constant juke box in my head. Every morning, just about, I wake up with some song playing in my head; or just a melody maybe. I sometimes find myself hearing (within my mind) a song I haven't even heard for twenty or more years; yet I still remember it as though I heard it just last week! It's pretty uncanny, my capacity for memory of music. (I can't say the same for lyrics; I often can't remember more than fragments of the lyrics to many of these songs.)

I actually see music as a great catalyst to my initiative to work at, and accomplish all that I have endeavored during my lifetime; which amounts to a pretty impressive background in some ways; although certainly a bit troubling in various ways, at times perhaps, too.

But just today, for example, I have been wondering, throughout the day, about where this music, playing in my head, really comes from? Is it stored subconsciously; played back through my conscious by subconscious prompts? Yeah, probably; but since it is so pervasive, and there are many times when I can't shut it off (like sometimes when I need to go to sleep); I am inclined to identify this as a conscious problem; although these things can often be a bit tricky, in terms of becoming able to feel any greater certainty about.

However, tonight, as I lay awake, trying to get some sleep, I was reflecting that I have "some" conscious control over the music playing in my head, when I want to exert it. For example, tonight I found I could slow the speed of the music playing within me, way down; I could also make it just pleasant tonal chords; I could exert conscious intention to play the same three chords over and over, at a slow pace; and this had a calming effect tonight.

So, maybe the conscious can't shut down the subconscious thinking mechanism, which is always ticking; but I found myself wondering how many processes are possibly going on at once, within my subconscious thinking mechanism. Is music perhaps constantly playing in my mind at all times, even though I am quite unaware of thinking about music for several hours at a time?

It is obvious to me that music plays an important role, in inspiring my subconscious mind to continue with productive and inspired mental activity. For example, I was very productive today at doing some home repairs and painting, for several hours; which I had suddenly decided to do out of the blue; and I noticed, as often is the case at these times, that complex and spirited music was playing within my mind the whole time; and now I'm having trouble stopping it in order to get some sleep; so I got up to write about it a bit. I guess I'll go back and try to slow the music down again, and keep it very simple, perhaps consciously leading myself to repeat to myself some pleasant tonal progression, in order to try and gently relax. When I consider this kind of problem to be of a conscious nature, I can often effectively shut it down for the night using these kinds of strategies.

CHAPTER 15

INTUITING THE PROBABLE ORIGIN OF CONSCIOUS-VERSUS-SUBCONSCIOUS LINES OF THINKING AND FEELING

I was thinking today that it would seem sensible to assume, that since physical pain is a conscious phenomenon, then if you realized that you were fighting with yourself, over whether you will make it to the gym today, for example, and one voice in your head was saying "you're going to go;" while another voice within you was saying, "no way, you're not going;" perhaps it would be reasonable to assume the probability that the voice saying you're not going, would be the conscious mechanism; whereas, the voice saying, "You <u>are</u> going; you need to get there and do your exercises today," I picture that this would logically be coming from the voice of my subconscious thinking mechanism.

I say this because the subconscious mechanism seems more likely to be somewhat insensitive to the degree of physical pain I might be apt to feel the next day, as a result of working out today. I was thinking that therefore, perhaps we don't ever feel pain, as a physical phenomenon, within our subconscious thinking mechanism; although we undoubtedly will feel the emotional pain of heartbreak, for example.

We could say that at least theoretically, the subconscious thought mechanism is more concerned with inclining the individual to engage in activities which would pragmatically be ideally good for you in the long run; or in other words in this case, to consistently be getting regular daily exercise.

While this may not appear initially to be of much help, in trying to arrive at your ultimate decision; whether to go to the gym or not today; at least this theoretical probability might well provide some beginning insight to consider; as your two inner voices argue back and forth over the issue; possibly coming to believe, in some greater overall magnitude, that you might intuitively understand the identity of each of the two inner voices involved in this internal discussion.

Then again, the ultimate decision you had made, possibly at the moment, might then also then proceed to change, at different points throughout the day, as you develop various future inclinations over the course of the coming hours. For example, in my case today, I had decided that it would be best for me to make myself go to the gym anyway, even though I realized that I would undoubtedly feel an appreciable amount of pain the following day; and at this particular time of consideration, I felt good about having made that decision.

Yet, I then ended up doing some shopping for a couple of hours; and by the time I was to head to the gym as planned, my foot hurt and my body ached a bit all over. However, at this point I realized that I had already done quite a bit of exercising, in my having walked through several large stores, for a few hours, finding and picking up what I needed to buy; so my strongest inclination at this point became to skip going to the gym; and instead head home and take a hot bath. -But the point is, that I felt good that I had made responsible, healthy decisions throughout the day; and then too, I actually did end up getting adequate exercise for the day.

Of course, with my family history of heart disease, I do realize that I need to get cardio exercise regularly too; so I plan to go to the gym tomorrow and work out on the elliptical machine as usual; as this heart-racing exercise is better for me than just walking, even for long distances. I cite this "real-life-experience" example merely to illustrate some of how I personally go about living with myself in a comfortable and constructive manner, as I continually do my best to hammer out a healthy and enjoyable existence, from day to day.

As the above example illustrates, ideally, the conscious and subconscious minds within you would most-advisably work together; even though, as I have suggested, the conscious mind might be apt, in beginning to think of itself as more of a servant entity; to its subconscious master, in effect.

Although the conscious mind's exclusive purview is its ability to sense the outside world; as well as too, having some ability to sense the emotional and intellectual world going on within the mind of the subconscious thinking mechanism; it also seems that the subconscious mind does apparently have its own separate brand of awareness; albeit more of an internal awareness of itself; on mental and emotional levels, perhaps.

It appears that somewhat often, what the subconscious thinking mechanism becomes aware of and takes into account, in its incessant churning, is intuited at a level beyond our conscious capacity to detect; at least not without conducting some further conscious-search initiative beyond what perhaps might more-commonly be included within the conscious mind's typical more- automatic functioning; before we might have grasped some of the concepts I have discussed here. It would probably be reasonable to assume that, minus the conscious mind's having become somehow made aware of the subconscious mind's current considerations, it would have no cause to search further.

So, it would seem apparent that, at the times it desires to enlist conscious resources and input, the subconscious mind deliberately chooses to make its conscious counterpart aware of certain of its current considerations; perhaps often including its own automatically-computed conclusions, which resultantly have culminated into its separate set of feelings of inclination and disinclination.

This seems to define the nature of our potential to work cooperatively together with our subconscious thinking mechanism. I would think that, at these times, as one paramount conscious priority, we probably owe it to ourselves to focus in on sensing what we might try our best to isolate, as detectably-strong subconscious inclinations of the moment.

Next, we might focus in on sensing any reservations we might have, that would constitute a reason why we would not want to act in accordance with what we are currently are sensing as the "strongest inclination" of the moment.

To cite a bit more of my "real-life-experience" as an example, it appears likely to me that; although it probably was mainly the strong inclination of my subconscious mind, to take us on an adventure to convert my favorite violin concerto into a transposed work for solo cello instead of violin; I sense that both of my thinking mechanisms have since come into agreement, that the project had turned out to be rife with overwhelming complications and difficulties.

What I had initially thought would be a fairly simple process of scanning and converting the individual instrument parts into an orchestral accompaniment for the solo cello part, did not go at all as I had imagined.

The software I have, did not have good ability to read the sheet music exactly as printed; which meant that I did not have the ability, as I had anticipated, to copy and paste each orchestral instrument part into the sequencer file, as it had been originally composed; so the parts became an hopelessly-incorrect jumble of stray notes.

For example, it left spaces where notes should have been in sequence; and I had to find where the spaces were in each part, and move the notes back together. Then, the mechanism I had put into place would sometimes convert sixteenth notes into eighth notes in places; and it didn't read triplets well; it usually made them into note clusters which were pretty-hopeless to decipher. So, although initially, I had been filled with a sense of great excitement and desire to accomplish my goal of transposing the piece; as I continued to struggle with these insurmountable unanticipated difficulties, I ultimately began to feel overwhelmed, and discouraged.

I can't be sure whether it was my conscious or my subconscious mind that first had newly developed the strong inclination to abort the project; but I sense it is more likely that my subconscious mind changed its mind about wanting to continue; and then it took some time to slow down the momentum behind my conscious inclination to continue-on, sort of blindly.

I also see this as a phenomenon that occurs within many of us, from time to time; and I suppose that at these times, we have to endure the consequences of continuing on inadvisably, once our smarter subconscious mind has yet given up the ghost; having intuited this was best, given the circumstances; but our conscious mind, slower to figure these kinds of more-important things out, has not yet been able to arrive at this more-intelligent conclusion.

I must admit that, a number of years ago now, this phenomenon once cost me quite dearly, resulting in dire consequences I must continue to endure the brunt of, still yet for years. However, I have learned to view it as my challenge accordingly, to accept the predicament I currently

Imagining Who's Telling Who

find myself in; and to still forge ahead, in the spirit of productively accomplishing what I remain having the ability to reasonably undertake; as far as worthy initiatives that I might consider continuing my ongoing pursuit of, regardless.

I was hopeful that the music project I've been telling you about, would be a worthy undertaking in this respect; so at first, it was difficult for me to abort this transposition project, that I had spent almost two months working on altogether; but in its place, I have already plotted out a few new projects to work on.

Then too, in the process of trying to accomplish completing this project, which I ultimately discovered that I could not; due to various obstacles and difficulties; I realized that I certainly had come to learn quite a bit more about the greatly-expanded features inherent in the latest version of the recording software I have been using for the past several years, that I recently had installed; which will now enable me to pursue creation of other new composing projects going forward, perhaps, much more effectively and easily.

Existing as evidence, that I have not become discouraged, in any larger way really, over this recent disappointment of having to abort this exciting undertaking, today I found myself already loading up a project I worked on last year; which I had left unfinished; into my new software format; my having newly-learned some improved methods of creating orchestral compositions, in an instrumental sound format.

I've also discovered I could also later import into my Finale PrintMusic software afterward, in order to produce a printed score and separate instrument parts; in case I might get lucky enough to find an orchestra that would be willing to perform one of my orchestral arrangements!

So, instead of feeling down about having to give up on what had been a pretty exciting and important goal, I found myself becoming newly-excited about picking up another project that I had stopped working on, pending the completion of my last semester of college, when my course-load had become too difficult and demanding, for me to continue working on any project which might consume any significant amount of time and energy.

Of course, in addition to this musical project, I am glad to be able to get back to writing this book; as regardless of whatever ability I may have to communicate these philosophical and scientific ideas, concepts, and suggestions on how to forge a better way of life for the individual, in some timely and profitable fashion perhaps, it is more important to me, to at least put forth the time and effort to get these ideas down on paper; because once I have accomplished this much, then at least there will be some potential for others to find value in reading and coming to understand what I am trying to suggest about the realities of the human condition; assuming the value of my ideas might come to light in some manner, at least at some point in the future, perhaps.

I suppose I felt that I had to suspend my continuing work on writing this book a few months ago, when my father became very sick and I considered that he was in great need of my daily presence and assistance; but thankfully he is doing much better these days; and I feel I owe it to myself to diligently get back to work on this most important project.

Most notably, I found myself thinking tonight, that if I am writing things like that this is no joke, and we might all be dead soon, if we don't pretty-quickly begin embracing conscious-subconscious theory; then how can I do as I have been telling my family and friends? I've been saying that I plan to wait three years until I can have internet again, to create a website and try to market this book; along with some other things I've written and recorded perhaps. (The Connecticut State penal system is restricting me; for reasons I would rather not go into, at this point.)

So, I suppose I am tying this book up (at a somewhat-early ending point, from what I had initially planned) and releasing the book as is; in the hopes of getting these kinds of messages out there sooner, rather than later.

This Second Section of "Imagining Who's Telling Who" discusses the contrasts between the traditional AA program ideology, and the theoretical ideas and point of view that I have been expressing, within this book.

In addition, I make further use of these contrasts to illustrate the practical nature, in terms of applicable day- to-day use, of my newer ideas and concepts; utilizing this new theoretical perspective, to pretty-concretely expose the fallacies and inconsistencies inherent in the messages and suggestions of AA literature. I have gone about this, in an attempt to dissuade us, from falling for this suggested method of disadvantageously orienting ourselves to become consciously self-directed, consistent with the dictates of the AA program; however, I see very little harm to rescuing yourself from ruin by utilizing the AA program; as a starting point. Any of my theories are still considerable after becoming oriented to AA ways of thinking. The only thing you will have to do in order to develop the capacity to open your mind up to considering my potentially-useful ideas, is to <u>not</u> continue to close your mind; which is basically what you have to do, in terms of embracing the <u>fundamental principal</u> of the AA program; which is that you are required to consider (and somehow "choose" to believe in) the contended "Factual existence of God;" and this necessarily closes one's mind to considering a host of other possibilities; such as that God may be merely a figment of our imagination, for example.

The term "pseudo-science" refers to various possible "contended" realities of life, which are not in any way based upon irrefutable scientific evidence, or strictly-scientific principals; such as is the case regarding astrology, for example.

Within this second section of the book, I discuss what many would agree to exist as the pseudo-scientific nature of the AA program; which for example, has yet, long-been courtroom-recognized, as a formidable, legitimate basis to begin guiding your life by; for those who have come before the court, with substance-use related allegations against them; and I ask, why must certain tenets of the modern-day legal system still be based upon a multi-generational continuing societal- embracement, of what we now could pretty-firmly- establish as a set of antiquated contentions, merely having been creatively dreamed-up out of thin air, in our yesteryear? Granted, we did the best we could, back then, with what we had at the time; but at this point, we seem to have a far more valid basis to operate by, I would suggest.

I make reference to the Alcoholics Anonymous program; comparing its principles with the set of ideas that I am suggesting we newly begin to embrace and utilize, as a basis upon which to guide our thinking and behavior, going forward; specifically because AA seems to serve as a very good example of a convincingly-powerful suggested program of "consciously-self-imposed," ongoingly-disciplined conditioning of oneself, to think and behave in its prescribed manner; which of course, runs quite counter to the ideas and concepts inherent in the theoretical model that I have put together, with respect to my own various alternate conceptions of the realities of life, and the human condition, as I have been discussing. AA is also a program that I have become quite familiar with over the years, due perhaps mainly to my own family's connections with it; which is another reason I would want to refer to it, in such a thorough and contextual manner.

To be clear, as opposed to forcing ourselves to follow some consciously-laid-out procedural process, such as AA written dictates, bowing to this externally-generated type of encouragement to think and behave in a certain externally-prescribed manner, I am suggesting that instead, we seek to become self-encouraged, and self- motivated; the source of this encouragement, of course, coming from our own inner person; once we have learned how to better-connect with this potentially-powerful, extremely-valuable component of our overall person.

I would like to clarify, however, that although I am speaking out against the AA program itself, I would never want to speak out against any of the people who go to AA meetings, making sincere attempts to better themselves; especially those reaching out for the intended help of this program, who have found that their lives have completely fallen apart; at this point desperate to try and save themselves even from death's door, perhaps in a number of cases.

My writing efforts in this regard actually started out four years ago, when I hatched the idea to develop a suggested alternative program of recovery, which I had called "AA for agnostics." I had created this program because I saw some serious flaws in the AA program's dictates and contentions, particularly centering around members' perceptions of God. I had long-observed that when a "mere belief" becomes instead a "definite reality" within your conscious mind, this appears as a most-disadvantageous, and potentially trouble-causing phenomena.

To illustrate, let's take the silly example of one of those TV movies where some couple's little girl is abducted by a psycho; and he tells you that unless you find him at the train station in one hour with ten thousand dollars in a duffle bag, your daughter is dead! So, you scramble to the bank, and talk the bank officer into lending you the money as quickly as you can; but you arrive at the station only five minutes before the deadline.

You see the psycho walk onto the platform as you are parking your car; so, in your mind, you <u>know</u> he is on the southbound side of the tracks. You scramble to the platform, and after two minutes of searching fiercely, you still can't find him. But you <u>know</u> that he is on that side of the tracks because you saw him go up there, and you just "feel it in your bones" that he is definitely there.

Just as the time runs out, you suddenly see him on the platform, on the other side of the tracks. He had walked across through the tunnel, to the other side; but you hadn't searched over there because you were absolutely certain of the psycho's presence on the platform you saw him walk onto. Whoops! Your daughter is dead because of how absolutely sure you were of something that you should have remained uncertain of, within your mind. Perhaps, it probably would have enabled you to save your daughter.

Do you see what I am getting at?! I frustratingly wonder, why couldn't we all possibly see that this is what happens when we somehow convince ourselves, and feel absolutely certain that God unquestionably exists?! We see the Muslims killing each other <u>precisely</u> due to this false degree of certainty. One says to the other, "We both agree that God exists; but I say that I also know that his prophet has always been Mohamed; and you say that the prophet changes every so often; Dammit; I'm going to kill you!" How absolutely stupid is this?!

And AA laughs this off. Oh, people have been pointing out, for years, that we kill each other off <u>precisely</u> because we make ourselves believe that God absolutely and unquestionably exists; So? Why should this affect our further following-of-our-inclinations to yet develop a sense of absolute certainty about the (unprovable) existence of God?

But, if we were instead to acknowledge that maybe it <u>looks and feels</u> like God is real and present in our lives; yet, at the same time, it would only be reasonable to acknowledge that many others certainly have their doubts about this; and indeed, if this were to be paramount to our human existence, for example, perhaps it doesn't seem very likely that God would not put absolute certainty of his existence into all of our minds, every last one of us; right?

As I should think that any reasonable soul would be able to see, one huge consequence of feeling unquestionably certain of God's existence, is that it would have the tendency to incline us to ignore the paramount importance of acknowledging and working with the great force of intelligence that evidently exists within almost any person's own subconscious mind. (Yet, it seems that AA's say, "Sure, maybe we occasionally sense that we have a subconscious mind; we have dreams, and underlying feelings at times; but of what importance is any of that? All I ever need to focus on is God!) I say Wow! Are you missing out on your own HUGE greater potential, for thinking this!!

It seems pretty obvious to me that trying to make ourselves feel entirely certain of what is apparently uncertain, would naturally have the effect of closing our minds to entertaining any other possible alternative explanations for why things appear to us as they do; whereas, I'm pretty sure that in order to see the truth more clearly and completely, we need to keep an open mind regarding how "what we are seeing as real " may or may not actually be a true reflection of reality; at least in some instances. In order to have any confidence that we are remaining somewhat reasonable and sensible, don't we need to appropriately correct our misperceptions, in some ongoing fashion?!

We shouldn't even <u>want</u> to develop a mindset which may not be a true reflection of reality; as this could really send us quite detrimentally astray, in my estimation; and having attended years of AA meetings; perhaps knuckling-under to family pressure for the most part; I saw that those who made God a reality within their minds, had often appeared to suffer great disillusionment for this; even though, at the same time, they may actually have been considering themselves quite fortunate to have developed this conception of being cared for, by such a powerful and benevolent external force, or being; as God is, at least, contended to be conceived of, by many AA members.

The focal point of the trouble, is that although we may have consciously convinced ourselves that God is real; I should think that, deep within anyone's subconscious mind, this must surely be concluded to be a delusion; formulated within the separate thinking mechanism of their conscious mind; to believe in the reality of God quite so convincingly; when it has in no way been proven, nor is this even being more-widely contended, by more than a fraction of the population; certainly not in the current day and age!

Within this writing, I have attempted to theoretically establish that the subconscious "you" is far more intelligent and knowing, than the conscious component of your overall being, which maybe, is trying to sell your collective overall person, this "quite-possibly- false idea," undoubtedly in the subconscious mind's eye. It becomes rather obvious that, not only would the subconscious mind fully realize that the definite reality of God is impossible to prove; at least this has never been unquestionably established, to date; but logically, this would also represent a significant conflict within this person's thinking, between their conscious and subconscious entities; and this can't be good either.

Of course, in addition, there are many other beliefs which can become facts within a person's mind, and they are accompanied by varying degrees of detriment perhaps; but the "God" belief-become-fact has probably been the most troubling for me to sit and listen to, at meetings. It really rubs me the wrong way; as it seems pretty evident to me that we seem to become so badly misled, by clinging to this apparent misconception.

Holding onto this idea simply constitutes a refusal to acknowledge the significant role that our subconscious mind will play, in pretty-much all of our endeavors. Again, here is more evidence pointing to the "dirty pool" that the conscious mind will characteristically play, as it clamors to remain in control. I interpret these indicative displays of defiance as pretty-hard evidence, of the nasty competition apparently taking place between the conscious and subconscious divisions of self, continually at play within so many of us.

Having embraced the alternate type of underpinnings I have been discussing, I should think that any of us would agree, that we really need to continually and more-extensively become aware of the great inner resource available to each of us; existing as such a capable subconscious force of intelligence; perhaps continually providing us with the greatest amount of help and assistance, which it seems that we also may consistently rely upon, for that matter; throughout the entirety of our lives, as we daily forge our way.

Anyway, as far as what has happened to the "AA for Agnostics" program that I had earlier designed, I eventually abandoned the initiative, after having written it three years earlier, and rewritten it in the summer of 2017; as no "staunch" AA member (these longer-term members are the centers of influence who can command, pretty much without exception, newer members they are the sponsors of; as new members are made to feel they must follow the prime directive of, "You must do everything the sponsor asks, if you are to be successful at saving yourself") with whom I had subsequently shared my newly-written program with, really had any kind of positive response to it; nor did anyone show up at the first Alcoholics for Agnostics (AA4A) meeting I had set up with the church.

I have since come to realize that whereas, AA members may, or may not eventually become a target audience for my ideas and theories at some point in the future, I should probably instead begin thinking more along the lines, that it would be of much greater impact perhaps, to write more-universally, to the world-at-large, about these seemingly-pretty-important ideas I have stumbled across.

I also realize that if I were simply to term these ideas as a "recovery program," in the midst of many other recovery programs, across many types of common out-of-control behavior problems that humanity often might face, undoubtedly the literature would only get lost-in-the-sauce of the many millions of self-help books, that are already out there, in the world.

In any event, I had initially written out a group of steps, I suppose in order to mirror the AA program structure; But having reconsidered, I decided that perhaps steps aren't the best way for people to begin employing my particular suggested methodology within their lives. So, in keeping with my modified objectives, below, I have pasted sections of the text I extracted from this scrapped book otherwise. I then edited, and added further to these excerpts:

I'm thinking that maybe it might be better for readers to become exposed to these newer ideas by first reading all the way through this material; and then they might begin to grasp this improved method of self-directing their thinking and conducting of themselves, at their own pace. I suppose the only first step in this process is really coming to realize that there is another greater part of us which, in many ways, actually exists as almost a whole different individual than the awake part of us. Although at first this may be somewhat difficult to swallow, once we have grasped this notion, I would say it seems that it's pretty much all downhill from there.

To offer a few clarifications, from the outset; first, unlike the contentions made within the AA program twelve-step literature, for example, I can assure you that I will be diligently endeavoring to refrain from making contradictory statements; however, here is one exception: This book <u>is</u> <u>not</u> simply an addiction recovery program; and yet this book could indeed be considered as an addiction recovery program; but additionally, the theories and concepts presented herein are intended to help an individual learn how to more-effectively deal with perhaps a whole host of other troubling problems and dilemmas, as well.

The book will suggest what I consider to be a vastly-improved method of dealing with just about <u>any</u> of our personal problems; and to clue readers in a little, many of the solutions involve becoming more trusting of ourselves, in at least a few important aspects.

Before we continue, let me further-address what might otherwise be a huge stumbling block to exploring conscious and subconscious theory; having to do with different people's conceptions of God; and for those of us for whom thoughts of God are more of a rarity, and they are not really a part of their considerations while negotiating their daily affairs, to any extent; what I will be commenting on in the next few paragraphs could still be of good value to read and think about; at least it could be useful in a conceptual sense.

First, I would not want readers to feel as though the further development of conscious-subconscious theory might be an entirely Godless endeavor. In fact, as I see it, the ideas discussed herein are very much respectful of, and in accordance with all that God is said to be, and to represent.

Of course, many people in Twelve step programs commonly refer to God as their "higher power." Yet, certainly for them, and for any long-time churchgoer who constantly hears, on Sundays, different readings offered as quotes from a great many religious figures, for whom God's presence does appear to them, to be a true reality; the wisdom inspired by their mental images of how God interacts in our lives, certainly characterizes God and godly ways as infinitely good; and as quite-definitely being the "highest power" in the universe.

Therefore, I would ask, shouldn't all those who believe in the absolute reality of God as a being, regard him and speak of him as being the "highest power," and not just a higher power? Perhaps, this is just another incongruence existing within the minds of confessed firm believers we might hear speaking out at an AA meeting, for example.

I have observed that true Twelve-step program followers certainly do seem to sense the great importance of impressing upon themselves, and each other, that we, as consciously-aware individuals, are not powerful; and that it could be dangerous to think of ourselves in these terms. Perhaps, this could be seen as the most important reason why we would want to embrace the concept of powerlessness; which of course, is a great focal point of the AA recovery program.

Like many other God-related principles that I have been exposed to, over the years, as a regular weekly churchgoer who has sung in the choirs of many different church denominations, I certainly see the great value we may derive; in common among all of these denominations; in that so many religious teachings seem to have great utility for us to embrace.

Yet, as older ideas often seem to be, I look at many religious ideas in the context of being on the right track, but not-quite-accurately-reflective of true reality, perhaps. -And of course, it is very common for us to first become somewhat-on-the right track to begin with, as we hone-in more-gradually on a more-full understanding, which eventually becomes a more-completely accurate reflection of reality perhaps, in time. This, of course, is a very common phenomenon observed in scientific study.

Apparently, the truth must slowly unfold for us, as we make continual efforts to flesh it out.

Relating the "powerless" idea to conscious- subconscious theory; in this context, the great value of impressing upon ourselves and each other that we are not powerful, could simply be seen as an alternate way of acknowledging that we must not be so bold as to act hastily when we become in touch with powerful feelings within us, at the level of our conscious awareness; but instead, we should be looking to a more powerful source, realizing and acknowledging that we really need to be guiding ourselves by something more powerfully- intelligent and wise, than merely our awake thinking mechanism.

But, to draw an analogy related to the manner in which we may skip acknowledging an important helper, if we consider that God alone seems to be the one "higher power" that grants all we may receive, of which we cannot provide for ourselves; let's suppose that a powerful financial source were to provide a large sum of money which you will ultimately be the receiver of; if there is a middleman who first takes in the gift, and then bestows it upon you, if we then only acknowledge and express our gratitude and appreciation directly to the financial source, then aren't we doing somewhat of a disservice to the middleman who actually handed us the money?

Taking it a step further, suppose this middleman actually takes in, even a much larger sum of money coming from this financial source, and then goes through some painstaking research process, to identify those community members who would be most deserving of a financial reward, or perhaps to identify those in most need of financial assistance; and as it turned out, you had actually received the money you were given, only as a result of the wisdom and fairness which the middleman has employed, in aptly identifying you as an appropriate receiver of this gift; wouldn't it then be even <u>more</u> of a sin if you gave no acknowledgment whatsoever to this middleman?

But this is actually what I see happening, when people only acknowledge God for the goodness they have received, while not even having a thought, for a second, of owing any debt of gratitude to their own subconscious mind, which could certainly at least be seen as an important middleman, who has worked very hard to provide much goodness for us, too; even if the original source of the gift doled out, actually was God.

I have attended years of AA meetings where members, at times, will recite their gratitude list of that day; but never once have I heard a person say that they were grateful for their subconscious mind's wisdom and assistance!

Then too, I think we could all agree that God does not interact directly with our conscious mind; at least we haven't heard of this being the case, since Moses went up the mountain and stood at the burning bush! (well, maybe with the rare exception of a deluded extremist, such as Mike Pence!) So, even assuming that God does truly exist; it would appear that he interacts more-directly with our subconscious mind; as apparently, many of us do gain a true sense of God's presence within their lives; yet of course, there is no conscious conversation with God involved.

-And, in the case of anyone for whom God's existence is seen as a firm reality, for that matter; I can only imagine that God would not be the least bit upset with our further individual and collective learning, regarding the workings of the human mind; in fact, I can only imagine that God would probably be quite pleased that we were taking the initiative to further-explore our inner essence.

Whereas, I should think God would be much more upset by all the terrible things that we have done, due to such a greatly-misguided personal reliance on more- exclusively utilizing our conscious thinking resources, as a basis for the deliberation of even our most important and consequential actions and initiatives toward each other; especially as this has obviously resulted in quite ungodly, and extremely unjust acts; in so many cases, in the modern world; as always.

I can also only imagine, that God would not want us to neglect acknowledging any significant source of reliance and assistance; certainly not one which has helped us in countless ways, as the subconscious mind of each of us undoubtedly has.

I should also offer that religious teachings have very-much connected with me, on a conceptual level; I have learned of, and grown a great appreciation for all that is offered, in this sense, during the typical Sunday service, in church. I have heard many ancient stories, the stories of Jesus's travels and interactions with the people of his time; such as when he arrived at the pit where a woman was to be stoned, and suggested that he who is without sin, may cast the first stone; and everyone walked away. I have heard Paul's letters to the church recited and talked about, by many ministers, for example; as well as some contemporary offshoots, such as a sermon I once heard where the minister started out by saying that you can't "un-say" something; the message being that we must be careful of what is about to come out of our mouth, because once it has been said, perhaps it's too late sometimes, to provide any remedy for the harm we have done by saying it.

Another contemporary sermon I once heard was delivered by a minister of a church, in a city where gay people made up a reasonable percentage of the population; including some churchgoers in the congregation. It was a very insightful entreaty for him to read several conflicting passages within the Bible; some suggesting that being gay was an abomination, and some more-welcoming and accepting of anyone as a child of God, whatever they thought or did; as long as they remain seekers of the wisdom of religious teachings, and are observing of Godly ways.

Within this particular sermon, the minister's ultimate message to us, was that the Bible was impossible to understand according to the "literal wording" of any single particular passage; but that understanding the overall messages which we are to glean, must involve interpretation. I suppose it's a little like the IRS tax code!

But certainly, I have heard many ministers; spanning the 40 years of my churchgoing experience; who collectively have given quite a variety of interpretations of various passages of the Bible and other Scriptures, of which I thought many of these lines of thinking were often significantly helpful to follow, or at least to otherwise consider; and which I certainly count as having added richly to my perspective. -And I certainly am in no way a God-less person; I just focus more on the middleman, being the subconscious mind within each of us.

I can't imagine that God would look down on me, for my many years of considerable thought development regarding the workings of the conscious and subconscious minds. Rather, I should think that he would laud my long- standing and considerable efforts to turn our attention toward what we have eluded to see as our greatest ally and benefactor; besides anything else that God, perhaps as a primary source, may have ever provided us with, more indirectly. I should hope that having said all of this, might help readers to let their guard down more, so that they might comfortably allow themselves to consider the possible benefits of all I have to say, on the subject of achieving greater understanding, regarding some (perhaps) lesser-known, yet truly-important aspects of the workings of our minds.

Avoiding Damaging Forms of Self-Control

Returning to the topic of out-of-control addiction, self-control certainly is a major topic of this day and age; and of course, it is at the center of everything we do or overdo. There are many plans, guidelines, and programs to deal with specific areas of self-control; and we assign terms like "addiction" to represent our current belief that, minus subjecting ourselves to serious controlling outside forces, or at very least perhaps subjecting ourselves to strict behavioral conditioning regimens, we have come to strongly believe that our lives would continue to remain quite unmanageable as they are, indefinitely.

Even though we can definitely establish this as <u>merely a theory</u> which any of us might be presently holding, many of those who have been suffering from what seems to be an indefinite plight, in terms of their lack of ability for self-control related to their possible future-ingestion of any type of mood-altering substances, would never allow themselves to entertain the thought, even for a second, that the way they historically have totally-lost-any-control to stop themselves from a drunken frenzy, once they took a single drink; this may not always continue to hold true, concerning their own personal case; like perhaps if, for example, they were to go through an effective-enough learning process of some sort.

Taking the AA pledge, so to speak; committing to yourself, to hopefully not ever take a drink again; and to stay wedded to a program that will enable you to stick to your resolve; regardless of even the most extreme potential costs or other harms you would possibly be opening yourself up to suffering, as a result of sticking to these hard and fast decisions unquestionably, for a lifetime; this certainly is a prime example of how we might desperately begin employing a level of conservatism which may be quite excessive; which could perhaps even seem more damaging than helpful, upon our closer inspection.

Likewise, we certainly could think of many other areas of our lives where taking extremely conservative measures could be quite consequential, in terms of potentially amounting to a considerable level of self- deprivation, injustice, or oppression; in one of their many different forms.

For example, Arizona Police stopping every car having Mexican-looking passengers, and imposing lengthy questioning upon each of them, in order to find a small percentage of illegal immigrants, would certainly amount to a significant unjust disruption unfairly for a great many, perhaps. -Or on a much larger scale, we could think of how Hitler implemented the atrocity of killing off all Jews, because he found the behaviors and thinking of some of them objectionable, and he arrogantly felt quite certain that dangerous attributes were inherent in all Jews; this certainly illustrates the possible detriment of moving forward with many more-extremely-conservative initiatives.

In-keeping with our various programs for daily living, throughout the world and in countless settings, we give ourselves slogans to live by; but perhaps many of these may be quite contradictory; from group to group. At an AA meeting, the slogan might be don't drink and go to meetings, and Think, Think, Think! – While at the local bar, the slogan might be, Don't think; Drink!

When it comes to addiction, as well as a wide variety of other problems we face, perhaps it is our very beliefs themselves, or at least the way we may tend to hold onto certain beliefs pretty indefinitely, that could be a big part of the problem. -Or at least the strength of some of the beliefs we allow ourselves to grow within us could possibly lead to big problems for us; to the extent we may be operating on false assumptions.

This all ties into the idea of proof. Perhaps, what we may or may not be able to prove to others, is nowhere near as important as what we might feel we have proven to ourselves, at any point. Yet, when we <u>are</u> able to become completely certain of something, of which others around us cannot concur, the arguments that can ensue may render us roundly distracted from directing our energy toward progressing further, in what just may be our superior thought development.

On the other hand, if we do know something (that seems to be elusive to others) is true, then we may not need to put forth an abundance of energy all the time, to convince others at every turn.

The development and application of theories may potentially bring us into a world of much "mental-related" research potential. Theories tie concepts; possibly among other observations and ideas; together; by nature, suggesting that it may be a good idea for a particular theory to enter the realm of possibility, within our minds. It seems that, quite factually-speaking, AA closes our minds to many possibilities which may be of much importance for us to alternatively consider, as explanations, for example.

For instance, the AA program communicates to us that God's existence and intervention into our lives explains why everything occurs as it does, how it came to be that we became insane; and how God might fix this, provided we can embrace the AA program; among other things we are entreated to consider as certainties.

One of the cornerstone theories we might embrace, within the domain of conscious-subconscious theory; and unlike AA, we are specifically warned <u>against</u> trying to sell this as an absolute certainty to ourselves; but conceptually and <u>possibly</u> even real-ly, it may be most useful for us to consider ourselves as two pretty separate individuals, having some potential to work together; and the inner individual of this team could well be thought of as holding all of our information and memories; additionally possessing a much-more-vast computing capability, and thought-organizing ability, as well.

Assuming we can grasp this idea, and suspend any disbelief at least temporarily; then, as the very existence of God cannot be unquestionably established, we could imagine that perhaps we would be well-aware of this inside, within our much-smarter inner self; and therefore, if we have merely a conscious awareness that we actually <u>do</u> feel utterly certain that God exists, and He is truly involved in our lives; then obviously our conscious mind will be trying to sell this idea to our subconscious; but of course, this inner component of our being could never really buy this. – And conceptually speaking, wouldn't this have potential to result in inner turmoil? –And isn't it perhaps possible that most of our mental illness stems from conscious false ideas, of which it is continually trying to foist them on the much more intelligent and knowing inner self; the subconscious mind? This is but one of perhaps many possible explanations for why, each of many different things, may be happening to us, and to others at various times; one of but many possible explanations for how things came to be as they are; for why things are different than they seemed before to us; or even to explain such things as what happened to something I placed on the counter yesterday, which has now gone missing. Of course, in reality, we can only guess at any of this; nothing more!

A firm subscriber to AA's philosophy would not allow even the strongest inclination, to drink, to move them into action in this direction. This, of course, is an example of a conservative strategy, imposed by our conscious entity, if you will. It is well-reinforced by the great fear that drinking again would really be detrimental to our cause, as a going human concern.

However, this firm belief become a certainty in our minds, also inclines us to rule out the real possibility that we might be able to learn how to enjoy a drink without doing ourselves significant damage in these respects, perhaps at some point in the future; should we undergo some unforeseen effective learning process, for example.

Here again, I don't think we should be roundly ruling out any possibility which could perhaps become a reality for us in the future; especially if it involves obtaining a rewarding and enjoyable benefit, of great perceived value to us. Perhaps, almost anyone considering that they have an out-of-control drug or alcohol addiction, had earlier found significant enjoyment in using their "drug-of-choice"; and in fact, it was the fact that it <u>was</u> so enjoyable, that led to the uncontrollable compulsion to use more and more; more and more-often.

Certainly, while someone is desperately trying to end the drinking and drugging nightmare their life has become, as a member of AA, this is the last thing you would be inclined to allow your conscious mind to get in touch with; (the "conscious-mind-directed" confining of your thoughts appears to be a big part of this antiquated program's "suggestions") but pushing things like this under the rug actually constitutes creating an inability to look squarely at the most pertinent truths surrounding the problem you are facing; it is , of course, quite literally employing the principal of ignorance, isn't it? Should we be practicing this principal in all our affairs? Probably not.

And perhaps it leads to further ignorance, of the fact that you would certainly wish to be able to continually enjoy some feelings of intoxication at times; indefinitely going forward, right? So this, right here, is the first problem with embracing the concept of "addiction;" in that without honestly knowing whether it is actually true or not, we are consciously trying to force it upon our whole being, of course including our more-knowing subconscious selves, to develop a feeling of certainty that the only sure way out of our drinking or drugging problem, is to plan to never have another drink, for instance.

You are not really going to sell this idea with any level of comfort, to your greater inner self; it's just not going to accept this possibly false contention. We cannot control our inner beliefs, try as we might! We can't really force ourselves to believe, that which we simply don't believe within the fiber of our being. We cannot possibly "will" a belief; we either believe something, or we don't; although this may change, of course, over time; and of course, we probably cannot predicate our current plan of action on beliefs we don't actually hold, with any good effectiveness.

Perhaps, a great many of us have it backwards; we probably shouldn't be trying to consciously impose different ideas, that go contrary to the ideas that are just naturally and unavoidably held within the fiber of our subconscious mind. This just leads the way toward another "sweeping the problem under the rug" practice; it is the very denial process which simply defines immaturity and self-deception. Should we be practicing this principal in all our affairs? Again; probably not.

To confuse matters further, we have to then grapple with reconciling the idea that we may never have another drink, with that the program is a daily reprieve; and we must tell ourselves we only need to resolve not to drink or drug, for one day at a time.

Which is it? I can never safely have a drink again? Or I just can't have one, for one day? It can't be both, can it?! –Then perhaps this puts our minds on "tilt." How can we truly better ourselves by putting our minds on "tilt?" True however, for many of us, imposing this level of confused thinking on ourselves may somehow effectively allow us to keep ourselves from drinking; at least temporarily.

But it seems quite obvious that the inner self of a self-proclaimed addict doesn't really want to keep from drinking; and based on the ideas that we have just been discussing; at least theoretically, our subconscious mind certainly isn't going to like the probable atmosphere of confusion we would be feeding it, by further-embracing the AA program's possibly- false contentions.

Although it may sound too good to be true, before undergoing further learning; again at least theoretically, in order to appropriately serve the inner self within us, ideally we would aim toward figuring out enough about ourselves to try and solve the problem of our incessant inclination to drink too much, and too often; in a manner that would also allow us to have a drink at times, without having to experience this compulsion and obsession problem any further.

Perhaps, only some more-seriously disadvantageous form of arrogance would assume this was definitely impossible.

After all of its honorable intentions over the years, I wouldn't wish to step on AA so hard as this; but possibly assuming the program actually creates several other significant mental problems for many of us, while merely getting some smaller percentage of those who work at it, sober for any long stretch; I would say this very badly needs to get addressed, at this point.

Our inclinations toward engendering AA fellowship are probably a great idea; but perhaps we must now begin to aim toward exchanging and supporting ideas and behaviors, which maybe we have newly come to believe, would be considerably more- relatively-healthy and intelligent for us to embrace; in order to hammer out a more satisfying lifestyle; assumedly, therefore forming a better world for ourselves personally, and maybe for all of us, eventually.

So, taking into account all of what we have so far been discussing, ultimately, the objective onlooker could easily see, just as yet another contradiction within the AA literature; that even though in the preamble, it states AA neither endorses or opposes any causes; yet by the writings within its twelve steps, it inherently not only endorses causes; but its causes actually appear to be pretty toxic, in some pretty concrete ways.

Ultimately, although we can be sure that the AA program's authors had it in mind purely to be of good help to apparent addicts, and to save them from possible ruin, or perhaps even death; and although we can also be sure that any possible detrimental side- effect was not in the least bit intended; either by its authors, or by those individuals who have become proponents of the AA program; it appears that, speaking from a relative-mental-health standpoint, many of the ideas and dictates of the long-established AA program may-well unfortunately be considered to be pretty toxic in nature.

Again, beliefs are not facts; and unfortunately, perhaps we may often be hurting ourselves whenever we have falsely converted certain types of beliefs, to instead occur to us as facts, within our conscious mind's eye.

Those of us going to AA meetings regularly may likely hear the testament of a reasonable percentage of longer-term members of AA who contend that, since they began to stop denying they had a drinking problem, and started making a sincere effort to recover via "working the steps" of the AA program, they have had a wonderful life ever since. Yet, the concept of "wonderfulness" seems to be another possible illusion in the making; being that, similar to the concept of "healthiness," the concept of "wonderfulness" is merely a relative term; there is no such thing as perfectly wonderful or perfectly healthy, in a literal sense.

True, someone who had been literally killing themselves drowning in a sea of alcohol might easily begin to feel more-than-satisfied with any lifestyle change that could end this type of very troubling, even potentially deadly nightmare; and at least initially, we could hardly argue with marked improvement, on this level.

However, again, it seems that working the AA program basically amounts to making continual attempts to assert consciously-contended false ideas upon the whole of your being; including of course, your subconscious mind. Perhaps, this exists as the crux of the conditioning process employed, in offering its solutions to our daily problems. Yet, within the mind of someone who has more-newly become open to consider that, in addition to their "awake" form of thinking, they seem to have another pretty-separate, and much-more-sophisticated mental machinery within; which can also be seen to have a much better handle on which ideas may be "possibly believable;" versus its knowing, as well, of things we are trying to sell ourselves, that are wholeheartedly <u>not</u> to be (unquestionably) believed; perhaps we have now aptly become enabled to begin seriously questioning the validity of some of AA's contentions; no longer concretely thinking of them as unquestionably-valid reflections of true reality.

Of course, in addition to what we theoretically could assume to exist, as at least <u>slightly-uncertain beliefs</u>, that may be held by people working the AA program, there are also some <u>indisputable facts</u> which would appear quite pertinent, regarding its longer-term members who claim to be having a wonderful life since they started accepting the ideas and dictates of the twelve steps of the AA program. At least some of these people have been taking various psychiatric medications; either for depression, or perhaps to better cope with different forms of otherwise-serious mental conditions;

continuously for years; yet while they have been professing, week after week, that their lives have become wonderful!

-And there are factually still others of these AA members professing of the wonders of the AA program, and all the positive things that working this program has done for them, who have yet continued to remain stuck in very unfortunate business situations for years; or who come to meetings continually complaining of somewhat plaguing family and marital problems, year after year. Of course, they would rationalize that in any case, a variety of troubles and painful experiences are bound to occur, even in sobriety; but what if many of these perhaps excessive troubles are possibly recurring as a result of the disadvantageous "conscious conditioning process" inherent in the ideas and dictates of the AA program which they have been continuing to "work?"

Here, we can see that, even with the unspoken contentions of certain definitely-and-exclusively-true explanations, such as that there will be nothing further of any help, that may be done by the individual to reduce or eliminate the recurring themes of some of these ongoing problematic cycles; except for some relief afforded by talking at meetings and with their sponsors perhaps; but that, in order to have the absolute best life possible for us, we must pretty- exclusively just keep continuing to try and practice the principals laid out within AA's twelve steps, in all our affairs; these kinds of assertions will perhaps inevitably incline AA's followers to completely close their mind to any possible alternative explanation, for why so many members of AA continue to disclose and lament persistent problems they have long been suffering from.

Within the text of my earlier-developed "AA For Agnostics" Program Step-Book, I had further written:

As we might properly consider it, the ideal of employing liberal strategies basically amounts to allowing ourselves a maximum of liberties and enjoyment; as opposed to the conservative ideal, in which embracing it at the extreme, we might approach becoming so protective against the occasional suffering that may ensue; as a result of disallowing ourselves this greater degree of liberty and enjoyment; that we end up making sacrifices which may relegate us to living in a poor-spirited state of frustration, a sense of inability to adequately be getting our needs met, and perhaps a significant sense of inconvenience, or unnecessary deprivation.

Still, on the other extreme, to give an example of when our strategies may become extremely liberal, to a fault; excessively drinking and drugging is probably a good example of the possible detriments that may often ensue, in this case.

We typically use the terms of compulsion and obsession to characterize why we need to stop ourselves from carrying through with any strong inclinations toward ever drinking again; or to get ourselves to stop persisting in any of a variety of other excessive behaviors any further, for that matter.

However, addiction, obsession, and compulsion, these are all merely concepts that we have invented, or in other words, that we have created as concepts; and the embracing of these types of concepts represents a good example of certain theories we have decided to live by; in terms of their hinging on stronger beliefs we have developed within us. We might have come to believe that our mind has entered into a state of hopeless obsession with getting drunk or high; or that we have developed such a compulsion to continuously pour massive amounts of drugs and alcohol into our body; that we are alarmed with great fear, with great frustration over not being able to control ourselves, and with serious physical sickness, to boot.

When we really get serious about giving our intense regard to the disadvantageous thoughts and behaviors we can't seem to escape, consciously we might-well commence to project that this will always be the case; that we will remain obsessed, or compulsive to our extreme detriment; unless we effect some conscious form of intervention and attempted control over our whole being, aimed at effectively quelling these troublesome inclinations and behaviors, which somehow seem to have become natural to us.

However, this also may-well incline us to close our conscious mind to considering any alternate possible solution which might otherwise occur to us; such as that even as apparent addicts, we cannot be entirely certain that if we began instead to become more beholden to what we sense as our strongest inner desires and inclinations, that we might, at least eventually, become cured of these seriously- problematic, perhaps once seemingly-perpetual detrimental tendencies.

Lack of sleep is often said to be self-correcting, for the most part. There may be other problems we could be experiencing that are also somewhat self- correcting in nature. Perhaps, we may be able to effect a much better outcome, if instead of trying to "come to believe" that a regimen of consciously-led self- conditioning is our most effective option, we consciously work to better understand and provide a more subordinate form of support to what we could become better-aware of, as our more-enlightened subconscious thinking mechanism.

Even though AA seems to dictate that we consider we should have no confidence in ourselves, only concerning controlling our drinking, we still may potentially find this to be quite a destructive line of thinking; in terms of accepting a "defeatist" attitude, in this sense. This, of course, is quite disempowering in itself; and many of us can probably be pretty certain that this is not what we should be attempting to impress upon our whole being; even though it may seem like a successful solution in the short run, to act in accordance with the dictates of a program contending to be quite effective at keeping you from drinking.

Regarding the very-firmly impressed AA concept that we may gain the power to drown out any stronger inclinations to drink by consciously confining our focus on keeping from having a drink just for today; and don't think about tomorrow until it comes; if indeed we take this route, deciding each successive day, that we can't drink because we definitely can't trust ourselves to act according to any stronger sense of inner inclination; instead trying to consider that living by our inclinations is quite dangerous to our well-being; we can see how this amounts to making constant daily attempts to condition our subconscious thinking mechanism to accept a subordinate position, to that of its conscious counterpart.

Yet, giving ourselves the constant message that we cannot trust ourselves to guide us effectively, this seems quite detrimental to our well-being, in itself.

Accepting this idea would snuff out our greater potential for self-discovery; by closing us off to the possible validity of our subconscious understanding and reasoning, at points.

For example, it would give us a tendency to avoid attempting to focus on becoming aware of the groups of thoughts that are apparently responsible for causing any particular one of the many different strong inclinations that we would more-typically otherwise be able to sense; to have formed within us; of which, minus the conscious mind's conditioned squelching, we might otherwise find greater value in bringing to mind; or in other words, summoning it to come to the forefront within our conscious mind; so that we can look to these sources of thought giving rise to our feelings.

We may learn much from these introspective experiences which can influence us to modify our approach; in perhaps what will become our future, relatively-more-healthy attempts to "follow our nose," so to speak; perhaps beginning to assume an infinitely more satisfying lifestyle of paying ourselves much respect, by living via making more-consistent attempts to serve our greater sense of what we may feel to be our deeper inner inclinations.

In the final analysis, we should probably invest some amount of trust in ourselves; trust that at least eventually, once we have realized enough about just why we would've become inclined to believe we would be serving ourselves best, by drinking and drugging to extreme excess, for example; this may engender great potential for us to find an effective solution to this, and other of our behavioral-control problems.

As we might do well to consider, there's probably a good possibility that there could be <u>quite a few</u> psychological issues that we seem to have been struggling with, in the mix; which also may largely- embody the main contributing factors behind the out- of-control feelings and behavior we are now trying to address.

Relating even to <u>many</u> areas of sickness, medical experts have learned, from quite a variety of types of professional experience; that simply treating the symptom (in this case stopping the problematic drinking) often does little to cure the underlying problem ultimately responsible for the <u>emergence</u> of that symptom. Alternatively, once the underlying problem becomes effectively addressed; and subsequently solved via some effective form of treatment; perhaps a whole group of previously- troubling symptoms may no-longer be suffered.

One thing that many of us have learned over the years, as a result of our association with the AA program, is that most people who call themselves addicts to alcohol and/or other drugs, have somehow blocked their own development of maturity, in many different respects. The Twelve and Twelve book outlines many of the ways in which we have held ourselves back from being able to grow up; as well as some of the most important reasons, for just how and why reaching maturity may be continuing to elude some of us, to date.

But once we realize that we have finally succeeded, in substantially growing, in our maturity; in ways which are well-outlined for us to strive for, including giving us guides to measure our own progress at working in these problem areas; perhaps it may be entirely possible that we could even be able to use mind-altering substances once again, to enhance our life experience; adding to our enjoyment, without causing detriment perhaps.

Although this may definitely be seen as a dangerous form of liberal strategy; by anyone affiliated with the AA program for any significant length of time; perhaps this is just another example of the variety of possibilities which we may, at least eventually, feel we owe it to ourselves to consider; in the pursuit of providing the best life we can, for ourselves.

Pushing against the formerly suggested conservative strategy of depriving ourselves, why don't we now consider embracing a more liberal perspective as an alternative? It's your life; do what you think is best; but remember that we only have one life to live, and plenty of people have termed it "but one short life to live;" regardless of some people's beliefs in possibly being granted eternal life, upon satisfying certain contended conditions.

We may ask, what about the difficult time we may go through as we are potentially learning how <u>not</u> to remain problem drinkers, while also trusting that we might be best off embarking on a new mission to carry through with our strongest inclinations at any point, as a continual process?

But as an alternate consideration, perhaps you could see it, that you may not even legitimately have the right to interrupt or pass judgment, (at least theoretically) on the very subconscious entity who would seek to create "the conscious you," as a necessary level of consciousness, perhaps having intended for this conscious entity indeed to serve its more-intelligent and knowing purposes. At least in the most advanced evolutionary sense; thinking further, we could now consider that we should primarily be making conscious efforts to consistently serve our inner selves; in terms of becoming a conscious servant entity, to our vastly more intelligent personal subconscious master. Ultimately, I suppose this begs the question, can you engender enough trust in yourself to become more internally-led; trust that your inner self not only has considerable wisdom, but might you also believe that your inner self's ideal objectives mainly involve harmless constructive tendencies?

Actually, this may not be too difficult for most of us to imagine, eventually.

It can be seen as our chief responsibility, as a conscious entity, to make certain that we are allowing ourselves to be carrying out whatever becomes our strongest desire; after our more careful consideration; at each moment of decision. If we sense stronger reservations, we might try and bring these to our more-full awareness, so that we might also give them our careful consideration; to the extent we have possible inner concerns. This perhaps becomes a major aspect of the effective teamwork we can potentially employ within ourselves. Employing teamwork between our conscious and subconscious entities seems to be what better living is all about!

Perhaps, these are some examples of the common false assumptions contended by AA's: I must be working the AA program well, because I am successfully not drinking; and in working the AA program according to its terms; I am doing the best I can possibly do for myself. I apparently have been working the steps effectively, as far as I can see; and doing my best to practice all of AA's principals in all my affairs. Therefore, I must be doing great; and living the most wonderful life I could possibly bring about for myself.

But what if none of these assertions are actually true except that we are not drinking; due to following the AA program's dictates? What if this fairly- exclusively is the main benefit of working this program; and we later come to find that we are actually hurting ourselves, and our greater potential to have an exponentially better life; in having dedicated ourselves to become, and remain, beholden to the AA program's dictates? Would it only be then, that we might begin striving to further open our minds to some possible alternative explanations for what we have been perceiving and experiencing?

Yet, for those of us familiar with the AA program who would initially take offense, perhaps we could not even aptly consider the ideas discussed within this AA4A step book to necessarily constitute an affront to AA, as several aspects of the AA program's contentions have been endorsed throughout this book. We are not attempting to throw the baby out with the bath water, as it were. We are simply being asked to consider AA possibly in a different light. Once having become introduced to the ideas within these pages, we might consider the AA program basically as a somewhat questionably-effective conditioning process; whereas, the objectives of the AA4A program might be seen to constitute a suggested <u>un</u>winding of perhaps more- disadvantageous forms of conditioning.

The idea of sanity, or lack thereof, comes into play in the second step of the AA's "Twelve and Twelve" book. There, we are asked to consider ourselves insane at the outset, and to come to believe that only some power, perhaps outside ourselves, could possibly restore us to sanity. However, this is merely a belief that one could possibly embrace; and of course, it could be seen as unwise to substitute any belief, for a fact of life.

Alternately, we might consider mainly trying to embrace a strong belief in <u>yourself</u>; that, provided you truly commit yourself to serve your own subconscious entity, which attempts to provide direction via making you aware of your strongest inclinations; this will work out best for everyone.

Making a commitment on this level inherently requires you to extend trust that, as you work in this direction, you will lead yourself toward more- constructive and fulfilling ends as an individual. To the extent that we may possibly feel insane at the outset, we may assume that working toward becoming increasingly-more-relatively healthy; with the help of having made this paramount commitment; will probably have good potential to move us away from a possible state of insanity.

The word "insanity" really has no clear definition, does it? Much like the word stupid, we use it as a catch-all, to describe what doesn't make sense to us; the only difference being that one whom we are considering as being insane, we might also consider to have a somewhat-dangerous degree of intelligence perhaps; whereas the concept of calling someone stupid pretty much infers that you are of the opinion that there is no real sense of intelligence, which could either be associated with a particular act; or sometimes even a particular person as a whole, perhaps.

Similarly, we associate the concept of "stupid;" to describe either an act or an expression, as being what we could define as both something someone is doing that doesn't make any sense to us; nor to be the least bit sensible. Yet, sometimes we come to believe this to be so, only because we haven't yet learned enough about the possible reasons that their behavior may actually make some sense; and once we find out more, then perhaps to the contrary of our earlier opinion, it might actually occur to us to be a perfectly rational way to negotiate or respond to the situation, or circumstance.

We do have other definitions of insanity; such as that it is represented by carrying through repeatedly with the same process, yet expecting a different result than the last five times you did this, for example.

Further on the subject of insanity, or wild madness, the Twelve and Twelve characterizes anyone who is unwilling to believe in the definite existence of God as "savage;" which is perhaps the first major departure from its earlier contention that the AA program does not demand that you believe in anything at all. -And it says that if you "won't believe…".-but belief is not a question of will, is it? We cannot believe what we simply don't believe, at any moment, of course.

Perhaps what has been left out is the idea that if you won't say you believe… and of course given the major emphasis of this long-ago-written program, it would seem to make some sense to try and get everyone in the room to voice a belief in God at regular meetings; as this might encourage more cohesiveness; whereas, saying that you certainly don't have any strong belief in the existence of God, this represents a pretty serious form of dissent from the AA program guidelines, perhaps. —But maybe the authors realized that they couldn't really write that we must at least say we believe in God, as to do so would be suggesting right away that some of us perhaps be dishonest. —And wouldn't calling non-belief "savage" incline many AA members to act dishonestly right from the start; by hiding their unbelief, and telling other members falsely that they do believe?

However, concerning the suggestion that it might be savage to take the position that you won't believe in God as a being; as a fact of reality, couldn't we instead, reasonably contend that it is the other way around? –that those examples of the personification of utter dependence on the suppose-ed factual existence of God; such as Sunni militants in this day and age, can pretty easily turn "savage" in their thinking and actions toward others, due to this strong-belief- become-fact within their mind; for example finding it reasonable to be killing others; and pretty surprisingly, even those who also share having this same utter sense-of-factual dependence upon God; too considering that they truly stand completely convinced of God's existence, as a reality of being. Yet, they kill each other because they simply don't concur, on a few other aspects of possible religious belief-become-fact? Perhaps this could <u>clearly</u> be seen as insanity, and more insanity in the making as well.

The AA4A program does not contend that you must jump through any hoops; but that you may pretty much think and do whatever you are inclined to, on a perpetually-continual basis. Speaking of perpetual, here's a possibility for us to consider: the word eternal was used earlier, and it may occur to some of us that perhaps if we learn how to take care of ourselves more consistently and completely; as we evolve into the future, death may not continue to be quite so inevitable; maybe only having to pay taxes will remain as a certainty!

However, having any ability to conceive of this as a real possibility for the future, of course, may be quite well beyond just about all of us at this point! –But if God does exist, perhaps this is what he meant for us when he tried to fill our heads with the idea of life eternal. This seems to be just one other example illustrating how at times we could possibly think in these God-like terms, and at other times many of us might agree en-mass that this is a completely ridiculous idea! –and this in itself is an example of why it seems clear that in order to have an better life; in any more optimum sense; it seems that embracing a conception of God, or at least the idea of God, reasonably must come and go, in the matters of our lives; in the sense that possibly for a great many of us, we are not focusing on the idea of God, quite certainly as we deal with each and every ongoing situation in our daily lives.

Gaining the ability to expand our consideration of the different real possibilities that will occur to us, may often deepen our perspective, as an overlay, to whatever else you were experiencing at the time you were considering a particular possibility.

At one point, we may be going-about in a spirit of optimism, or hope; and at another time when our minds seem to be preoccupied with an area of frustration; or when we find ourselves dwelling on repeated failed-attempts at trying to accomplish something of importance to us, for instance; we might then be going-about our activities in a more pessimistic spirit, or with a sense of hopelessness as an overlay.

These could be defined as different forms of spirituality. Perhaps we should confine the formation of our concepts of spirituality to within more tangible concepts such as this; and lose the idea of spirituality as some nebulous force. It seems that it may be unwise to predicate our more important thoughts and activities on anything we cannot more-clearly define; and it could appear to many of us that spirituality has never been clearly defined.

Perhaps, in the interest of our possible greater sense of well-being, we might realize that it is <u>only</u> our sensing of the more-tangible ideas and inclinations occurring within and around us, that would truly be most-advantageous for us to focus on; this, as well as the spirit with which we go about our day; which may often change at different points, of course. It might appear that grounding ourselves in more solid, tangible, indisputable realities may give us the strongest foundation for continued sanity, for that matter. Maybe these are the new directions we should be working in, from this point on Certainly, in order to deal with our various perceptions of cold hard reality in its many different nasty forms; we may find that we owe it to ourselves, to work at acceptance; yet how can we really expect ourselves to come to accept the unacceptable? Perhaps we should not be working at <u>this</u>!

These kinds of thoughts could bring us to reconsider the Serenity Prayer. I'm thinking that perhaps we shouldn't even be praying anymore, because we must consider the possibility that there may be no one out there we are praying to, after all; or couldn't it also be possible, if we were to assume that God <u>does</u> exist, perhaps he may not want us to think we can turn to him, when he knows damned well that we can potentially solve our problems for ourselves; provided we work wholeheartedly at applying ourselves, in the most advantageous ways.

Maybe it's high time we started simply voicing our hopes instead; and especially to ourselves; our inner selves, that is. Perhaps, related to the Serenity Prayer, we could think of the historic emphasis to be on the first stanza of the prayer; but perhaps maybe it could be reinterpreted as I hope, that within me, I can somehow come to accept what seems somehow unacceptable to me at present, concerning those aspects and events which at this point I have come to believe I cannot change.

This certainly could be seen as the major focus of the prayer, as cited within the AA program. At times, this kind of serenity is perhaps indeed the hardest type of acceptance we could imagine gaining; and perhaps we should not actually be gaining it, in some cases!

Within the newer AA4A program, the emphasis might be more on the second stanza; perhaps reinterpreted as I hope that I may find it within myself to effect changes to whatever I firmly believe is most important to work at changing, at any given moment of thought or decision. –Maybe instead of saying prayers; let's say our hopes instead.

As for the third stanza, it might be newly interpreted as I hope that I can summon the internal wisdom to incline me in the most relatively healthy and constructive directions, and that I can avoid falling prey to expending my time and energies in any other unproductive direction.

This certainly seems to say so much more than "the wisdom to know the difference;" and as we continue to evolve, some of our other old sayings, too, probably need to be continually updated at various points; perhaps partially to serve also as "yardsticks to measure our progress by," as well.

As we possibly consider some new directions we might take, in terms of managing our conscious thought processes, let's talk about the acronym HOW; open honest and willing. It is said within the AA program that this is the way to get sober. But this could get a little confusing, because regarding honesty, openness and willingness; each could possibly be thought of on a number of different levels; or in other words, they have at least a few dimensions that we might consider.

The AA program mentions two specific examples; both being rhetorical questions; which seem to have obvious answers. They both assume that an individual has finally found a way to stop themselves from drinking, which seems to be working. One of these questions being, do we unload a detailed account of our extramarital affairs on our husband or wife? –and the second being do we confess to our boss, that over the years we padded our expense account by thousands, buying drinks, and basically stealing company money for our personal benefit; while finding ways to hide this at the time?

So the question becomes, who should we be honest with; and about what sorts of things should we perhaps not be so open and disclosing; and of course, what should we become willing to do on our own behalf, in these respects? This is perhaps a good example of when we might rely on our strongest inclination from within; -and here let me suggest another good rule of thumb that we might employ more consistently; to often consider that our best guess is our best bet, as individuals.

When we possibly give ourselves this conscious suggestion, at a point where we need to accomplish deciding on a strategy to employ, or a direction we might head in, we are not necessarily relying on our conscious thinking processes to wade through every possible scenario, and ruminate as to when we might do, or avoid doing something; or to say, or avoid saying something in response to different people's possible lines of questioning of us, in order to satisfy their apparent curiosities. Alternatively, we might, from this point on into the future, more-be using our conscious processes, mostly to search ourselves; in an attempt to become aware of our greatest desires or fears; related to how we might answer questions regarding the topic in question; coupled with considering what may further develop as our strongest inclinations; at any particular moment when we might have to make a decision, as far as what we might do, in a given situation or circumstance.

The AA fourth step starts off with a bold statement that we are here because of Creation, and as part of this creation, we were endowed with instincts. However, whether we came into being, more instantaneously-developed, in terms of our thinking capacity, or whether the complexity of our thinking instead more-gradually evolved, over many thousands of generations; as would seem far more likely; it seems we have always had the idea that we are instinctual to some degree, and who could argue with that?!

However, we could also consider instincts simply as inclinations we sense within us; and perhaps this is the most meaningful and constructive way to look at what we have always considered as instincts. To suggest that any of our instincts exceed their proper function seems to be just another way of suggesting that we must use our conscious processes to over-ride our inner inclinations.

This is exactly the opposite of what this program suggests, of course.

If we are to develop more faith in ourselves, it seems we must define ourselves by the emotions within us. If we come to believe that some of our emotions are wrong to have, we could eventually come to believe that there is something very wrong with us. Maybe we could encourage ourselves instead, to get away from thinking in terms of right and wrong in this respect; perhaps learning more to look at our world from the standpoint of the advantages and disadvantages of any action we might consider taking; or any present position we find ourselves in, at the moment.

As far as our potential reactions and behavior, going to the extreme; in almost any sense; usually has some pretty unhealthy disadvantages, whether it is being miserly, or extravagant; or whether it is being a social butterfly in every circumstance or becoming an isolated recluse. Dwelling on sexuality and sexual matters, or denying yourself any sexual thought, are two other extremes that most of us should probably try to avoid as well.

We might also consider our level of dependence, in our most important relationships. It may be that, at the point of your beginning in this program, you find that you are pretty dependent on at least one other person for either strong emotional or financial support. We may want to ultimately think in terms of eventually becoming more independent in these ways; but again, getting away from thinking we are <u>wrong</u> to be in any particular position we might find ourselves in, is probably a good starting point, in the battle of learning how to feel relatively good about yourself, regardless of what your predicament may be at any current moment. It is most-definitely a major aim of this program to help you achieve and maintain this psychological position.

During the course of our concentrated written effort at viewing your past, I should think it probably also would be important to examine our personal values; <u>both</u> apparent sets; consciously-held ones, and those apparently held by your inner self, as well. Anything that potentially gets in the way of our ability to feel okay about ourselves seems fair game to consider abandoning; as a major striving. If you value being top-dog in any venue, whether it is related to your position in work, or in terms of having strong inclinations toward dominating and controlling the events of your family or intimate personal relationships, it may be well-worth considering more carefully, the disadvantages of following unchecked inclinations to attain and hold this position. If you are in a position of leadership or dominance, you may want to weigh the importance of exerting yourself; in terms of intervening in the lives of others; against the importance of respecting the beliefs and the needs of others around you; and in so doing, engendering their feelings of appreciation for having taken their interests and objectives into account. Even the long-ago-written AA program literature puts it that "Every time a person imposes his instincts unreasonably upon others, unhappiness follows."

The AA program literature also aptly observes that "Instincts on rampage balk at investigation." I would certainly agree that it is a very meaningful activity, to utilize your conscious resources to run down exactly what seems to be behind these strong inclinations, when they are in obvious conflict with someone else's strong beliefs and values, whom you are dealing with. We should probably be very careful of "going on rampages," in any event!

One of the aims of the AA program is to encourage humility, and it said that we must develop perspective in order to develop genuine humility. One of the new ways we can develop perspective is to use the greatest measure of objectivity, when viewing ourselves. Much mention is made that pride can be quite problematic for us, especially when it blinds us to our various liabilities. If you think you don't really have any liabilities to speak of, in terms of your personal tendencies and characteristics, this might be a good indication that you have found ways to blind yourself in this manner; through getting in touch with feelings of pride, as a block to any sense of utter objectivity. Lowering your guard in this respect could possibly better-enable you to recount various negative ramifications which, more-objectively-speaking, could perhaps aptly be associated with your past actions or thinking processes. Engaging in this type of more-humble reflection would probably provide much potential to mend relationships and avoid troublesome thinking and behavior on your part.

It is perhaps very common for many of us to have developed falsely-protective devices, such as excessive self-justification, or having become quite overly-prideful; and since in many cases, this seems to result in somewhat-persistent difficulties, in our dealings with others who can't agree with our self-justified viewpoint. But we might do well to consider, from this point on, that it's probably a good idea to do whatever we can to "let the light of reason shine in;" as it is said in the Twelve and Twelve; that we might more-often be making good attempts to try and revise our thinking, in the spirit of greatly reducing the number and magnitude of our clashes with those we are dealing with, on a day-to-day basis.

Another part of becoming more mature involves reviewing our sense of justification, of countless thought processes and behaviors we have indulged in over the years. What we are really looking for here are what we refer to in this day and age as cognitive distortions. The AA literature keys in on at least a few of these, such as in thinking that maybe we drink too much and we know it, but we are not half as bad as plenty of other souls we can think of, in this respect.

In reality, for example, it doesn't matter if you once saw a guy at a bar hit a police officer five times, and you only hit an officer once; you still are going to jail for assaulting a police officer! Using your best sense of utter objectivity, along with input from others regarding your past communications, expressions, and actions, this can probably help you to stop looking at yourself and your situations through a lens which may be distorted with various rationalized justifications, in a relatively unhealthy manner.

One other important area of justification for many of us is in placing blame on others for bad things that have happened, where we were somehow involved.

Whereas, I don't believe we need to drop the word blame from our vocabulary, as the Twelve and Twelve suggests, this is probably a good area in which to begin opening our minds more to the possibilities, in terms of considering that some trouble or difficulties have arisen, possibly due mainly to a disadvantageous manner we had behaved in, in given situations; where we have heretofore only attributed them to what we could blame others for.

Of course in some matters, the gaining of perspective does not necessarily lead to a gain in humility. Suppose that some worker who regularly visits your house whom you've gotten to know pretty well, seems to really appreciate it when you simply treat them with common decency; you later find out that some past act they had committed has soured them in the eyes of the public, and yet you decide, upon gaining perspective on why they might seem especially grateful that you will not shun them as well; assuming you could still find it within your heart to be as-nice to this person each day, this might lead to a gain in pride, for being able to rise above the petty judgments of most others.

However, if you were the worker in this scenario, you might have come to take it for granted that this homeowner will probably have continual good regard for you, and gotten quite comfortable in your relationship with him; but upon finding out that he just became informed of your checkered past, you might now feel more humble, and treat yourself-more on a less-than an even keel with him, resolving for now just to keep your head down and do your work.

As another type of example, of a gaining of perspective which may lead to a gain in humility, suppose that you believe unquestionably in the existence of God, and you tend to look upon anyone who doesn't, as somewhat lost and misguided; feeling prideful, or above them. When you go to church, passages are of course read which speak in terms of God and other aspects of the supernatural as a definite reality. However, then you read a book such as this one, and come to understand that others keep their mind open to additional possibilities, other than just God being the only true reality, or in other words they entertain possible alternate definitions of the realities of life as we know it. Perhaps you will now come to realize that as an unquestionable believer in God, you are looked down upon to some extent by these others, as not having the wherewithal to open your mind to consider all conceivable real possibilities, other than a single contention, for which there has never been any definitive proof. Perhaps, this could have a humbling effect on your previously-high- and-mighty sense.

Indeed, even if we were to assume that God exists, he may no longer want us to depend on this, in ways which might possibly alter our own human sense of becoming inclined to work hard, at bringing about what is decent and fair and just; whereas, if we believe that God alone, will bring about ultimate justice, in his own scheme of time; we may not be as inclined to feel that it is personally "on us," so much, to bring many good developments about.

Another essential aspect of our stock-taking activities involves the concept of "levels" of thought. It is probably of importance to classify our various lines of thinking into what we could refer to as different levels of thought. One example might be pertaining to your thoughts regarding your intimate lover. On one level you may deeply value and appreciate this other person, but on another level you may feel angry toward them because of what they have recently done, or because they betrayed your trust in some circumstance, for instance.

The above example identifies characterizations of your feelings toward another, but let's break them down further, as we seem to have established that, other than sensory feelings, such as physical pain for example, we may consider the formation of our feelings as being the computed end-product, of the pertaining groups of thoughts behind that particular feeling. This is where levels of thought apply. For example, on one level you may be in touch with an inclination to break it off with this person for something they have done which angers or otherwise upsets you. Yet, on another level you may be reflecting on how you have enjoyed so many encounters and experiences with this person whom you have grown very close to; and a conflicting thought may develop; so on this level you are thinking that you would really like to find ways to stay more well-connected with this other person.

Eventually you will have to integrate these two conflicting lines of thinking in order to decide what you will or will not do under your circumstances, however, it is probably most helpful if you can examine each level of thought, isolated in and of itself first. It seems that only after having thought through the levels of thought pertaining to a particular situation and the people involved, can you develop a better conception of your strongest inclinations. This is an example of how you may start to utilize the teamwork between your conscious and subconscious thinking mechanisms in more advantageous ways.

Some of these stock-taking activities, where we follow our natural inclinations to recall different events, across the span of our lifetime, are bound to fill us with an overwhelming sense of upset. At the times we sense, that we have sufficiently lost our ability to remain rational and objective, as far as our current thought processes will allow; just as AA suggests, we should probably concentrate instead on quieting our disturbance. The concept of homeostasis, a principal where, even on a physiological level, we generally seek to maintain balance, or equilibrium via striving for a minimum level of satisfaction and peace, through whatever means seem to be available at the moment; this may be most useful.

Maintaining our sense of objectivity is probably pretty important, as we reflect on our most impactful memories.

I wonder how useful it is to assume an attitude that there is a lot wrong with you which will require monumental efforts to change in significant ways, as AA literature suggests. Even some of the most difficult changes we might make during the course of our lives could be seen to require less-than-drastic amounts of change in our thinking processes. For example, stopping smoking is seen as quite difficult; for some impossible even. Yet, if instead of viewing it that we must turn our thinking in an opposite direction entirely in order to stop smoking cigarettes, we could get in touch with our inclinations regarding the subject, and realize that the fact it can kill us, or render us quite ill and incapacitated, to suffer a short and miserable later life, we can be pretty well-assured that somewhere inside of us there must exist an inclination to stop this dangerous habit. If we search further, we can probably find several other disadvantages we may find ourselves with, related to our smoking; such as that we are setting a poor example for young ones who will see you smoking and think it's alright for them to start; people you are romantically enamored with, may not even want to kiss you; and they may keep from getting involved with you specifically due to the way it makes your breath and your clothes smell; you can't smoke at work or any public place, and this renders you in a state of uncomfortable withdrawal for hours at a time, during the work day, etc…

Then of course, there are the inclinations to smoke due to how good it tastes, it relaxes you, etc… If you think about it after processing your thoughts more carefully, isolating your concentration on the most important aspects of these different, sometimes conflicting levels of thought, it could become more clear to you that you don't really have to entirely change your thinking at all; you just have to find a way to tip the scales, so that the inclinations to stop begin to outweigh the inclinations to keep smoking. It may not require that much energy after all, yet this is a huge step towards becoming significantly more relatively healthy, I think we could all agree.

It probably doesn't help to think of ourselves as being defective, as AA suggests. Quite to the contrary, in a manner of speaking we are each perfectly human. On the other hand, no matter what we show others on the outside, at times any of us may feel like we are less than what we should be, as people. This is what most-likely needs to be combatted; not that we should feel defective, but more that there is merely something temporarily wrong with our perception of ourselves, if we do feel that way. We are human and imperfect, but that doesn't mean we can't work to effectively-become very humanly good.

That being said, it's also true that some of us have said and done things which have turned out to be quite hurtful and damaging, to ourselves and others, and in a spirit of working toward continual improvement, it would probably be best now if we begin to take steps to look at these troublesome behaviors and those aspects of our own thinking which led to them. It does no good to cry over spilt milk, but if we can look back and realize that we held the milk carton in a way where it easily slipped out of our hands, this can be more useful to us in how we will handle the milk carton in the future.

Some of us may reflect on things that we did which have rendered us unloved by the public at large, thinking that this a great undo-able loss; but we can comfort ourselves by coming to new realizations, such as that perhaps being loved deeply by a few is as valuable as being, to some much-lesser degree, more-widely loved.

Perhaps, everyone doesn't have to love us, in order for us to have a good life, or even in order for us to have the potential to make meaningful contributions to many of those around us.

It does seem useful however, to categorize our areas of vulnerability. Perhaps, not much trouble can come out of our altruistic motivations to do good things for others, with no expectation of further rewards; however, if we know that others are well-aware that we have been doing well, and this inclines us to try and hide our mistakes, for instance, this kind of pride can blow up in our face, by keeping us from receiving help with what we have difficulty with, and are therefore making mistakes because of, for example. Perhaps, many of us somehow come to feel as though we will be seen as much-less-of-a-person if we have weaknesses or areas of little or no personal development, and others were to become aware of this. We probably shouldn't be quite so self-conscious, in this sense.

Certainly, we may not want to run around showing everybody our weaknesses, but there probably are times when it would be best to let-on, to key people at key times, about various areas we are struggling with. We may be well-advised to ask for help from those who we believe might be able to supply it, at times when we most seem to need it. So it follows that we don't need to turn away from feelings of pride, but rather we might consider valuing a different type of pride, for those times when we have done our level best, to the greatest extent of our human ability at each moment. It also follows that if you feel inclined to try doing something new; where you would normally stop yourself because you fear being poor at this new activity; this may be a time to summon your courage to follow a stronger inclination to go ahead and try it. To the extent that the spirit of adventure may grow within you, life can become more of an adventure, and this, at least eventually, can be satisfying and fulfilling, even if you initially suck, at something new you are trying.

Next on AA's list of the seven deadly sins is greed, and what we think of as greed. To break it down to its base components, we might consider it as the thought that I'm going to get as much as I can, and I don't care what happens to anyone else. This type of thinking has some pretty obvious serious disadvantages to harbor within you, as an idea. If you haven't yet learned the importance of maintaining respect and regard for others, it seems you have probably suffered some impedance in gaining perspective on at least one important level of maturity; and of course, this is actually quite common for a number of us. In a similar spirit, to that you can't have your cake and eat it too; you can't take from everyone else in order to hoard it all, without bringing upon yourself more-serious consequences for having done so.

Unfortunately, the way the material world works however, those who have amassed great fortunes can use these resources to insulate themselves, to some extent, from any harsh consequences. Therefore, they may take on a devil-may-care attitude, and keep right on pushing their luck.

It seems pretty obvious that we cannot consistently rely on God to even the score, so instead we must work cooperatively together perhaps, to work at taking away this damaging ability from others, even if it is merely to be accomplished, taking down one sick and hurtful individual at a time. Particularly for a novice, at being effectively offensive, this is one of those endeavors we may suck at, when we initially try; but there sure seems to be adequate motivation for us to keep working individually and collectively, at helping those who have not yet learned critically-important tenets of maturity; and in the process, we may stand to garner more resources for everyone.

Although this could be thought of as a socialist ideal, by some, I would rather say it is an alternately- successful entrepreneurial ideal. Why should those who have amassed fortunes, have a corner on being considered the only entrepreneurs? It seems "entrepreneurial" for groups of us to collectively take advantage of a few rich immature and unbalanced targets of people, in order to bring about a state of greater-well- being in the world. Why wait for government to levy taxes on the rich; this will probably never happen, of course; as the rich pay for this to never occur. Almost any exploitive method, that this small percentage of the population has typically employed, has been fair game, as far as they are concerned; why should this not be so, for the rest of us? We certainly don't seem to need to make any of these people richer!

Many of us tend to think of money as the chief resource, but perhaps it is instead people. For example, a good lawyer can relieve a rich person of some of his money in an above-board manner. A lawyer can be motivated by their sense of justice, as well as being promised a percentage of the award won in court.

Perhaps if we can learn to more effectively tap into our subconscious resources individually, this may, in turn, lead us to join forces with one another in much more powerful ways, which could help us bring about more fairness in the distribution of resources such as money. These are some of the kinds of possibilities we might begin to open our minds to, as we progress into the future.

We might view all categories of what has been historically termed sin, as not inherently bad to have at least a touch of. In order to stay objective in our thinking, it seems we must abandon the labels of right and wrong, and replace them with thinking in terms of sets of advantages and disadvantages, associated with each choice; or each position, or each situation we find ourselves in. This way, no one gets to lay a guilt trip on themselves, or anyone. If we had half-seriously considered doing something terrible to someone else, for example, under the right and wrong principal we are supposed to feel terrible about having had these thoughts. Launching these kinds of guilt trips on each other seems to just cross up our emotions, to where we can't possibly maintain any reasonable amount of objectivity in our thinking. Trying to get ourselves and each other to think of everything we might think or do in terms of the ideas of right and wrong, we just cripple each other and lash out at each other, back and forth endlessly, perhaps.

Let's take that club out of everybody's hands.

There really doesn't seem to be any need to feel bad about any particular thought that happens to come into our head; ideally, we want to feel as good as possible about ourselves during the entirety of our one short life, as it were. Instead, with a more-clear conscience and our best objective thinking, let us consider an accompanying set of advantages and disadvantages for each of our various apparent options, as they naturally occur to us, from one situation to the next; and serve our inner selves, quite well.

Perhaps, a little anger can help you more- effectively get across a salient point, to another who seems to miss a reasonably-important aspect of your current situation; or it can demonstrate that you are being <u>completely serious</u>, in a given matter. It may fuel courage to do or say something which is beyond your normal "offense-taking" abilities, or otherwise beyond the scope of your usual repertoire of available-and-ready behaviors.

Yet, I'm sure we could think of at least as many cases where anger might be associated with significant <u>disadvantages</u>. Getting angry at your boss can easily get you fired. One angry sentence uttered, could end a relationship, and leave you sorry for saying it, for years possibly. Speaking of anger in this manner, it's almost as if anger is a tool like a knife. Used skillfully, it can help constructively sharpen your tongue; used carelessly it can cut you quite deeply, in an emotional sense.

A little envy can spur us to strive for greater achievement for ourselves; a little laziness can help us enjoy a day off, and so on. Let's not call our inclinations sins, but rather sort through them, as they hold our interest. We can probably trust that the conflicting natural inclinations within us will generally keep us in check, so that we don't act too impulsively and without consideration. Of course, if this doesn't seem to hold true in your case, it may be time to see someone for help.

Imagining Who's Telling Who

Once having examined pretty-much all of our troublesome past thoughts and experiences in a thorough-stock-taking fashion, we may-well feel a sense of relief and accomplishment, that we have more-fully faced the monster within us; if that is what we feared we might discover we are, to some extent; at the outset.

With all of these efforts to examine ourselves still fresh in our mind, it is probably the best time to share and discuss what we have recorded during the process of taking this step, with our sponsor, or a trusted good friend otherwise.

In almost every case, the sponsor will inevitably become impressed with your thorough and sincere efforts to look at yourself and your past, and there is usually quite a lot they can identify with, within your story.

Sharing parts of yourself and your past experiences more with others, may also develop into more-of-a habitual practice; as you learn to develop true partnerships with those whom you come into greater contact with. Use these resources wisely, and you might undoubtedly be well on your way to <u>much more</u> of the fun, loving, exciting, fulfilling, and productive life that you were perhaps hoping to live.

The sad truth about a perpetual AA phenomenon, perhaps for the foreseeable future:

The problem is that pretty much any and all of these ideas and suggestions fell on deaf ears when I gave out this literature and talked about it at meetings. There was absolutely no interest, as far as I could see, in the eyes of staunch AA members; and due to the hierarchy of the organization, the newer members who did seem pretty interested in some cases, all reported to me that their "sponsor" had told them not to get involved. For those who are unfamiliar with how the program works, by the time a newcomer is to attain a sponsor, invariably he or she has been oriented to consider that, in order to best-ensure that they <u>will</u> get sober, and stay sober in the AA program, they must follow every suggestion the sponsor is to make.

This represents the ultimate unfailing resistance to any change whatsoever to the ideas or structure of the AA program. My trying to break through this resistance apparently was a hopeless cause; so I let the initiative go dormant; but I do believe that, at least at some point in the future, people acknowledging that they seem to have an "apparent addiction" will perhaps commonly find their way to help through embracing the types of ideas I talk about here.

I have pasted below, the remaining excerpts from my former AA4A step-book, which I consider meaningful and constructive to include in this work:

The Fallacy of Consciously "Taking Control"

The problem with "taking control" in a situation is that it has the potential of forcing others out of control by this action. Consider for example, that you just became the new owner of a property where neighbors have been coming to swim in a river that crosses through your property for years, and the previous owner did not exert any controlling forces in this matter. If as the new owner, you now show up where they are swimming and tell them, "Get off of my property; you can't swim here anymore," if one of these people gets overly upset, and acts out in some retaliative manner, we don't look at it, that by exercising our prerogative to exert our control in the situation, we may actually have a tendency to force people out of control, as a byproduct. This is perhaps just one of the ways in which we don't take responsibility, as individuals and as a society of people.

Instead we say he is out of control, and it is entirely his fault and his responsibility, if he acts out in some harmful way.

-Not that it wouldn't be totally reasonable for a new property owner to want to make his own new rules regarding the use of his property. The point is that whenever we are in a position of power, such as in the previous example, we should probably realize that, in imposing ourselves and our self-centered agenda on others in this manner, we may have significant potential to cause upset; and so it seems that you owe it to yourself to act carefully, so as not to cause yourself and everybody else involved unnecessary grief and trouble, perhaps.

It also appears to me that your intellectual focus on God must come and go from time to time, in your mind and in your affairs, as suits both yourself and whomever people you may be dealing with. How paramount could God be, if this is the case; as it certainly is for many agnostics? This gives rise to the idea that perhaps the existence of God is not a reality we can depend on, like the ground we stand on, for instance. That being said, I don't want to "harsh anyone's mellow" in the case that the existence of God is such a strong belief in you that it has become a fact of life, within your mind; and especially if in your mind, you think we should all believe this.

However, should we really be idealizing the idea of exclusively placing blind faith in God to bring about whatever goodness he might provide us with, if in doing so, consequentially, we might naturally be inclined to avoid placing much well-founded faith in ourselves to bring about goodness, utilizing the fine minds we each apparently possess?

Perhaps, in order to get along with others in an optimum fashion, we may consider that whatever others believe is theoretically tolerable to us, unless it leads to an action or inaction which causes any significant degree of detriment; and only then would we have a problem with it, if we disagree. Up until that point, perhaps we may usually say let's just agree to disagree, and go our merry ways.

However, as innocuous as believing in God can sometimes seem, it is all too evident that this has been a huge source of conflict and destruction all over the world. Why don't we let go of an overpowering conception of God for a while, and work within the confines of our conscious and subconscious minds; and see if this might possibly be a more effective way of life?

There seems to be a wealth of power and capability there in itself; why must we seek more than we can depend on that we have? This seems unrealistic and immature. Certainly, one formidable feature of the Twelve Step program is that it heads us toward maturity. Why don't we let that be our guiding light, instead of merely placing blind faith only in God?

We have learned, from coming to understand the Muslim terrorist's way of thinking, that in some ways, it seems that firm belief in God may well be a troublemaker. We probably need to stop making such trouble for ourselves, with arrogant forms of contended certainty; even though we may have very strong beliefs within us.

As the AA program suggests, it would also probably be arrogant, perhaps even savage to maintain a firm belief in the nonexistence of God; because if for no other reason, others have so strongly believed in this perhaps possibly imaginary being, and it would, at very least, be discourteous to arrogantly insist that He does not really exist. But even more importantly, it would probably be best for us to try to consider any possibility which might be a reality; whether it is imagining that we may someday live on other planets, or that a being God may in fact exist, although we have not yet found any way to prove this with undeniable certainty. The very closest we can get to this would still amount to at least a vaguely uncertain belief. Calling the existence of God an out-and-out fact, without being able to establish undeniable proof, is a prime example of how we may falsely substitute beliefs for facts, within our minds.

Harboring a strong belief in God may be constructive at times; but although the AA promises suggest we may find that God will be doing for us what we cannot do for ourselves, what seems wrong with striving to learn how to do more for ourselves, as well?

Further regarding the possible existence of God, certainly, the thought has occurred to many of us, at least occasionally, that things seem to be too coincidental to be mere coincidences, in a given circumstance; although some of us would publicly deny this. It may certainly be an uplifting feeling, which we would miss out on assuming we felt dead sure that God did not exist. In fact, getting the feeling that what has just occurred within our lives is no mere coincidence, can be the very phenomenon that changes someone from a pure atheistic bent, to having suddenly become open to the possibility that God does exist; and is involved in their lives.

If the existence of God remains as a possibility within our minds, at times it can make a huge difference in how we behave, and in how we think; and it can sometimes bring us abundantly good feelings of joy, or relief; and as long as we can keep ourselves from converting, this sudden strong belief in God, into a factual certainty within our minds; perhaps it usually may not hurt us, to any extent. So, here we can see that it may actually be disadvantageous for us to not even try opening our minds to the possible existence of God. –And really, could any of us, by our adulthood, truly assert to ourselves that we have never gained the sense, even for a minute, that God just might actually exist? On the other hand, who among us hasn't ever thought, at least for a moment, that God, as a being, doesn't truly seem to exist.

On the other hand, maybe we shouldn't be praying to a possibly nonexistent God, because it seems that this would bring on a tendency to all-too-easily make the notion of God into a firm reality within our minds; which we must remind ourselves that absolute certainty of this has not been unquestionably established among us.

We probably need to be extremely careful of being tempted to act to extremes based on any belief that cannot be proved pretty much beyond a shadow of a doubt, to all of us, in general. Belief in the existence of God, for example, is most definitely not something which is universally accepted by everyone, even in general all across the world any more, these days, for that matter; although certain larger bodies of people may, in common, see this as a fact of life within their minds.

Within others of us, it can seem pretty obvious that this may well be an illusion. We probably need to be on guard for any possible illusions that we may become subject to, especially when we realize that an overly strong belief may lead us to significantly harmful acts of imposition on others. We have certainly seen how these types of apparent illusions can potentially cause big problems for many.

Leaving the subject of God for now, let us turn to the subject of other potential forms of empowerment.

Certainly, a scientist's <u>curiosity</u> can empower them to potentially make important discoveries which may impact many people's lives. There are those of us who may become quite curious fairly often; and over time, this curiosity has often helped shape us into increasingly better scientists. Curiosity can be a big help in making discoveries of all kinds. It may help us to gain new insights, and to come up with important new ideas, as a result of having inclined us to search for knowledge, pertaining to whatever it is that we have begun to wonder about; especially so, over longer periods of time.

Curiosity-driven research paves the way for ongoing developmental learning; which seems essential for our growth, and for our further evolution as a race, even.

Anger is another mental force that can empower us, and fear can empower us too, of course, but perhaps we should be careful of great anger or great fear, as we know they can empower us to think and do harmful and destructive things, by overcoming our sense of rationality at times. It might better serve us if we try not to hold onto, and build our anger; but instead get curious, as a replacement for our anger.

Perhaps this may work well with great fear as well. Curiosity seems to be able to convert our destructive thinking and acts into more constructive and benign internal forces; so we could think of curiosity as potentially being even more powerful, in a constructive sense, than anger or fear. For example, we may realize that we are angry at someone; but then instead of going in the direction of an angry tirade, we may begin to wonder how it is that this person became inclined to do what they did that angered you.

Maybe you could try having a civil discussion to try and satisfy your curiosity further. These kinds of measures seem to have much potential to resolve conflict; through coming to understand what is behind another's point of view; possibly using this information to develop respectful compromises, for example.

Trying to stay objective and calmly rational also seems to have potential to empower us. Whenever we can keep from flying off the handle, or giving in to a sense of becoming overly vulnerable to possible inflammatory remarks, for example; this is something that would probably be good for all of us, of course.

Our memories can empower us, and again this can be dangerous too, especially since it has been observed that the characteristics of our memories of events, and what we or others have said to us in the past, may change with successive memory recalls, especially over longer periods of time. It has been noted that in some cases, our memory of a given event may change at least slightly each time we attempt to recall it.

Further consideration of the possibilities that occur to us, can be empowering as well, it seems. We may become empowered to explore potentially useful new ideas and theories stemming from some possibility which occurred to us, such as that for many of us, our conscious entity possibly has, in many cases, grown to overpower and dominate our being in relatively unhealthy ways; when it seems that our primary guidance, and our most important thought development probably should be coming from the more intelligent subconscious component of our being instead.

And although many of us may think of mental illness, such as depression, to be just a pretty- permanent condition; and the possible cure is nothing that may perhaps only involve coming to understand a more-purely psychology-related explanation; and which could perhaps effectively be cured via talk- therapy; we might do well, at this point, to open our minds to the possibility that this may be a false impression we have latched onto.

There seems to be a few main reasons why most of us might think of mental illness in these terms. One is that apparently, with very little exception, once someone has become diagnosed with a mental disorder of any kind, this diagnosis will invariably follow them throughout their whole life; meaning that every mental professional whom that individual will ever see, will list this same diagnosis in their reports and any insurance claims; usually making persistent attempts to treat it as though it continues to be a threat; in addition to any other possible further disorders which may be added; again permanently.

Although many of us may never become aware of this common practice, individuals seeking professional treatment will become labeled with a disorder first by a mental professional; and perhaps subsequently by most of the people they will come to know better, at least. For example, anyone who is known to have ever suffered depression, also is thought to be an ongoing "sufferer of depression;" as if this will always be a continuing tendency; regardless of any efforts in treatment; no matter how successful.

And that leads us to another major component of the public's apparently-common strong belief that mental illness is permanent; that so far as perhaps most of us recognize at this point, we have not really had much success in curing the many different types of mental disorders we have come to diagnose, within various people seeking treatment. We generally see only some improvement; some relief; or possibly remission in rare cases; possibly due to hospitalization, or maybe to medications, talk therapy, or some possible combination of these.

Yet, perhaps we would do well to consider the possibility that much of our mental illness may form and persist due primarily to the conscious mind's refusal, or inability to face important aspects of reality, that are yet quite well-understood by this same individual's subconscious self. If so, we could imagine what a terrible, frustrating, defeating war we would be fighting internally for many years; assuming this has been going on without the person's subconscious mind having ever been effective at bringing their conscious entity to realize some terribly-consequential false ideas it has continuously been embracing for many frustrating and distressing years. As we could also probably imagine, in some cases, this would lead to quite a quite maddening effect!

Maybe by this point, we then call ourselves or each other insane; which is yet another nebulous concept that may well do us more trouble than good; to the extent our conscious thinking has become significantly distorted.

To underscore the benefits of embracing brilliantly-developed concepts and theories, let us consider that although within this country, we might generally tend to think in terms of having become successful in life, as mainly having obtained control over financial wealth, having a rewarding and enjoyable intimate relationship with a partner, maybe having children and raising them properly in many cases; and perhaps being at least somewhat popular. These achievements have proved attainable, at least, to a smaller percentage of us; perhaps due to individual development, coupled with calculated reliance upon more-successful past theories and concepts which have become imagined and embraced.

Actually, we might consider that some people's definitions of success may not even involve either raising children, or necessarily even having a close intimate partner; so it might be safe to assume that perhaps money, more than anything else, is the main universally-held attribute defining our conception of success these days. Yet, beyond having enough earnings and savings to provide good ongoing comfort; let's call it $200,000 per year to support a family maybe; access to more money than this, as an individual, would probably not have any greater potential to add further exponential value to your quality of life.

Yet, plenty of us idealize having great wealth of many millions; and we can be sure that a considerable percentage of the work force will also work twice as many hours per week, as others, who still might be somewhat-adequately supporting their more-modest, but somewhat satisfying lifestyle. We can see that time, to do what we please besides generating adequate earnings, could also be seen as a measure of wealth, in real terms.

But if we think more carefully about it, we may realize that there are so many other aspects that we typically do humanly-value; which we might aptly consider as a form of wealth, that we could not only attain; but possibly be able to hold, indefinitely, in some cases; such as knowing that we have uniquely created an art form; be it paintings, or original songs written, or a new widget that makes life easier; maybe because it is newly-much-more-effective at doing some of people's dirty work for them; and in these instances, you have created wealth for yourself, in terms of knowing that what you have created brings pleasure, or other value, to many others.

Or maybe you wrote more of a "one-hit-wonder" song; which will be appreciated now, but it becomes forgotten once the current fad is over; such as the song, "Have you got cheating on your mind," by the Union Gap, in the 1970's. In this case, you would have less wealth of this type.

The point is, that in this sense, relatively-greater wealth can be seen to have been developed by first embracing concepts; such as those taught to a budding young artist learning to develop a talent for making greatly valuable paintings, for example; and then formulating theories; such as that if I were to dab my brush, using this technique I have come to understand conceptually, in the following projected pattern I am imagining; it would seem to create an "impression" of a flower I might be attempting to capture in my painting; and this might look interesting; let's see… And thus, Monet or some other artist first develops "impressionistic painting;" and we all know how valuable an original Monet painting is today. Of course, the high price tag is also indicative of how Monet's paintings bring great pleasure to look at; maybe we should be looking more at this aspect, as a yardstick of what constitutes wealth. In some senses, "wealth" is equal to "value."

We are asked to think in these terms, in order to gain a sense of the exponential increases in wealth that we might generate, as a result of having simply grasped new brilliant concepts and theories that become dreamed up. This potentially-exponential increase in our own wealth not only could add value for those who will benefit from our creativity and intuition; but we can gain exclusive personally-appreciated value, such as feeling as though what we have just done amounts to our making of a fabulous contribution to mankind perhaps, in some cases.

So, when we ask ourselves and each other, "What really greater value would there be, to doing anything beyond working the AA program; as it keeps us sober, and I seem to be happy enough…" well the answer is that we would potentially be sacrificing such a huge wealth, of which we could be feeling exponentially-enriched by; by possibly having thought up something of unique value, for example, with the unique mind that we surely have; just like everyone else has a unique set of experiences and learning, leading to their own uniqueness; and if we begin to think more constructively, and less closed-mindedly as to consciously condition ourselves; we will probably gain much potential to become infinitely happier and more fulfilled personally.

And the world will probably become a much better place too; to the extent that we can teach others about some brilliant more-newly-developed ideas and concepts that we have picked up along the way because our minds had become more open to consider an expanded variety of possible explanations and answers, to our questions of wonder.

Unfortunately, in order to bring this most- necessary transformation in our theoretical understanding of ourselves into the public eye, there will pretty undoubtedly be some collateral damage, in the form of people, such as long-time AA members, becoming incredibly floored by the contentions herein; and although we will almost certainly feel heartily sorry when certain people that we know and love may-well suffer some trauma and confusion as a result of the rolling out of this newer program; it seems far more important that humanity become introduced to these types of ideas and ways of expanding our thinking.

It appears to me that subconsciously, we are always ready and willing to learn something new; on just about any subject of interest to us. Our subconscious mind is never filled up it seems. Other theorists have expressed this idea. One important figurehead of psychological wisdom is Abraham Maslow. His pyramid, of a hierarchy of needs that he assumes we would be best off working at achieving, puts self-actualization at the top of the pyramid of our growth and development; and he explains that no one is really ever fully self-actualized. Maslow asserts that this is merely an ideal, which the most relatively healthy of us, psychologically speaking, will continually strive for, and this is also what renders them the most self-fulfilled among us. This theory is well-recognized in the field of psychology.

Perhaps, we can't stop someone from being too scared to try trusting themselves, in terms of carrying through with their strongest inclinations at any particular juncture, on a consistent and continual basis; and granted, this could seem awfully risky; especially for some of us. -But life is an adventure, and talk about becoming in a bad place of no spirituality; who are we, in terms of our puny little conscious entity; of which perhaps we could ideally consider it most appropriate, as an ideal, to properly relegate ourselves to continued servitude, of our master subconscious entity; to put a damper on our spirits of adventure?

Highly spirited of soldiers in the Revolutionary War once proclaimed, "Give me Liberty, or give me Death!" Maybe we could begin to live our lives more in this same spirit; except that we would not be fighting anyone but ourselves, of course; in the war of conscious versus subconscious self-control.

Of course, it is very meaningful to discuss conservative versus liberal thought processes and strategies; in their many possible degrees of magnitude; however, at this earlier point when we are first attempting to interrupt our seeming compulsion and obsession, to remain caught up in an endless cycle of self-destructive behavior, we may develop a clear need to rely on some conservative strategies, at least at the beginning. In order to squarely face and come to terms with our out-of-control thinking and behavior issues; such as excessively drinking; it seems that we must first become willing to remove ourselves from any immediate environment which we have come to believe we may-well become vulnerable to a weakness in our resolve. It seems we must do this, in order to interrupt the apparently addictive behavior we are trying to avoid, in our own best interest.

If it is non-prescribed drugs and/or alcohol that we wish to not be a problem in our lives any longer, we realize that at this point, we certainly owe it to ourselves to make a commitment to refrain from putting any mood-altering substance into our body; possibly for at least a year, as a start; under the guidelines of this program. Working with a sponsor may-well additionally be helpful; and this should probably be someone whom we are not inclined to desire romantic or sexual involvement with; as we have generally discovered that sponsorship relationships involving two people attracted to each other in this way, has potential to relegate either party to a level of emotional upset which may render our attempts to embrace a program of recovery to be quite ineffective.

In terms of the conservative stances that we may consider taking, many people in the AA program have discovered that an ongoing indefinite commitment to refrain from ingesting substances, unless prescribed by your doctor, still leaves them with a satisfactory lifestyle; and of course it is seen as an effective way to avoid addiction-related problems. Many people may come to believe that life is just great without substance use, and that any potential substance-related enhancement is not, in any way, necessary.

Certainly, we can learn through taking in external messages, in any of a variety of different forms of potential presentation of these new ideas, such as by reading, or via different forms of media we are subjected to. In order to avoid being thrown off track, we will probably want to consider with some amount of skepticism, any message such as a contention, offering new and potentially important information that we have not yet made a more thorough effort to verify, as being a valid reflection of truth.

For example, much of what is reported or contended these days over the Internet may be false or without basis, and we must be careful not to be led astray, in order to avoid relatively unhealthy ideas from rolling around within our minds, which are only masquerading as representations of the truth.

At this point in our new journey to gain a more- full conception of our own potential goodness, at this point we might also consider the existence of God as a possible reality; listening carefully to those who offer contentions of testament to this idea. Even if you find that you do not believe in God as a being, the concept of God is most certainly a long-established reality, and certainly even one of great potential value, when we consider some of the ideas behind "Godly ways of thinking and acting," as an ideal.

Perhaps we can find much value in the many teachings and contentions of Jesus; not that we should consider Jesus as the son of God necessarily, but perhaps we could at least regard him simply as one real human being who once existed in the distant past. His apparent discoveries, and his acknowledgement of many significant aspects of our humanity, can perhaps be of great value for us to embrace.

The somewhat advanced, and quite civilized thought developments which apparently formed within Jesus, seem to offer us, even today, quite valuable ways to think in terms of; especially concerning how we might view and treat ourselves and each other in a more relatively healthy manner. Of course in addition, the ideas of any of those whom we have come to see as the most intelligent and insightful of us, can certainly provide us with quite alot more food for thought than we might be capable of drumming up, using purely our own mental devices, as an individual; and of course, it seems necessary to at least embrace the <u>concept</u> of God, in order to constructively interpret and gain a more useful sense of understanding regarding the ancient ideas of Jesus; which perhaps may-well be associated with his incredibly strong conception of "God," as being an absolute reality.

This perhaps is a good example of how making use of concepts we might embrace, can give us great leverage to develop our thoughts into more complex lines of thinking. For that matter, it seems there are almost an infinite number of concepts that can be thought up, by different individuals, and possibly then embraced by many more of us; and as is perhaps often the case; the more validity we can associate with any particular concept, the more potentially useful to us that it may also become.

The field of psychology seems to consist almost entirely of conceptual ideas and other thought processes, leading us to formulate various theories related to how our minds work. As our thinking becomes more complex, overlaid with different theories and ideas which we might string together just naturally within our minds; to form variously-developed feelings, intuitions and inclinations within us; this, in turn, may often incline different individuals to develop further new, valid, meaningful, and useful concepts; which of course, again, many more of us may possibly make good use of.

It is quite apparent that this kind of developmental thinking has the cumulative effect of increasing our knowledge and our potential intelligence; and we even seem to gather momentum, as a people, to develop and evolve faster and faster, as time goes on. Just as technological ideas have grown in leaps and bounds; causing exponential, or fast and furious development of new technological breakthroughs in more modern times; so this seems to hold true regarding our growth in potentially useful <u>conceptual</u> thinking, which perhaps chiefly fuels all of this development.

But we also know, as a body of people around the world, that human nature and human development does still seem to have many inherent impediments and imperfections, in terms of falling way-short of our greatest possible degree of integrity; resulting in disadvantageous amounts of selfishness and greed, for example.

Would any relatively healthy individual want people to go hungry, or suffer unnecessarily? Perhaps not; but we also know that there are those having vast sums of money and other forms of financial wealth in their accounts, who would disagree. It seems that in their minds, what is theirs must remain theirs, unless it is traded for something which they might perceive of, as at least of equal value. Meanwhile of course, many people around the world go hungry and suffer in any number of ways associated with a lack of financial or other material resources. This is just one example of how our generally-conceived human ideals could be quite different from some of the unfortunate realities, of the actual workings of the world, at any given time.

The word "seems" is used heavily throughout this book; and this is so because it takes note of the fact that our perceptions not only can change over time, but even the ones which don't ever appear to change, in our own view, are often merely our own ideas; and others' ideas about things could be quite different. The other reason for staying within the realm of "seems," is that it may well help us, as we try to remain open to any "considerable" possibility; as opposed to those other contended possibilities which have been suggested to us perhaps, of which we feel wholeheartedly that we should not give any further thought to.

Then, we may consider that there is of course, one true reality of our existence; and perhaps knowledge or realization of different aspects of ourselves and the world around us, in this light; may only be attained somewhat questionably, over a longer period of time, as we gain more life experience.

By making current reviews of our most important historic life events, and the formation of our many different attitudes and viewpoints, what we can potentially learn from this may be quite helpful in forming updated ideas and beneficial resolutions within, which may improve our future behavior, and therefore our quality of life on many fronts, perhaps.

We might consider the following; it could be, that a large share of the types of problems we have been facing may be developing chiefly because; perhaps ultimately; how we have thought of ourselves, and conducted ourselves, has been pretty devoid of our hearing and processing feedback from the people in our world of surroundings; and even devoid of our own <u>internal</u> feedback; considering that we have been consciously- pushing-ourselves-around.

Maybe a bit like trying to drive down the road without continually looking out at the road in front of you; it seems that many problem addicts have lived pretty exclusively by their own short-sighted and boxed-in ideas and perceptions. We may almost <u>always</u> be better off, in taking into more careful consideration more-often, the apparent actions of others towards us; as well as listening more carefully to what others have to say to us along the way, as we move forward.

At this point, I would suggest that we should probably concern ourselves with how we view and understand <u>ourselves</u>. Somewhat mirroring the AA fourth and fifth step sequence of priorities and suggestion plan of action early on in recovery, it might be best if we first sit with our own thoughts, and write an accounting of where we see that we have gone astray; in having ended up, somewhat-unwittingly, behaving badly, in our relationships, and in our dealings with others in general.

Next, it might be most helpful to seek out those whom we could perhaps trustingly confide in, to share our written insights, in their more intimate detail; with at least one other closer acquaintance or friend. It well-may be at this point, that we begin to gather fresh perspective, which we can draw upon, in making future periodic ongoing re-assessments of ourselves; for more- purely constructive purposes.

We might pay particular attention to the resentments and other bad feelings we harbor towards others. These festering wounds may well keep us from maintaining a somewhat more constant state of objectivity, which we will need to rely on; in judging the validity of our own sense of inclination, at various times.

At different points going forward, the subconscious entity we serve may often call upon our conscious to dig deeper into what is behind any given more-significant- inclination we may be sensing within us. Perhaps, we can probably come to trust that our inclinations themselves will steer us to the most important information we need to have at hand, as we naturally-analyze, and measure the strength of our various inclinations, as they successively occur to us.

In many instances, we may be best advised to consider at least a small number of alternative behaviors we could select from, before charging ahead with our most instantaneous inclination; which of course, may certainly <u>also</u> have current potential to move us into action. We must better learn to use our inner senses, and try to avoid blocking our awareness of any of them, if we are truly to keep our ongoing commitment to conduct ourselves in accordance with our inner conceptions of: Who we are and what is happening, along with our deep inner values, and what we can discern as our relatively healthy desires.

Besides our resentments, our fears are probably also of paramount importance to examine, at this time of taking stock of ourselves. We could view our fears in two categories perhaps; some of them in terms of their irrationality, and also from a standpoint of those having any true and rational basis we might associate with them. Although there will almost certainly be times when we wouldn't be well-advised to disclose <u>some</u> of our fears, we must probably learn to communicate our fears to others more, in general; if we are to move beyond our fears' perhaps-often-immobilizing effect over us, at different points. James Taylor writes, in a song about taking a chance on love, "It's okay to feel afraid, but don't let that stand in your way…" Perhaps this points up a flaw in the idea of pretty-consistently utilizing more-purely conservative strategies.

If we truly want to be happy, it seems we must become willing to learn to take at least some number of calculated, and perhaps even some uncalculated, risks at times, when we are perhaps pretty strongly moved to, on a deeper level within us. It also seems relatively healthy to live in a spirit of adventure; at least to some extent; as a means of maximizing our own personal fulfillment.

As we look back on our lives at this point, in this most thoroughly-analyzing manner, it might probably be helpful to consider lost opportunities, and any strong degree of our own sense of loss associated with some of them; especially in those cases where we tend to believe similar kinds of opportunities may-well arise again for us, in the future. Thankfully, we do seem to get second chances, and building this type of hopefulness within, perhaps breeds a relatively healthy sense of optimism. It may also help heal some of the deep hurt associated with our greatest losses we have suffered in the past.

It <u>is</u> clear however, that leaving-unchecked, our first strong inclinations; in a given situation; can certainly be problematic, to say the least. As we mature, we may learn to develop increasingly better ability to sense the nature and degree of our own internal conflicts; in terms of the different conflicting inclinations we can sense within us at any moment. Expending some of our time and energy considering what may be the reasons and motivations, behind our different conflicting inclinations, is probably one of the more-useful functions that we can make of our conscious thinking processes.

In the final analysis, dissecting the thoughts which appear to have formed our feelings at any moment; of course, only when we feel somewhat inclined to; ultimately gives us a much better understanding of ourselves; and this can often help us considerably, in our ongoing struggle of trying to figure out what to do, or what not to do; as the case may be.

REFERENCES

Grayling, A.C., (2016?). "War." *Yale Press, Boston, MA*

Kleese, D.A., (2001). Nature and nature in psychology. *Journal of Theoretical and Philosophical Psychology, 21,* 61-79. Kolb, B & Whishaw, I.Q., (2015). *Fundamentals of Human Neuropsychology.* New York, NY: Worth Publishers.

Lindeman, M., Tapani, R. & Svedholm-Hakkinen, A.M., (2015). Individual differences in conceptions of soul, mind, and brain. *Journal of Individual Differences. 36,* 157-162.

Pinel, J.P.J., (2014). *Biopsychology.* Upper Saddle River, NJ: Pearson Education, inc.

Plomin, R., Reiss, D., Hetherington, E.R. & Howe, G.W. (1994). Nature and Nurture: Genetic contributions to measures of the family environment. *Developmental Psychology, 30,* 32-43.

Sigman, M., (2017). "The Secret Life of the Mind." *Little, Brown & Co. N.Y., New York*

Zimbardo, P.G., John, R.L. & McCann, V., (2012). *Psychology: Core Concepts.* Boston, MA. Pearson Education, inc.

www.ingramcontent.com/pod-product-compliance
Lightning Source LLC
Chambersburg PA
CBHW072001110526
44592CB00012B/1166